THE OTHER SIDE OF THE MOUNTAIN

Leon Lui

TALISMAN

First published in 2022 by

Talisman Publishing Pte Ltd

talisman@apdsing.com

www.talismanpublishing.com

ISBN 9789811857249

Copyright © 2022 Leon Lui Yuen Leung
Editor Sng Siok Ai
Designers Stephy Chee, Wong Sze Wey
Publisher Ian Pringle

As far as possible, the author has used currency exchange rates relevant to the periods
mentioned, although there may be instances where accurate information is unavailable.

All images in the book, unless otherwise stated, belong to the author's collection.
Every effort has been made to trace copyright holders for images used. In the event of
errors or omission, appropriate credit will be made in future printings of this work.

For my wife, Kwan,
my son, Pak Seng, &
my favourite only daughter, Oi Leng

CONTENTS

FOREWORD

I must say, I'm terribly excited. If you're reading this, it means Pa's book is finally finished and published. For the longest time, all he could talk about was the opening scene. It was to be his funeral procession, with his coffin carried in the belly of a garbage truck, his portrait mounted on the truck's grille, and his family sombrely marching behind. He never clarified if he was to be buried, cremated, or compacted.

Many years, drafts, digital rip-ups (including, thankfully, his original introduction), and rewrites later, I dare say, it is almost done. We are all proud of the huge effort it has taken him to complete his magnum opus. He should be too. It is my pleasure to share my thoughts on what his work means to me.

From a personal perspective, the book totally resonates. After all, I have known the author all my life. The voice, tone and language are a part of me. For example, in addition to my grey hair, I have inherited from my dad a love of long-distance road trips. Any journey that takes less than twelve hours in a car is fair game. Passengers enjoy deep conversations and meaningful face (to face) time while ensconced in a car for these periods. I love that sense of closeness and comfort in tight proximity. To me, a long road trip is a welcome reprieve from our normal frenetic lives, where we are always shooting off in different directions. The journey matters, not just the destination.

For others, this must be quite a unique collection of stories. When I consider other parents I know, or autobiographies I have (been forced to) read, I cannot think of many people who have experienced as much as my dad. Most tend to live in one country their entire life, and therefore may only live through one or two intense periods at most. They may experience a war, a period of racial riots, a revolution, or an economic crisis, but not all of them. They may know one or two different cultures, but not a plethora. My dad, on the other hand, has travelled so extensively that he has a kaleidoscope of contemporaneous events and cultures woven into his life tapestry. My dad brings his keen eye for detail, an excellent memory, a witty sense of humour and a flair for drama to record these stories. It is much more meaningful to experience these events through his perspectives, than to read about them in a textbook. Pa's stories impart a strong sense of what it was like to be a person on the ground, the grout to a historical mosaic.

This book is Pa's version of Roald Dahl's *Boy* or *Going Solo*, two of my favourite childhood books. Not only are the stories fascinating in themselves, but they come from my favourite father (one of his favourite jokes). With this book, my children will have the opportunity to really know their grandfather.

How many of us only have a thumbnail sketch of our grandparents? I lost my last grandparent when I was twenty-four, and only spent sporadic moments with them since I was fourteen. Although I still hear my grandparents' stories told by my parents, aunts, and uncles, they do not form a complete picture. I can no longer remember my own grandfather's voice. What a shame he did not take the time to write his story down.

With this book, Zack, Sam, and Max will always remember Ye Ye's voice. Even better, because Pa finally got around to writing the book, they will be able to discuss it with him in person! If they are lucky, the stories will provide wisdom and knowledge they may draw upon later in their lives. If nothing else, the boys will have plenty of fodder for conversation when they see him in person, or more likely on Skype these days. After all, there is a limit to debating who is better: Arsenal or Liverpool.

Please fasten your seat belt, sit back, relax, and enjoy your flight.

Pak Seng Lui
London, October 2022

PREFACE

In the fall of 2013, I visited my former boss, Mike McWherter, in Oklahoma to attend his 70th birthday party. I have known him for years, and he has always been a mentor and a friend. Sipping cold beers on the porch of his house, we recounted many of the trips we took together to try and sell some helicopters.

Those included a trip to Phnom Penh, Cambodia, to meet with the prime minister, a trip to the Philippines to meet with the president, and a trip to Bangkok to meet with the Thai army chief. We also made numerous trips to India. As it turned out, India became our biggest market in those years. Of course, I also recounted some of my experiences when I visited Iran and Afghanistan before I joined Bell Helicopter. We had a good laugh over them. Then he said, "Leon, you should put all these stories into a book!"

I thought that it could be an interesting project. I have always had a lot of travel stories to share with my family and friends. Maybe it is because I am someone who has the desire and passion to see what is on the other side of the mountain. I want to experience as much of the world as I can, visiting every place, trying every new type of food (and beer), learning new things and making new friends.

In my early years, the ebb and flow in life circumstances brought me from my birthplace in Hong Kong to Sabah, then across the oceans to America and back to Asia to settle down in Singapore. As a grown-up, work and personal interests have also led me to different corners of the world.

Mike was adamant that I should write the book so that my grandchildren would get to know me better. He even hired a ghostwriter for two days to jot down some notes to kickstart the project. Then, on my own, I prepared a draft structure by listing down the 50 states in the US that I had been to. This was followed by a list of all the places that I had set foot on – close to 80 countries around the world, 18 provinces in China, and 17 different states in India.

To be honest, the journey of writing a book turned out to be more challenging than I had expected. I had to dive into my memories to recount the events and incidences that I had experienced. As I typed out each chapter, the world continued to change: some countries that I had visited have since split (for example Yugoslavia) or merged due to war or revolutions, some countries used to exist but no longer do, yet others face existential threats. Cities and entire countries have been renamed, while regimes have risen and fallen.

I also began to write about aspects of my family history. However, I faced some roadblocks, for there was a fair bit of unknown information. Where should I start my research? Vital records and documents were woefully lacking. Most of my elders had passed away, and for the surviving ones, memories were fading over time.

The deeper I looked, the more intrigued I became, including how my surname and middle name made connections when I met total strangers. There were surname variations too. Among my grandfather's 10 children, some are Louie, some Lui and some Luie. It all depends on the registration officer when you tell them your baby's Chinese surname is 雷.

I also had a remarkable encounter with someone whom I found vaguely familiar, as if we had met somewhere before, in the distant past. In the 1980s, while having lunch in a restaurant on one of my trips to Hong Kong, I noticed a gentleman who bore a resemblance to my father, both in looks and in mannerisms. Curiosity came over me, and I walked up to his table and enquired politely in Cantonese if his surname was 雷. He turned out to be a younger brother of my father – Uncle no. 8. Later, I found an old photo taken during my grandfather's 76th birthday back in 1952, and it showed that Uncle no. 8 and I were at the same party, when I was merely 3 years old.

When I was tracking down the village where my grandfather came from, there were many twists and turns. It was definitely not an overnight project, but something that took years and a whole lot of determination. Even my father's surviving siblings had never been to the village where my grandfather was born. However, through the photos of some distant cousins who had been back to that village, and a slightly mis-remembered district name from my uncle in Vancouver, I finally located our ancestral village in Taishan, where everyone had the same surname as me.

When I entered the ancestral hall (or lineage temple) in the village, I was expecting to find ancestral tablets that embodied the ancestral spirits, and a genealogy book listing down the lineage of the Lui family. Instead, all I found was a simple altar and a ping-pong table sitting in the middle of the hall.

Throughout my writing journey, I was also fortunate to receive help and inspiration in many ways. Family members and friends lent their generous support by checking facts, loaning their travel albums and giving useful feedback and ideas. I am grateful to my Aunt no. 9 Lui Sau Mui, the only surviving sibling of my father as I am writing this book, for some insights into my grandfather's character; my cousins Grace and Katherine Lui who shared with me some of my grandfather's artefacts; Mike McWherter who urged me to start on this project; fellow Hardship Group travellers Leen, Beng, and Jerome who gave permission to use their photos of our trips in my book; and an old friend, Bill Gartshore who actually penned a few passages of my unique experiences in some of the off-the-beaten-track places.

To my publisher Ian Pringle, thank you for taking an interest in my stories and putting them into print with the Talisman team of designers. Many thanks to the book cover's creator Kevin WY Lee, who generously offered to design the whole cover, all for a few bottles of killer chilli sauce from Sabah. To my editor Siok Ai, my thanks for contributing so much to this book, by giving me suggestions on how I should present my material, and continuously asking difficult but relevant questions which I had to trawl through my memory to come up with the answers.

In addition, I would like to thank Columbia University Libraries and the National Library Board of Singapore (the staff of the Lee Kong Chian Reference Library: InterLibrary Loan and Document Delivery teams) for their assistance.

At home, I managed to unearth a trove of resources – there were many old family photographs in my personal archives. My penchant for keeping every single one of my passports since day one came in handy too, except for the one stolen from my car when it was parked in the carpark of a five-star hotel in Singapore.

During the COVID-19 lockdown, I was stuck at home and looking for things to do. I finally cleaned up all the notes I had taken over the years and submitted them to my publisher. The result is a book of stories that I have been carrying with me, and stories that I want future generations to carry forward. Wisdom comes from travelling, and I hope to give my descendants some insights about life. A knowledge of our family history will help them discover their place in the Lui clan and appreciate their unique cultural background. This book is also a gift to friends who have travelled with me over the years and friends whom I have yet to meet. I hope that the stories will entertain and inspire everyone to enjoy the freedom to explore the planet, just as I have.

Because of COVID, I have not been travelling as much as I used to, although I managed to record a new territory on my post-lockdown travel logbook with a visit by a light aircraft flight from London to Jersey, the biggest of the Channel Islands. I also accompanied Oi Leng and family to Sabah where they climbed Mount Kinabalu while I waited for them at the national park since I have already done the climb three times. Now that restrictions are loosening and more borders are re-opening, I am excited to jump on a plane again, and go somewhere, yes, just somewhere, to see the other side of the mountain.

Leon Lui
Singapore, October 2022

THE LUI FAMILY TREE

■ Male
● Female
m. Married
? No further info
① Birth order
.... Family line
continues

● *m.* (1) ?

● *m.* (2) Chiu Hung Yung
趙杏容 (?–1948)

■ Lui Yum Suen
雷蔭蓀 (1876–1953)

● *m.* (3) Ho Yuk Keng
何玉瓊 (?)

● *m.* (4) ?

■ Lui Chak Lau ①
雷澤榴

● Lui Sau Heng ②
雷秀馨

■ Lui Chak Chiu ③
雷澤劍

■ Lui Chak Yung ④
雷澤鏞

■ Lui Chak Chuen ⑤
雷澤荃

■ Lui Chak To ⑥
雷澤燾
(1920–1997)

● *m.* Eleanor Kwok
Wai Bun 郭慧斌
(1921–1988)

■ Lui Chak Jun ⑦
雷澤榛

■ Lui Chak Gwing ⑧
雷澤炯

● Lui Sau Mui ⑨
雷秀梅

● Lui Sau Fong ⑩
雷秀芳

■ *m.* Jang Yun Yaw
鄭允耀 (1935–)

● Trudie Lui Shuk Tak ①
雷淑德 (1947–)

■ Leon Lui Yuen Leung ②
雷元亮 (1949–)

● *m.* Tan Kwan Siu
陳娟秀 (1951–)

● Patricia Lui Shuk Ping ③
雷淑苹 (1950–)

■ *m.* Liew Kwok Leung
廖國樑 (1949–)

■ Fred Lui Yuen Fai ④
雷元輝 (1954–)

● *m.* Connie Moy Won
Man 梅蘊雯 (1953–)

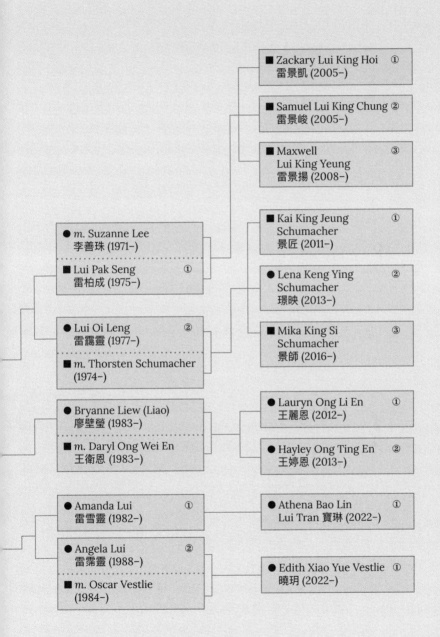

■ Zackary Lui King Hoi ①
雷景凱 (2005–)

■ Samuel Lui King Chung ②
雷景峻 (2005–)

■ Maxwell ③
Lui King Yeung
雷景揚 (2008–)

● m. Suzanne Lee
李善珠 (1971–)

■ Lui Pak Seng ①
雷柏成 (1975–)

■ Kai King Jeung ①
Schumacher
景匠 (2011–)

● Lena Keng Ying ②
Schumacher
璟映 (2013–)

● Lui Oi Leng ②
雷靄靈 (1977–)

■ m. Thorsten Schumacher
(1974–)

■ Mika King Si ③
Schumacher
景師 (2016–)

● Bryanne Liew (Liao)
廖壁瑩 (1983–)

■ m. Daryl Ong Wei En
王衛恩 (1983–)

● Lauryn Ong Li En ①
王麗恩 (2012–)

● Hayley Ong Ting En ②
王婷恩 (2013–)

● Amanda Lui ①
雷雪靈 (1982–)

● Athena Bao Lin ①
Lui Tran 寶琳 (2022–)

● Angela Lui ②
雷霈靈 (1988–)

■ m. Oscar Vestlie
(1984–)

● Edith Xiao Yue Vestlie ①
曉玥 (2022–)

Chapter 1
INTRODUCTION

A journey of a thousand miles begins with a single step.
— Laozi, *Dao De Jing*

千里之行，始於足下
— 老子《道德經》

I can still remember taking my first steps in life. I couldn't have been much more than a year old. I recall hearing my nanny joyously proclaiming, "Look, Ah Dee (my childhood nickname) can now walk!"

We were playing on the driveway of my family house in Kowloon. I took a few steps forward, then flung myself onto the steel gate – and from my newly elevated stance – peered through the grille to the big world outside…and a journey that was to be somewhat more than a thousand miles.

That was the beginning of a wanderlust that was to lure me to almost every continent, including all 50 of the United States and over 80 countries, and still counting.

When friends learn about my colourful travel history, they often ask me two questions. The first is: "Aren't you afraid of getting injured or killed going to some of those off-the-beaten-track places?" Indeed, there is a Chinese saying: "When you hike up the mountain too many times, you will surely run into a tiger" (上得山多, 終遇虎). However, I would respond, "Well, you have to be in the wrong place at the right time or the right place at the wrong time to have problems; but, if you are in the wrong place at the wrong time, nothing will happen to you". Well, almost right.

So, armed with this attitude and as a zealous, adventurous youth, I ventured forth with no concern to my personal comfort or safety. Certainly, I have had my share of close calls; these incidents can even be conceived of as life threatening. When I was a toddler in Hong Kong, the train that I was travelling in derailed, but fortunately I suffered only light injuries. Then, as a 14-year-old passenger flying from Singapore to Hong Kong, I witnessed one of the aeroplane engines catching fire mid-flight...but thankfully, we were able to return safely to Singapore before things worsened. The next close call came when I was 17, driving a cousin's car from Kansas City to Dallas, when its crank shaft pulley broke and caused engine failure in the middle of a highway. And before I turned 21, I had been robbed in Mexico and encountered gun-toting bank robbers face-to-face in Indiana.

When I became an adult, I encountered more hair-raising emergencies because I travelled a lot for work. This included venturing into war-torn countries like Iran and Afghanistan, and flying during violent thunderstorms, both as a passenger in a commercial flight, and later as a pilot of a single-engine light aircraft.

Friends are also surprised to know that travel became second nature to me from a relatively early age. So the second question that I often get asked is: "What led you to move around so much since young?" Well, that had a lot to do with my family history, and the best way to answer that question is to go back to the starting point, where it all began with my grandfather.

My grandfather's name was Lui Yum Suen (雷蔭蓀). He was born into a prominent business family during the Qing dynasty in 1876. His birthplace was in Taishan (台山) county, Guangdong province, and he had three brothers. A child prodigy, he passed the imperial examinations at the age of 16.

Subsequently, he entered the Qing imperial court which appointed him as an administrative service[1] official. According to one of my uncles, my grandfather had to attend many banquets every night and then get up early in the morning to attend the daily reading of the royal decree. In order to sustain such a hectic schedule, he took to smoking opium.

Some years later, he studied law at the Imperial University of Peking (京師大學堂), in a faculty that admitted court officials and was known as Shi Xue Guan (仕學館). The Qing dynasty fell in 1911, and the Republic of China was established thereafter. On 22 February in the second year of the Republic of China (Minguo[2]) (1913), at the age of 37, my grandfather was conferred certificate no. 624, officially qualifying him to be a lawyer in the republic. In fact, he was among the first batch of lawyers to graduate from the university, which later became Peking University (北京大學). He was appointed as the chief of staff in the Canton provincial government, and also served as the advisor to the Canton provincial treasury.

After his public service in China, my grandfather relocated to Hong Kong, involving himself in a group of diverse businesses left behind by my great-grandfather. These included provision stores and other interests in the Chinatowns of New York City and Vancouver; and steamers that hauled tea and other commodities between Hong Kong and North America. There were also other business interests in Hong Kong and Macau.

Like his father, my grandfather was a natural entrepreneur. He was invited to sit on the board of many shipping associations and was one of the founders of the Hong Kong Chinese Chamber of Commerce (香港中華總商會). He was a co-owner of Sze Yap Steamship Company (四邑輪船有限公司) and Sun Kwong Hup (新廣合金山莊), a trading firm specialising in the American trade. He also personally owned Yan Vo

---

1 One of his colleagues was Xu Shiying (許世英), who later served as the premier for a brief period in the 1920s, when China became a republic.
2 The first year of the Minguo calendar was 1912, the year that the republic was founded. The months and days follow the Gregorian calendar system. China used the Minguo calendar until 1949, when it became the People's Republic of China.

Tong (仁和堂酒莊), a liquor distillery and became the first chairman of the Hong Kong & Kowloon General Association of Liquor Dealers & Distillers (港九酒業總商會).

From 1940 to 1953, he co-owned a tin mine (元朗大棠錫礦) in Tai Tong, Kowloon. The mine closed down following his death and the death of the other owner-managers. The company's mining licence was eventually revoked by the Hong Kong government because of environmental issues raised by the local villagers. In any case, it produced only 27.8 kg of tin in 1953! It is unfortunate that the story of the tin mine has been lost to time, and the mine is now overgrown with vegetation.

My grandfather took a special interest in education and philanthropy in Hong Kong, as was the tradition of successful and prosperous business families at the time. He sat on the board of many schools, and founded a school which became the present-day Confucius Hall Secondary School (孔聖堂中學) at Caroline Hill Road, Causeway Bay.

Welfare projects, orphanages, hospitals and schools for the poor also received much support from him. Amongst his appointments, he was a director of the Tung Wah Hospital (東華醫院) and Po Leung Kok Welfare Association (保良局), and he also served as the chairman of Chung Sing Benevolent Society (鐘聲慈善社) and Sham Shui Po Kaifong Welfare Association (深水埔街坊福利事務促進會). He was also actively involved in numerous fundraising activities.

As an imperial and Confucian scholar-official, my grandfather was known for his calligraphic talent. He was often commissioned to write the names of many business establishments and other organisations on their signboards. The signboard over the main entrance of a Chinese business or shop was as important to the owner as the significance of the company name itself. It could make or break the fortunes of the company. A well-made signboard that features striking characters by a renowned calligrapher is not only auspicious, but also a work of art.

In the 1980s, we were amazed to find a signboard calligraphed by my grandfather, over a shop entrance in Chinatown, Chicago. We were even more excited when we found a business signboard in Tawau, British North Borneo, calligraphed by him. In Hong Kong, his calligraphy can be seen at the gateway of the Confucius Hall Secondary School.

On a more personal level, he wrote a tribute to my grandmother on her memorial portrait. That may well be the only sample of his brush lettering that my siblings and I have, and it is on the ancestral altar in our family home in Sandakan, Sabah.

My grandfather had four wives and ten children. His first wife bore him a son (whom I address as Uncle no. 1, 大伯). His second wife bore him a daughter (Aunt no. 2, 二姑媽) and four sons, my father Lui Chak To (雷澤燾) being the youngest of the four sons. His third wife bore him another son (Uncle no. 7, 七叔) who was just one week younger than my father. His fourth wife bore him a son (Uncle no. 8, 八叔) and twin daughters (Aunts no. 9 and 10, 九姑姐、十姑姐).

According to Aunt no. 9, after she was delivered from her mother's womb and being washed by the midwife, someone exclaimed that there was another baby on the way. Everyone was so excited that they left No. 9 in the wash pan and forgot all about her. She almost drowned.

Many of my uncles, aunts and cousins ventured abroad and experienced a wider world. As a result, they put down roots overseas and their descendants are still living there today. My grandfather sent three of my uncles to North America in the 1930s to help manage the family business interests on that side of the globe. Uncle no. 3 (三伯) died at a very young age, but had two sons who both migrated to Canada in the 1950s. Uncle no. 4 (四伯) was sent by my grandfather to Vancouver before the Second World War, and held a degree from the University of British Columbia. Uncle no. 5 (五伯) ended up in New York City managing one of my grandfather's provision stores in Chinatown.

Over in Asia, Uncle no. 8 (八叔) managed the Macau branch of a distillery owned by my grandfather. Remaining in Hong Kong were Uncle no. 7 (七叔), a manager in the local branch of the Bank of Canton; Aunt no. 9 (九姑姐), a teacher; and Aunt no. 10 (十姑姐), a Hong Kong newspaper editor.

My father was born in Hong Kong in 1920. He completed his secondary school education at King's College, and enrolled in Far East Aviation Technical School in Kowloon. He had never been back to his ancestral village in China. When the Second World War broke out and the Japanese army invaded China, he joined the Kuomintang Air Force as a flight mechanic and was sent to Calcutta (now Kolkata), India. He was involved in the "Hump" operation that was flying supplies between India and Yunnan, China, to fight the Japanese invaders.

My mother, Eleanor Kwok Wai Bun (郭慧斌), grew up in Shanghai and joined the China National Airline Corp (CNAC) as a stenographer. During the war, the headquarters of CNAC was based in Calcutta. It was there that she met my father, and they were married in 1944. According to an invitation card that I found in our house years later, the wedding reception was held at the Nanking Restaurant, 22 Blackburn Lane, Calcutta.

TRACKING DOWN MY PARENTS' WEDDING VENUE

In 2016, I was in Kolkata and managed to locate 22 Blackburn Lane. I learnt that the Nanking Restaurant was started by the Au family in 1925, on the ground floor of the Toong On Temple. In 2008, the family tried to sell the building for redevelopment, but the trustees of the temple laid claim to the ownership of the building and won the case. Five years later, the municipal government moved a garbage dump right into Blackburn Lane, so the building was sealed up. The whole road was literally a dump when we found it, but the temple (the red building) was still standing.

In 2022, I was in Kolkata again. This time, I managed to get inside the building, and a caretaker showed me around. On the ground floor, there was a statue of the Chinese god of war Kuan Ti, and on the second floor, a statue of the Buddha. Among the relics lying around was a stove which might have been used to cook some of the dishes served during my parents' wedding reception.

Although I wanted to make a donation to the temple, the caretaker told me that no one knew who had the key to the donation box. So I just gave him the cash and he promised that he would hand it over to the secretary of the temple trust.

After the war, my parents left India and moved back to Hong Kong. With some start-up capital from my grandfather, my father incorporated a car dealership, Continental Motors (大陆汽車公司), distributing Pontiac and Peugeot cars. In 1947, my parents welcomed the birth of their first child – my elder sister Shuk Tak (淑德), Trudie.

My Early Years

In 1949, the Year of the Ox, there were leap seventh months[3]. During those two months, Uncle no. 4, my father (who was sixth in the family) and Uncle no. 7 had a son each. I was the youngest of the three baby boys. My grandfather, who was 73 at that time, was so happy that he had three rectangular gold pendants specially made for my cousins and me. The face of each pendant bore the respective grandson's name, while the upper part of the pendant was engraved with the same phrase: "Three outstanding descendants compete for excellence (三桂競秀)".

My cousin, Philip (Uncle no. 4's son), who earned a PhD from Juilliard School of Music, won that competition hands down. I do not have much of an impression of my grandfather because he passed away when I was 4, but I have been told by my elders that he was particularly fond of me, the youngest of his grandsons during his living years.

The Chinese tradition of having the same middle name[4] among all the sons of the same generation is practised in my clan, and yields some amazing tales. For my father's generation, the shared middle name is "Chak" (澤). For my generation, it is "Yuen" (元). I was acquainted with a gentleman who recounted striking up a conversation with someone on a flight to Canada. When he found out his fellow passenger was named "Lui Yuen Shun" (雷元信), he asked Yuen Shun[5] if he knew

---

3 As the Chinese lunar calendar month is shorter than the Gregorian calendar month, an extra month (*run yue*, 閏月) is added to the Chinese calendar approximately every three years to keep it in sync with the latter.

4 A typical Chinese name consists of the family name and a two-character given name. The first character of the given name (or "middle name") is usually generational, thus all children of the same gender in the clan share this name. An alternative tradition is to have the second character as the generation name.

5 Yuen Shun is one of the sons born to Uncle no. 1.

"Lui Yuen Leung" (雷元亮), that is me. Yuen Shun said, "Of course, he is my cousin".

My father's car dealership business went into receivership the year I was born. My younger sister Shuk Ping (淑苹), Pat, was born a year later. We had to move around mostly on the Kowloon side. My grandfather had a villa in the New Territories in the middle of a lychee orchard, where I would spend my summer holidays.

I started kindergarten before my third birthday. My parents tried to sneak out of the house with Shuk Tak to enrol her in a kindergarten, while my nanny was minding Pat and me. I caught them, threw a tantrum, and insisted on going with them. So they gave me a change of clothes and brought me along. I even remember that I wore a yellow T-shirt and red dungarees on that day.

We went into the office to see the head mistress, and she showed Shuk Tak a picture book with illustrations of animals and flowers. When she pointed to a morning glory and asked Shuk Tak what the colour of the flower was, my sister did not know the answer but I piped up, "Purple!" The head mistress convinced my parents to let me start kindergarten even though I was not quite three years old and below the enrolment age.

During the three years of kindergarten, I joined the 40-member percussion band. I rose through the ranks, from playing the triangle, *muyu*[6], tambourine, cymbals, and bass drum before I finally became the conductor of the band. I remember being packed into a windowless cigarette van with my band members, to take a cross-harbour ferry to an auditorium for a competition. We did not win because a band member struck the triangle when he was not supposed to.

---

6 Literally "wooden fish", the *muyu* (木魚) is a wooden percussion instrument that keeps rhythm in Buddhist rituals and Cantonese opera. It has a hollow body and is struck with a mallet.

On one occasion, I was onboard a train in Kowloon, Hong Kong, en route to my grandfather's villa, when the train parted company with the tracks. All I could remember was that I ended up with a huge bruise on my forehead. Later, the adults told me that I had bumped against the back of the seat in front of me, and the impact resulted in the bruise. I was only 3 or 4 years old then, so the seat back was taller than me.

After my father's business went bankrupt in the early 1950s, he took up a job in Sandakan, British North Borneo (now the state of Sabah in Malaysia), hoping to pay off his creditors. At that time, I was 4, and my brother Yuen Fai (元輝), Fred, was just born. With his aviation background, my father was hired by Borneo Airways as a mechanic. Borneo Airways was later absorbed into Malayan Airways, which was renamed as Malaysian Airways after the formation of the Federation of Malaysia.

Meanwhile, we moved into a two-star hotel owned by my grandfather on 30 Nathan Road. It was called the Rose Hotel, and was where the Imperial Hotel now stands today. Weekends were spent with my maternal aunt (五姨媽), Frances. She was my mother's elder sister, and lived in a big villa by the beach in South Bay, Hong Kong Island.

In December 1953, my grandfather passed away after a bout of illness. I don't have much memory of the funeral rites, except that we entered the house through a window and not the main door, and a white cloth was draped over his body. My father rushed back from Sandakan to pay his final respects.

Years later, my mother showed me an album that she had meticulously kept. It contained news cuttings of my grandfather's obituary notices and articles extolling his life's achievements. The funeral condolence money was to be donated to the victims of a fire[7] in the Sham Shui Po district, in accordance with his last wishes. Also in the album were photographs taken of the elaborate funeral procession along the streets of Hong Kong. Hundreds of people lined the route to view the procession carrying his coffin. Influential and famous people such as community leaders, merchants and the literati all turned up to bid their farewell.

---

7 The devastating fire at Shek Kip Mei rendered almost 60,000 people homeless.

Shifting To Sandakan

When my father's job in Malayan Airways was secure and he could support the family, my mother prepared to uproot us from Hong Kong to join him in Sandakan. I was almost seven years old then. Our nanny (more like a governess because she was authorised by my mother to cane us, and she did) had a son living in Hong Kong, so she did not want to go with us. My mother swapped her for Yue Jie (月姐), who was one of Auntie Frances's *amahs*. An *amah* is a domestic helper and nanny, easily identified by her uniform of a white blouse and black trousers.

On 14 July 1956, the four of us plus Yue Jie and my mother, filled with anticipation, travelled on a steamer to Sandakan to reunite with my father.

TRIBUTE TO MOM

My mother was an amazing lady. Although she did not even complete her secondary school education, she had many talents and an enormous capacity for learning. Her general knowledge gleaned from reading was phenomenal.

During the years when my father was away and based in Sandakan, she practically raised us as a single mother would. Sometimes, she would put the four of us to bed, but wake me up again later to accompany her to attend classical music concerts and operas.

After we moved to Sandakan, she subscribed to *National Geographic* and *TIME* magazines. She bought a set of *Encyclopaedia Britannica* and the *Book of Knowledge* published by Grolier Society. We also had the two-volume *American Encyclopaedic Dictionary*. She attempted all the crossword puzzles she could lay her hands on, so her vocabulary was simply immense. She could even explain to me the difference between an American crossword puzzle and a British crossword puzzle.

She encouraged us to learn Chinese, so she subscribed to juvenile magazines from Hong Kong such as 《兒童樂園》 to keep up our interest in the Chinese language. When I became interested in Chinese sword-fighting or wuxia novels (武俠小說), she bought them for me. I read almost all the novels by Jin Yong (Louis Cha) and Liang Yusheng. Later, I progressed to classics such as *Journey to the West* 《西遊記》, *Romance of the Three Kingdoms* 《三

國演義》, *The Water Margin*《水滸傳》and *The Generals of the Yang Family*《楊家將》.

My mother adored music and her vinyl record collection was impressive. While my father liked to listen to Chinese operas, she preferred western classical, pop and jazz music. Among my mother's prized classical music collections was a set of vinyl records compiled by *Reader's Digest*. After dinner, as we prepare for bed, she would listen to these records while attempting to solve a few crossword puzzles.

There were also albums by Paul Anka, Pat Boone, Mario Lanza, and Nat King Cole, and an album on the musical *West Side Story*, just to name a few. She could name each member of the original Platters on the record cover.

She engaged a private piano teacher to teach us how to play the piano, and she would practise the pieces on her own. With her encouragement, I had seven years of piano lessons. She also bought an acoustic guitar and learned to play it "Hawaiian style": plucking the strings with one hand while sliding a steel bar along the strings with the other hand, with the guitar lying flat on her lap.

In her spare time (if she had any), she would gather my siblings and me around the dining table to complete a thousand-piece jig-saw puzzle for family bonding. She bought a few *Sing Along with Mitch*[9] record albums so that we could learn English while enjoying the songs.

Most of our meals were prepared by Yue Jie who came from the Shunde district in Guangdong province, which was known for its culinary traditions. However, my mother would periodically make us doughnuts from recipes in the Betty Crocker cookbook; we would also get to eat her fluffy waffles or pancakes for breakfast. Her culinary repertoire was not limited to western food. Whenever she had a craving for her hometown food, usually during weekends, she would make her own Shanghai noodles and dumplings. She even fermented glutinous rice wine.

My mother was also good with numbers. When my father started a construction company just before he retired from Malaysian Airways, she handled the payroll and accounts. It was likely that she honed her bookkeeping skills during the years when my father was saddled with business debts. She was so determined to pay off the creditors that she would jot down all her expenses for the day in a little notebook, every day down to the penny.

---

9 Mitch Miller was an influential musician, singer and record producer in the 1950s and 1960s.

The population in Sandakan was only 20,000 in those days, and the port city was known as "Little Hong Kong" because many Hong Kongers migrated there. The main modes of transport were steamers, coal-powered trains and buses.

I had to switch from attending a Chinese school in Hong Kong to an Anglican missionary school in Sandakan where the medium of teaching was English. Luckily, I had just finished Primary 1 in Hong Kong so I managed to switch to the English stream in Primary 2, albeit with some difficulty at first.

The eight years from 1956 to 1964 were uneventful. I toured the west coast of British North Borneo with my whole class after our Primary 6 exams in 1960. The following year, we toured the east coast. I joined the Boy Scouts and climbed Mount Kinabalu, the tallest mountain in Southeast Asia (at 4,100 m), when I was 14 years old.

A few teachers during my secondary school years left a very deep impression on me. On the first day of her geography class, Ms Durrant said, "Civilisation taught men how to draw boundaries, and with that came war". Mrs Stally, our English teacher, was very strict and particular about how we learn and write English. She would not accept anything we turned in if it were written with a ballpoint pen. According to her, a fountain pen could be held at an acute angle whereas a ballpoint pen had to be held more upright, which would distort our handwriting. We were not allowed to start a sentence with the word "It" because "It" would not be referring to anything. Words like "nice", "well", "fine" were meaningless and therefore not acceptable to her. Then, there was my Chinese teacher, Mr Yang. On the front page of a Chinese essay that I had submitted, he actually drew a grave – complete with a cross atop a heap of earth – because he was so appalled at how bad my essay was.

In the winter of 1963, my mother took the four of us on a visit to Hong Kong. The trip was an eye-opener for us country bumpkins setting foot in a big city. Until then, I had never seen an escalator in my life. When I returned to Sandakan after the trip, I described to my classmates what an escalator looked like and how to get on and off the moving staircase.

I was so impressed with what I had seen and learned on that trip that I told my mother I would like to go to Hong Kong again. She told me

A SURPRISE FAMILY PET

One evening in the early 1960s, my father came home from work with a brown carton box. Inside was a little gibbon, curled up fast asleep. We gathered around the furry newcomer and whispered in excitement, trying not to wake him up.

Unlike most gibbons, ours was grey in colour instead of brown. Because of the sounds he made when he was excited, we named him "Woo Woo". My father explained that someone in the timber camp had probably shot the mother, hence the poor orphan was now looking for a home, and so we made him our pet. He had a birth certificate issued by the forestry department.

Woo Woo was a very affectionate pet. He was especially close to Pat who spent the most time with him, grooming his fur and playing with him. My father built him a cage downstairs (we lived on the second floor). Every day, when we came home from school, he would swing around his cage, crying "woo, woo, woo, woo". He would not stop until one of us went over to his cage to pat him on his head.

We could not let him roam around freely because he would leave a trail of destruction whenever he swung around, pulling on everything in the house with his long, outstretched arms. We also had to be mindful that he might wander out of the compound, climb an electric pole and be electrocuted.

He fed mainly on fruits and milk. Like all primates, he was very playful and would pull on the tail of any dog that walked by his cage. Sadly, while I was still in the university in America, I was told that he died after he became a victim of some epidemic that was spreading among the dogs in the neighbourhood.

that she would buy me a ticket on a steamer to Hong Kong if I would earn my own living expenses. So during the following year's summer holidays, I worked in my father's construction company as a labourer to save up for my trip.

Leaving Home To Study Abroad

Sometime in mid-1964, a life-changing event occurred. Before I had the chance to spend my hard-earned money on a trip to Hong Kong, my mother received a letter from her old friend, whom we addressed as Auntie Laddie. They were classmates when growing up in Shanghai, and Auntie Laddie moved to Hong Kong after the war.

Auntie Laddie was no stranger to our family. When we were still living in Hong Kong, she often came over to our home. Together with my mother, they would cook Shanghainese food for us. She would also join my mother and me to attend concerts late at night. Sometime after we moved to Sandakan to join my father, she married Uncle Wilson and they migrated to California.

In her letter, Auntie Laddie said that they were childless, and since my mother had four children, would she be interested to send one of us over, to stay with her and attend an American public school for free?

I was chosen as I was the eldest son in the family. There was no hesitation on my part – studying abroad was a dream come true. Within three weeks, I was on the way to San Francisco, turning 15 just a few days earlier. This marked a new and important phase in my life, where I spent seven years in the United States of America, a country that I had hitherto seen only on films.

I studied at Homestead High School for a term, before unforeseen circumstances led me to transfer to Menlo School, which was a full boarding school. Upon graduation, I was accepted by Purdue University, Indiana. Because of the very good education I had at Menlo (with its advanced placement courses), I was able to test out of a whole semester at Purdue and earned my first degree in 3½ years.

In between studying and working part-time, I strived to experience all that life had to offer. I represented the university on their soccer team and travelled around North America at every opportunity that came my way. This included meeting relatives from my paternal and maternal families. I also formed several lifelong friendships during this period. My buddies and I had lots of fun, getting into just enough trouble to keep things lively. Many of them also shared my love for travelling.

I was placed on the Dean's List every semester for my first two years, and was awarded a foreign student scholarship. This covered my tuition fees for the rest of my undergraduate education. Along the way, I was inducted into several honour societies at Purdue: Phi Eta Sigma

(Freshman honorary), Sigma Gamma Tau (Aeronautical Engineering honorary) and Tau Beta Pi (National Engineering honorary).

Due to the cost of plane tickets in those days, I couldn't fly home annually. I made my first trip back to Sandakan only after my freshman year in 1967. By then, my parents had moved into a big house situated on a hill, with a terrace from which we could see one of the islands of the Philippines on a clear day. As the house was built after I had left for my studies, I did not have a separate room for myself, so I shared a room with Fred during those few weeks.

My siblings were eager to hear about my experiences studying abroad, while my mother plied me with delicious home-cooked food that I missed a lot. It was great to be back home for the summer and I gained more than 10 kg.

Meeting Kwan

1969 was a special year because I met a girl who would one day be my wife. I was a senior at Purdue when Kwan showed up as a freshman. At that time, the male-to-female student ratio was five to one, so freshmen girls usually attracted a lot of attention.

Just like me, her family moved around a lot. She was born in Burma (now known as Myanmar), left as a refugee to Hong Kong, but moved to Thailand after only three years. Just before she came to the US, her family had relocated to Singapore.

She had three older siblings who also studied in Purdue. Her eldest sister, Susan, was my Engineering Mechanics teaching assistant (TA). She completed her postgraduate doctorate in Engineering at Purdue. Another older sister, Elaine, was in my German class. Her older brother Dennis was my senior in the School of Engineering and had graduated by the time Kwan came over.

There were only 200 Chinese students studying in Purdue at that time, and we had a Chinese Student Club that organised events so that all the Chinese students could be acquainted with one another. That was how we met and as the saying goes, the rest is history.

In 1970, I received my Bachelor of Science degree with distinction in Aeronautical Engineering. I was then 20 years old. With a mind to pursue graduate studies, I applied to several universities and was accepted to Stanford University. At the same time, Purdue made me an attractive offer if I were to take up their master's programme: a graduate teaching assistant post where I did not have to pay any tuition fees, plus a monthly subsistence allowance that would cover my living expenses. What's more, Kwan and I wouldn't have to be apart. After weighing all my options, I decided to complete my master's degree at Purdue.

After the first semester of graduate school, I made my second trip back home to Sandakan. As all doting mothers would do, mine made sure that I filled up on all the home-cooked food that I couldn't enjoy while studying overseas. Inevitably, I gained around 20 kg that summer. I was not sure if Kwan would recognise me when I showed up back on campus in September, weighing 85 kg, the heaviest that I had ever been in my life...

We had a whole year to cement our relationship further while I was studying for my master's degree. In 1971, I successfully graduated with a Master of Science in Aeronautical Engineering. With my new

MORE ABOUT MY SIBLINGS

My sisters and brother also went overseas for higher education. Shuk Tak went to the National Taiwan University (台大) because she was Chinese educated. Pat and Fred both went to the United States for their bachelor's and master's degrees.

After graduation, Shuk Tak went back to Sandakan to teach, and married Yun Yaw. Just like me, Pat and Fred lost their Malaysian permanent residence status for being away in college for six years. As Singapore welcomes foreign-born professionals who can contribute to its economy and adapt to its multi-cultural environment, Pat (who has a Master in Elementary Education) applied successfully for a teaching job in the Singapore American School, married Kwok Leung, and became a Singapore citizen after some years. She was with the school for 30 years till her retirement. Fred married Connie, an American citizen originally migrated from China, and so they decided to settle down in the States.

qualifications in hand, I contemplated my future. Because I had lived abroad for seven years, Malaysia would not extend my permanent residence status. And since I left Hong Kong when I was only 6 years old, I would have had to reapply for permanent residence if I decided to head back there.

Then I was told that Singapore would welcome qualified professionals like me. That sounded good. I could get a job there while waiting for Kwan to complete her undergraduate and postgraduate studies.

But first, I wanted to see more of the world, so I went backpacking in Europe for two months. Kwan would be heading home to Singapore for the summer holidays. I met her parents for the first time after my European trip and I also brought her to Sandakan to visit my parents.

Settling In Singapore

Soon, I found a job at Lockheed Aircraft Service Singapore as an engineer, mostly drawing up repair schemes for US military aircraft damaged in the Vietnam War. After working for a year, I applied for permanent residence in Singapore, which was swiftly granted in August 1972 because of my professional qualifications.

However, four months later, I was told by the authorities to register for National Service, and this took me by surprise. We were the first batch of male permanent residents who were called up for National Service. Singapore had been trying to build up its defence forces following its separation from Malaysia in 1965 and the withdrawal of most of the British troops in the early 1970s. Thus all able-bodied youths had to undergo compulsory conscription for about 2½ years.

At that time, I was barely 23, and sacrificing 2½ years of my life in exchange for citizenship was not something that I had thought about in great detail, especially since I had only lived in Singapore for less than 2 years.

However, I was simply not given a choice. When I reported to the Central Manpower Base and was inducted into the Army in July 1973, I was given a piece of paper that promised me citizenship upon satisfactory completion of National Service. That was how I became a Singaporean and made it my home.

Prior to this, Kwan and I had planned a Hawaiian beach wedding immediately after she finished her Master of Arts degree in the University of Hawaii in September that year. But basic military training lasted three months, so I was unable to get away to America. We ended up marrying in Singapore in November, as part of a triple wedding celebration with two other couples – Dennis (Kwan's brother) and Vicki; plus Precha (Kwan's maternal uncle) and Ivy. Our joint wedding dinner was attended by 600 guests.

While serving National Service in the first few months, I applied to be transferred to the Air Force because of my professional qualifications and working experience at Lockheed. My request was approved, and I was posted to the Air Force headquarters as a staff officer four days before our wedding.

In 1975, our first child was born. As I held my newborn son Pak Seng (柏成) in my arms, I felt an unspoken awe at experiencing fatherhood at 26 years old. Two years later, we welcomed another bundle of joy, this time a beautiful daughter, Oi Leng (靄靈). My father oversaw the naming process for his grandchildren, just like my grandfather did for my cousins, my siblings and me.

Balancing Family Life And A Varied Career

I completed National Service in July 1978 and gained citizenship. Although the military offered me a stable job environment, I wanted to try a different career so that I could build a better future for Kwan and our children.

Later that year, I joined my in-laws' palm oil business, which was based in Malaysia. Initially, I was supposed to set up a vegetable oil refinery in Indonesia. After some training in Malaysia, I spent nine months in the city of Medan, North Sumatra, but that project was abandoned for economic reasons.

In 1979, I came back to Singapore and became the general manager of a vegetable-oil refining and canning factory in Jurong owned by my in-laws' family. Our products were sold mainly to the Middle East, hence I made many trips to that region, including war-torn Iran and

Afghanistan. I also went to Nigeria to check out the market. Because we had to import all our raw materials – including crude palm oil with export duty from Malaysia, and crude corn and soyabean oil from the Americas – we were handicapped by our uncompetitive pricing, so we decided to close down the factory and put it on the market. I was involved in the sale and worked myself out of a job.

As the saying goes, when one door closes, another opens. In 1982, I was recruited by Singapore Technologies to start an aircraft charter operation with two helicopters and one turboprop commuter plane because of my engineering background and my pilot's license. Later, I also assumed the post of commercial manager, offering the company's aviation maintenance services to customers in the region. I made numerous work trips to Saudi Arabia, Oman, and the United Arab Emirates, and achieved some success in Nepal and the ASEAN countries.

In 1987, I was recruited by Bell Helicopter Asia to set up an office in Hong Kong. This would involve relocating to my place of birth, and was a fantastic opportunity that I looked forward to. I spent four months in Texas on an orientation programme to learn about all aspects of the helicopter business. While waiting for the final nod to go to Hong Kong, I dabbled in the sale of helicopters to Nepal and India.

I moved to Hong Kong with my family on 31 Dec 1987. From that office, I covered Nepal, India, China, and the ASEAN countries, selling mostly commercial and civilian helicopters to organisations, companies, and private individuals. Things were going well until the Tiananmen incident on 4 June 1989 threw a spanner in the works. The company, just like many other American companies, decided to close the office in Hong Kong, and so I worked out of the Singapore office again. Meanwhile, Pak Seng went off to boarding school in America, and Oi Leng came back to Singapore with us to continue her studies. I became the general manager for spare parts sale in the region, covering 13 countries. There was a year when I counted 204 days travelling for work-related matters.

In the early 1990s, Kwan and I began travelling with a group of good friends on a regular basis. Not only did they share our taste for adventure and sense of fun, they were also willing to brave the occasional rainstorm, landslide and altitude sickness. We called our vacations "Hardship Trips". For close to two decades, we admired beautiful landscapes, explored historical sites and met many friendly locals.

In 1995 and 1996, my director, Mike, decided to send me to the Texas headquarters for some corporate culture infusion. Oi Leng was sitting for her 'A' level exams then; Pak Seng was about to graduate from college and getting ready to come back to Singapore to serve National Service, so I lived in Texas on my own. Upon my return from Texas, I was made the marketing director for Bell Helicopter in the region.

Although work occupied a huge proportion of my time, I tried to find ways to fit in family bonding time and leisure travel. The years seemed to pass in a flash. When Pak Seng completed his National Service obligations, he tied the knot with Suzy in 1999 and settled down in America. One of Pak Seng's coursemates during his Officer Cadet training days flew to Virginia to be his best man. In 2005, the Lui clan welcomed the arrival of their twin sons – Zackary (King Hoi, 景凱) and Samuel (King Chung, 景峻). Kwan and I marvelled at becoming grandparents for the first time.

In 2006, I decided to resign from the company, even though I had worked there for close to 20 years, because I encountered value conflicts with my immediate superior that made me lose all respect for him. Given these unbridgeable differences, it was impossible for me to continue working in the company. I knew that it was time to part ways with the company.

Shortly after that, I started a small business in metal spraying. Although the technology behind the process was very advanced, the metal spraying process created a lot of noise and dust, and I had difficulty recruiting sprayers who were willing to work in such an unpleasant environment. We managed to secure jobs in Hong Kong, China and Indonesia, but having to send my workers there to complete a job was not cost-effective, so we shut down the business seven years later.

Pak Seng and Suzy had their third son, Maxwell (King Yeung, 景揚) in 2008, and they all moved to London two years later. Meanwhile, in 2009, we celebrated another happy occasion in the Lui clan – Oi Leng's wedding to Thorsten. They had their first child Kai (King Jeung, 景匠) in 2011, then Lena (Keng Ying, 璟映) in 2013, and Mika (King Si, 景師) in 2016. I appreciate that my children have maintained the traditional Chinese naming convention for their respective families, giving the same middle name (King, 景) to their sons.

Kwan turned out to be quite an entrepreneur. After spending a few years initially as a social researcher on national development initiatives and another few years in market research, she set up her own company to market various food products.

She has always taken on a "why not" attitude. She launched her own premium brand of soyabean oil in Singapore in direct competition to our neighbouring country Malaysia, which was then the largest palm oil producer in the world and had a transportation cost advantage.

She was also the first to introduce canned sardines immersed in a chilli-tomato sauce instead of the traditional ketchup sauce. She even owned a range of pre-mixed spices that was sold to more than 30 countries worldwide. That brand of spices is now owned by Kraft Heinz, a Warren Buffet company.

In 2001, she founded a chef training academy which has since grown to an annual enrolment of 2,500 students from 34 countries, with international degree partnerships. I am a technical adviser in the academy, which operates in a 45,000-square-foot facility housing chillers, freezers, induction cookers, security systems, and air-conditioning equipment. In the course of building the business, we travel often, exploring opportunities to work with other culinary schools and professionals, and attending food expos around the world.

In her wish to give back to the society, Kwan spent nine years as a director on the board of Spectra Secondary School, which is a specialised school for Normal Technical students. The school provides a more customised, skills-based and vocational education. She also served

21 years as a member of the Singapore Symphony Orchestra (SSO) Ladies League to raise funds in support of the SSO. She even facilitated an SSO cookbook that won the best fundraising cookbook at the Paris Cookbook Fair one year. In recent times, her agendas are promoting good gut health and upcycling of sidestreams normally discarded in the food chain.

My children have settled down in London and established their own careers – Pak Seng has set up a boutique investment fund and Oi Leng has founded a co-working ladies' club. And I have six grandchildren, some taller than me and at college age, and others a little younger. But the love for travel continues to burn in me, just like the day when I flew over the Pacific Ocean for the first time, eager to start a new phase of my life in America as a teenager.

Chapter 2
MY AMERICAN ODYSSEY

From September 1964 to June 1971, I spent seven years in the USA, completing my last two years of high school followed by five years of tertiary education. During my student days in the 1960s, airfares were prohibitively expensive, so most of my travelling was by car and bus.

Since then, I have been back and forth to North America and was even posted to Texas for two years in the mid-1990s, making my stay in the US a good nine years.

From Sandakan To San Francisco

Today, one can fly from Sandakan to San Francisco with a minimum of two transit stops, but back in 1964, I had to take a more circuitous route involving five flights. The first was a short flight from Sandakan to Kota Kinabalu on 13 September. I remember having dinner and spending a night with my parents in Borneo Hotel located on Tanjung Aru Beach. The following day was my 15th birthday, and my mother and I flew from Kota Kinabalu to Singapore. After an overnight stay, we made our way to the American Embassy on 15 September to obtain the US entry visa stamped onto my British passport[1]. From Singapore, my mother and I flew to Hong Kong so that she could buy me winter clothing which was not available in Sandakan.

Thus my American odyssey actually started with the flight on 19 September 1964 (five days after my 15th birthday) on a Pan American Airways Boeing 707 from Hong Kong to San Francisco. I was in the

---

1 I held a British passport because I was born in Hong Kong, a British colony until 1997.

window seat, with two Chinese ladies from Hong Kong allotted the middle and aisle seats. They did not realise that I was Cantonese, and as soon as they had boarded, they started arguing in my native dialect over which of them should take the less desirable middle seat – next to the stranger, a 15-year-old kid sporting a crew cut. Eventually, the elder of the two mustered up sufficient courage and sat down next to me.

Early during the flight, I had an urge to visit the restroom. I rose from my seat and said to my reluctant travel companions – in my best Cantonese – "Excuse me, may I pass through?"

They were both dumbstruck and red-faced as I edged past them. When I returned, I was greeted with profuse apologies. Perhaps it was my hairstyle that had led them to assume I was from a neighbouring country, the males of which were quite likely to molest them at the first opportunity, and of course, the seat next to me represented a danger zone!

It turned out that the ladies were emigrating to the US and were not proficient in English. The plane made a short transit in Honolulu, Hawaii, where I cleared the immigration formalities of entering the US, after which we continued to our final destination. Towards the end of the journey, I took self-righteous pleasure in helping them complete their customs and immigration forms.

Senior High School

Upon arrival in San Francisco, I was met by my guardian Auntie Laddie. She worked as a stenographer in Fairchild Industries, and her husband, Uncle Wilson, worked in the Hoover Institution and Library within Stanford University. They lived in a new house in the middle-class suburb of Los Altos, not far from Sunnyvale, the heart of Silicon Valley.

I was quickly immersed into the American lifestyle[2] on the day that I arrived, starting with hamburgers, hotdogs, French fries and sodas at the local county fair. My guardians also asked a neighbour's son to escort me to the school bus pick-up point on my first trip to Homestead High

---

2 I also had to adjust to the US customary units of measurement (e.g., inch, foot, mile, pound, degree Fahrenheit) and the American English vocabulary.

School on the following Monday morning. That was how I made my first American friend – Ted Thoman.

Although Ted was one year my junior in school, he invited me to join him and his friends on Friday nights to watch the Homestead Mustangs football team in action. We would go to an ice-cream parlour after the game for an ice-cream float and revel around town in his friend's small Renault car.

Much later, when I went to university in another state, I heard that Ted had taken a different route; he was drafted and sent as a US Army helicopter pilot to the Vietnam War. Preferring not to bear arms, Ted flew with Casualty Evacuation Helicopters. We kept in touch via post but about two years later, in response to a letter I wrote to him, I received a letter from his mother, saying that her son had died when his helicopter was shot down. Many years down the road, I visited the Vietnam Veterans Memorial in Washington, where I found his name. R.I.P., Ted.

I also made friends with an American boy named Mike, who lived across the street with his baby bulldog Malcolm. Mike introduced me to his hobbies of collecting coins as well as Pepsi-Cola bottle caps. Pepsi was running a promotional campaign then, whereby the inside of each cap featured a picture of a player from the National Football League (NFL) all-stars. At that time, there were only 14 teams in the NFL, made up of two Conferences of seven teams each. A full collection of the all-stars bottle caps would allow one to redeem a genuine football.

One day, when I was hanging about Auntie Laddie's house, I noticed some snow-capped mountains yonder. I asked Mike if he would accompany me to hike over to those mountains since I had never felt snow before. He agreed and we set off, with just the clothes on our back. After hiking for an hour over some open fields, it was obvious to us that we could never reach the snow on foot, since it had to have been more than a hundred miles (160 km) away.

To keep in touch with my family in the days before the invention of the Internet and messaging apps, I made the occasional (and very expensive) long-distance call. There was no telephone land line linking Sandakan to the outside world. My calls from America were so scratchy that my parents told me not to call home unless it was absolutely necessary, as my calls would only cause them anxiety when they were unable to hear me clearly. Instead, my father instructed me to write home an aerogramme once a week. The additional requirement was that it had to be written in Chinese, or he would not remit my allowance over.

Because of her failing health, Auntie Laddie was unable to take care of me, so after just one semester I had to transfer out of Homestead High School to a private boarding school. Little did I know then that a couple of years later, Homestead would have a new student by the name of Steve Jobs. Looking back, I found a photo of Steve Wozniak in my yearbook, so half an Apple was still a good omen!

The all-boys boarding school that I went to was Menlo School. It was very small, with fewer than 400 students spread over six grades. There were very strict rules for boarders; we were allowed to leave the campus only on weekends, and outings were restricted to just two nearby towns – with the proviso that we had to be back in the dormitory no later than 9 p.m. sharp. This meant leaving the local cinema at 8.45 p.m. even when the movie was still running. I remember the other patrons laughing as a group of around thirty of us stood up in unison and quickly filed out of the cinema hall whilst a Peter Sellers movie was still running.

I noticed a big difference between public and private schools. At Homestead, the students were there because education was compulsory until the age of 18; some of them really had no desire to attend classes. The teachers often made us grade each other's test papers. Once, someone in class raised his hand and asked the teacher, "How do I grade the true/false questions when Tom puts his answers as follows?"

1) A 5) A
2) B 6) B
3) C 7) C
4) D 8) D

It was obvious Tom did not even bother to read the questions when doing the test.

Over at Menlo, things were very different. As it was a college prep school, the tuition was very expensive (costing as much as a college education), and the students were there because their parents expected them to get a good education. Out of the fifty students in my class, only one did not graduate but he went on to be an actor in Hollywood. Close to 20% went on to graduate from Stanford University, one of the top universities in the country.

My first trip out of the San Francisco Bay Area happened over the Easter holidays in 1965, seven months after my arrival in America. I was invited by my roommate Bill to spend the holidays with his family in Colorado. Bill's father was a doctor and the family owned a log cabin up in the Breckenridge Mountains. That was my first experience with snow and there was a lot of it.

The cabin had no electricity, and to keep warm, we dug into the three-foot deep snow to retrieve some logs for the fireplace. We survived on sandwiches and milk. On the second day, Bill's younger brother suited me up and took me to the peak of the Breckenridge ski slopes by chairlift. Not having skied in my whole life, I only made it down to the bottom of the slopes just before they were closed for the day. On the third day, Bill decided to send me to the ski school for some lessons.

Soon, summer came. Together with three friends who were also from Sabah, we drove around southern California looking for summer jobs to earn some pocket money. We ended up in Santa Paula as citrus pickers for Sunkist. We stayed in wooden barracks-like dormitories for US$1[3] a night. For US$3 more, we could get three meals a day. This was my introduction to home-cooked Mexican food, provided by the foreman's wife. The spiciness of Mexican food reminded me of the food back home.

One day, we went to the orchard to work as usual, but no one was around. We realised belatedly that it was Labor Day, an American public

---

3   In the 1960s, the approximate exchange rate was US$1 to S$3.60.

holiday. So we filled the boot of the car with freshly picked oranges and drove to Los Angeles to visit friends, passing them dozens of oranges.

Later that year, I was invited by a maternal cousin, John Kuo, to spend the Christmas and New Year holidays with him in Phoenix, Arizona. He was 11 years older than me, and his father and my mother were siblings.

John was single and working as an engineer in Motorola. He treated me well and taught me how to perform household chores, such as washing dishes and vacuuming the floor.

During those two weeks, we took a road trip as he wanted to show me around his state. Firstly, we drove north to Monument Valley in southern Utah. Then we headed east to visit the Four Corners Monument, where the states of Arizona, Colorado, New Mexico and Utah converge – the only such place in the US where using your two hands and feet, you could claim to be in four states at the same time! On the way back to Phoenix, we passed through the Petrified Forest and the Painted Desert. Lastly, it was on to the Meteor Crater where one could still buy a small piece of a meteorite that impacted this exact spot on earth 50,000 years ago. Before I went back to school after the New Year, John also took me to see the bright lights of Las Vegas where we spent a night.

In the summer of 1966, I completed my high school education. Graduation day arrived, a happy occasion for all. We marched onto the lawn where the graduation ceremony was being held, but there was no music. Someone started humming the well-known "Pomp and Circumstance March" melody, and in no time we all joined in, bringing many a giggle and much laughter.

I had been accepted by Purdue University in Indiana and was due to start my college education in September. My plan for the summer holidays was to fly up to the Canadian city of Vancouver for a short stay with my father's older brother, Uncle no. 4 四伯 (Lui Chak Yung 雷澤鏞) – also known as Uncle Chak – and then head to Indiana after that.

Auntie Laddie and Uncle Wilson asked me what I would like as a graduation present. Quick as a flash, I replied, "A six-pack of Colt 45 malt liquor, please" – my favourite beer. This was a time that pre-dated US departure security checks. However, passengers arriving in Canada would be subjected to customs checks. So I hatched a plan to consume all six cans of the amber liquid en route, but as I was 16 years old and below the legal age of alcohol consumption[4], I had to drink my beer out of public view. This was accomplished by popping in and out of toilet stalls at the airport, and was greatly helped by a stopover in Seattle where I chugged the last two cans of beer in the toilet of the Space Needle, which had been built in 1962 for the Seattle World's Fair.

Uncle Chak migrated to Canada before the Second World War, so I had never met him before. Besides doing some real estate brokerage, he also owned a rice mill business packing rice into 5-kg and 10-kg cloth sacks. These sacks were printed with floral designs and the old folks in Vancouver actually made boxer shorts out of them after they had finished the rice.

Also in Vancouver at that time was Uncle no. 5 五伯 (Lui Chak Chuen 雷澤荃) – also known as Uncle Richard – who ran a provision shop in Chinatown belonging to my grandfather. He was a divorcee and had a daughter, Lorena, living in New York.

I met Uncle Chak and his family for the first time, and was introduced to his wife Auntie Irene, and my cousins David and his younger brother Philip, who was born just a month before me.

Philip was both a musician and a sportsman – he was an accomplished violinist as well as the wide-receiver on his school's football team. He was so musically talented that when his father brought home a second-hand piano, he simply sat down and began improvising and playing, without any training. After graduating from the University of British Columbia with a major in Mathematics, he went on to earn a PhD from the Juilliard School of Music in New York.

---

4 The minimum legal age for alcohol consumption in the United States is 21 years old.

Subsequently, Philip settled down in New York and started an educational software company that later also produced cyber security software. I have since lost touch with him, but when I visited him in New York many years ago, he mentioned that he would like to go back to composing music one day.

By way of contrast, and to keep me gainfully occupied, Uncle Richard offered me a part-time job as a delivery boy at his shop. The delivery truck was driven by a refugee from China who had escaped to Hong Kong by swimming across the river separating Shenzhen from the New Territories in Kowloon. I discovered that he was a *taiji* master who ran a studio teaching the martial art after his deliveries were done, so I took lessons from him. A few years later, I learnt that he had become the Grand Master of the North American Taiji Association.

During my short stay in Canada, I was pleasantly surprised that the people there were generally friendlier. One day, I found an old 1949 calendar hanging on a wall in the shop's basement. That was the year of my birth and I took it as a propitious sign of things to come into my life.

College Years

At the end of summer, I thanked my relatives for their hospitality and made my way to Indiana with two suitcases to commence the tertiary stage of my education. For the bulk of the journey, I travelled by Greyhound bus, first from Vancouver to Chicago. The bus made only a few stops along the way for us to take a toilet break or grab a sandwich.

The Canadian section of the journey took me through the southern part of British Columbia to Alberta, Saskatchewan and Winnipeg, Manitoba. Along the way, the bus passed through the Nicolum Valley in British Columbia, where the Hope Landslide had taken place a year earlier. In 1965, an estimated 47 million cubic metres of rock and mud wiped out a section of the Hope-Princeton Highway, burying four motorists.

From Winnipeg, the bus turned south, crossing the border into the US to Fargo, North Dakota and finally east to Chicago, passing through Minneapolis and Milwaukee. Upon arrival 56 hours later, I bade a fond farewell to the faithful plug of chewing gum that had kept me company for the whole trip. My final destination, Purdue University at West

Lafayette, Indiana, was just a few short hours from Chicago by another Greyhound bus.

On my 17th birthday, I attended my first class at the university. Freshman orientation was a novel experience for me: I had to know the number of seats in the Purdue Music Hall, the number of stone slabs around John Purdue's grave on campus, and even the number of holes in the urinals in the dormitory. I stayed in the same dormitory throughout my undergraduate years while I participated in intramural sports, playing table tennis and pitching on the softball team. I also worked part-time at the dormitory dining hall to earn some pocket money.

At the beginning of the first semester, I was contacted by Professor Will Schalliol and his wife Ilyff. They had signed up for a programme to be my "foster parents"; the aim was to make foreign students like me feel more at home as an undergraduate in Purdue. They invited me to their house for dinner periodically. Years after I left Purdue, they visited me in Singapore twice. I reciprocated their kindness by driving them up to Kuala Lumpur for a short trip.

As soon as the first semester had ended, I hit the road again, this time to Dallas, Texas. By then, my cousin John had moved there to work for his new employer, Texas Instruments. Once again, he kindly invited me to spend Christmas and the New Year with him, and I agreed readily.

I was exploring my transport options to Dallas when I learnt that our college football team had won the right to play in the prestigious annual Rose Bowl at Pasadena, California on New Year's Day. Thus I was able to share a ride with a fellow dorm-dweller who was heading out to attend the big match. As it happened, the road we took was the iconic Route 66, a.k.a. the "Will Rogers Highway", the "Main Street of America" or the "Mother Road". My driver was kind enough to make a detour and drop me off in Dallas before he re-joined Route 66.

In Dallas, John took me sightseeing, driving down the "main drag" and Elm Street. After parking the car, we walked over to the Grassy Knoll, then to the sixth floor of a building housing the Texas School Book Depository. This was the spot from which shots that killed the 35th President of the USA, John F Kennedy, were fired.

Alas, John did not consider driving me to nearby Fort Worth to the historic cattle market and stockyards or, better still, to watch a rodeo. Instead, he led me astray! One morning, he drove me to a deserted car park and told me to take the driver's seat. An impromptu driving lesson[5] took place on the spot. He showed me how to recognise the lines of the parking space through the rear and front windscreens, before watching me drive around the lot for a few more minutes. Then he declared that I was fully qualified to drive us north to Kansas City, Missouri, a mere 500 miles (805 km) away! At seventeen, those few minutes were the first and only experience I had behind the steering wheel of an automobile, and I was about to commit a criminal offence…

The journey to Kansas City, passing through Oklahoma City and Wichita, was uneventful, but the return run was a different matter. A loud bang suddenly erupted from the engine. From the rear-view mirror, I saw bits and pieces of engine parts scattered on the road. Then the engine cut out, so I had to pull to the side of the road. A check of the engine compartment showed that the crankshaft pulley that drove the alternator and hydraulic pumps had disappeared – there remained just a stump. We deduced that the pulley had broken loose from the external portion of the crankshaft and had bounced around the bonnet, knocking into and detaching various components. So, with no power driving the alternator or cooling fan, we were rendered immobile, stranded. Fortunately, a passing tow truck came to our aid and towed us to a nearby service station where we had a new pulley installed, so we could resume our drive back to Dallas.

During the 1966/67 school year, I was introduced to a special beer ritual during a weekend visit at a dorm mate's house near the Indiana–

---

5 Funnily enough, when I brought up this incident many years later to Marie, John's younger sister, she said that it was exactly how John had taught her to drive.

Ohio state line. This was basically a dash across the state line into Ohio where it was legal for 18- to 21-year-olds to consume beer, albeit no more than 3.2% alcohol. The alcohol limit was just as well, because the ritual also included road racing on the return trip, half-drunk. As we were close to the Kentucky state line, I hopped across to Kentucky for half a day. Before the school year was up, I had also explored the southern region of Michigan.

I was particularly close to a few Purdue students from Hong Kong. Wally was a year ahead of me. We had very similar interests in music and studies (engineering). We were both Bob Dylan fans, and we became very good friends quickly. David was another dorm mate who was a year ahead of me. His room was just down the hall, and he always had a bottle of whisky in his room. And there was Wing Kee. We were caught drinking beer in his room once, and were almost kicked out of the dormitory. But since we were both foreign students, they let us off with a warning.

In the summer of 1967, my parents decided that a trip back home would be good for me, as they had not seen me for almost three years. This would entail air travel from San Francisco across the Pacific Ocean to Hong Kong, then on to Sandakan by steamer. It turned out that Wally and David were heading home to Hong Kong on the same flight. We agreed to make separate arrangements to get to San Francisco, after which we would meet at the airport for the flight to Hong Kong, with a transit in Japan[6].

I shared a ride with several Chinese students who were driving from Purdue to San Francisco. They took an alternative way to Route 66, via what is now designated as Interstate 80. This highway runs through Davenport and Council Bluffs, both in Iowa; Omaha, Nebraska; Cheyenne, Wyoming; Salt Lake City, Utah; and Reno, Nevada before coasting down to Frisco.

As we drove over the Rockies, the car began misfiring, so we pulled off the highway and stopped at the first gas station. After a brief check, the mechanic advised us that the problem was a cracked distributor cap.

---

6   See Chapter 6 "East Asia" for my adventures in the Land of the Rising Sun.

As he did not have a replacement in stock, he drove to a nearby stockist, returned, duly replaced it – and handed us a bill that we felt was a grossly unreasonable sum. We rejected the new cap and told him to put back the old one, which he begrudgingly obliged.

However, as we continued on our way, the engine began performing worse than before. After another stop and upon close inspection, we found that the mechanic had replaced the sparkplug wires in the wrong firing order – no doubt out of a deliberate spite over the cracked-cap dispute. We corrected the fault and continued on our journey, mostly downhill. And this being the summer of '67 and at the height of flower power, we were accompanied by the radio blaring out Scott McKenzie singing "If you're going to San Francisco…"

I spent summer in Sandakan in the new house where my parents had moved into. After I returned to Purdue in the fall, my dorm mate Mick invited me to spend the Thanksgiving holidays with his family in Pittsburgh, Pennsylvania. The route there took us through Dayton and Columbus, both in Ohio; and Wheeling, West Virginia. To round off a great weekend, his parents treated us to a live Beach Boys concert!

In my second year at Purdue, I had a new roommate, Dave. He was a burly guy who would sometimes guzzle down a pint of vodka and go out onto the highway on a motorbike to chase semi-trucks. His family originally lived in Indiana, but his father, Mr Rogers, was transferred to the Bahamas to be the general manager of a cement factory.

During fall, Mrs Rogers came up to Purdue to visit Dave. In order to look like someone who lived in the sunny Caribbean, she applied suntan bronzer. The problem was, she did not wash her hands immediately after application, so her palms were stained with the bronzer too.

While chatting with us, she found out that the dormitory would be closed during the Christmas holidays, and I would have nowhere to go. So she invited me to spend the holidays with them in the Bahamas. My budget was such that direct air travel was not an option. I managed to persuade Dave to join me on a bus trip from West Lafayette to Miami, followed by a short flight from there to Grand Bahama.

The bus took us through Louisville, Kentucky; Nashville, Tennessee; Atlanta, Georgia; and Jacksonville, Florida – before arriving at Miami. During the journey through Kentucky, I communicated with an almost mute passenger who looked distressed. He signalled to me that while he was napping, someone had stolen his hearing aid. I was able to placate him via hand signals (although I would have had preferred using my hands on the creep who took his hearing aid).

At the Bahamas, I learned to water ski in the crystal-clear calm waters of the lagoons[7]. When the vacation came to an end, Dave's parents spoilt me by purchasing a plane ticket for the full return journey – which, of course, was very much appreciated.

Dave joined a fraternity a year later, and I heard that he dropped out of college after his second year and went to California to seek his fortune as a stuntman.

In the spring of 1968, Barry Green, who was in many of my aero-nautical engineering classes, invited me to his home in Detroit, Michigan. While there, we drove over to Ann Arbor to visit the University of Michigan campus, passing through Toledo on the return journey. We saw sand dunes along Lake Erie and made a stop to go skinny-dipping in the lake.

When summer came, I decided to head out to San Diego to visit my Sabahan friends who were studying at San Diego State University. They were the same friends who picked oranges with me at the Sunkist orchard three summers ago.

---

7 See Chapter 10 "The West Indies" for my adventures in the Bahamas.

By then, I had obtained my driver's licence[8], so all I needed was a car for the road trip. Wally told me that he had booked a flight to visit his brother Joe in Pasadena, a suburb of Los Angeles. I thought I would make Los Angeles my first stop and spend some time there with Wally, before I travelled to San Diego to see my other friends.

David decided to join me for the road trip. To save on transport and car rental costs, he contacted some "Drive Away" companies, asking if they needed a car to be driven out and delivered to California. One company responded, saying they had a car in Chicago to be delivered to its owner, an executive who had relocated to Las Vegas. And in Las Vegas, they would very probably have another car for delivery to Los Angeles. This fitted in with my plan to go to Los Angeles, and later San Diego. So David and I agreed to take on the "Drive Away" car project.

Wally asked us to help him deliver a rifle to Joe when we reached Los Angeles, since it was on our way and it was inconvenient for him to check in a rifle on his flight. We agreed readily, not knowing what adventures this special delivery would lead to.

After checking our driving licences, the company gave us US$100 for fuel and waved us off. The drive was uneventful until we came into New Mexico, when we were pulled over by the Highway Patrol. We were a soft target as our vehicle had no licence plates, and we were made to follow the highway patrolman to a nearby town hall. Here, we were slapped with nine charges, including the transporting of merchandise through state borders without a valid permit and having no valid medical certification. Fortunately, they did not search the car; the rifle would have had been the subject of an additional raft of misdemeanours.

The solution was to get the "Drive-Away" company in Chicago to remit the fine to the court, after which the car would be released to us. The lady judge, emphasising the seriousness of the case, told us of a similar occurrence the previous Friday when a college student was apprehended but was unable to get his "Drive-Away" company to remit the fine as their office was closed for the weekend. He had to wait

---

8 My foster father Prof. Schalliol had kindly lent me his car when I took my driver's licence test.

until Monday morning – and thus could not attend his own wedding scheduled for the weekend!

To rub it in, the lady judge told us that we should have been locked up while waiting for the remittance transaction, but that we were lucky because all the available cells were fully occupied by "drunken Indians", a.k.a. Native Americans. Thankfully, she was kind enough to allow us to wander off down the street to grab a bite while waiting for the fine to be paid. As we left the courtroom, I asked her where we could find rattlesnake meat, since, being Chinese we were known to eat anything. However, there was no restaurant serving rattlesnake in that town. After returning from lunch, I casually asked her how she became a judge, to which she replied, "By running for office and being elected." I learnt a lot that day.

After the money to pay the fine was received by the court, David and I were "released" and allowed to continue our journey. Having learnt our lesson, we decided to pull into a rest stop just outside of town and waited until nightfall. Under the cloak of darkness, our lack of licence plates was less likely to be spotted by the Highway Patrol. Arriving at the junction where we left Route 66, to head north to Vegas, we had a choice of two routes. One would take us to the Hoover Dam, whereas the other would take us further south, crossing the Colorado River.

We stopped at a gas station and asked the pump attendant which of the two routes was more remote, and less likely for us to encounter the Highway Patrol. He viewed us with some suspicion – I was sure he had decided that we were running away from the law (which we were) – but he recommended the Hoover Dam route nevertheless. Locals in this part of America were unfamiliar with, and had little contact with Asian aliens, to the extent that the so-called Chinese restaurant where we had lunch earlier that day did not even supply chopsticks!

Arriving at our Las Vegas destination, we discovered, as we had suspected, that there was no car available for delivery to Los Angeles. The company suggested that we hang around for a while, and...who knows...one might turn up? We opted to travel to Los Angeles by Greyhound bus instead.

To avoid unwanted attention, we obtained the bus driver's permission to store the rifle in the lower luggage compartment, and off we went. During the journey, we heard the breaking news that Robert Kennedy had been shot in Los Angeles that very night. As soon as we arrived at the Los Angeles Greyhound station, we immediately headed for the locker area where we planned to store the rifle.

Alas, the rifle was too long to fit into any of the lockers. So David and I were forced to take turns in nursing the firearm, making toilet trips, buying food and drink, and making phone calls to Joe until, to our great relief, he came to collect his rifle.

But the fun was just beginning. In the evening, we met up with Wally who was already in town. He brought us to his friend's house to rest for the night. Feeling really tired after the long drive and bus ride, I passed out on a comfy carpet in the living room.

Soon, I awoke to the sound of shouting and heavy footsteps – the house was being raided by the police! They were after drug dealers who were upstairs in a bedroom re-packaging dope before pushing it to local druggies. The dealers exited via a window with the cops in hot pursuit, leaving us alone – phew.

David did not remain in California with us; he went to Las Vegas to try his luck at the casinos, and returned to Purdue on his own.

In sharp contrast, for the remainder of that summer, I was a good humour man, driving an Eskimo Pie ice-cream van to peddle ice popsicles to kiddies in San Diego. I developed a very mechanical wave and stiff smile for every kid I met on my route, while listening to an electronic 15-second-long Eskimo Pie jingle over and over throughout the day….

One good thing that came out of this job was that hundreds of coins would pass through my hands every day. I was able to add some not-so-common coins to my coin collection, which started – thanks to my neighbour Mike – when I was living in Los Altos.

At summer's end, Wally and I drove back to Indiana in his newly acquired car, an Oldsmobile Cutlass. We decided to leave Los Angeles at 9 p.m. so that we would cross the Mojave Desert at night to avoid the blazing heat of the day. When in New Mexico, we came across a roadside stall selling watermelons, the size of which I had never seen before. I was

MEXICAN ESCAPADES

Of course, when one had spent a number of years in the US, it was quite impossible not to have travelled to the neighbouring country of Mexico. Being a 19-year-old young man, I too had to pay a visit to the notorious border town of Tijuana. After getting our pay on a Friday night, I drove down to check out the scene with Cheong Sang (one of my friends from Sabah) and a fellow ice-cream seller, a Mexican who could speak the language.

We hit a few bars and were lured into a compound by some *señoritas*, but a few burly guys appeared from out of nowhere and made us take out our wallets. They cleaned out most of our cash, but were kind enough to leave us with US$3 each, presumably for the bus ride back to San Diego (thankfully, they did not know that we had come to Tijuana in our car).

Since we were already in Mexico, we decided to make the best of the situation and drive down to the port city of Ensenada. While cruising on the foggy coastal road at 60 mph (96 kmh), the hood of the 1955 Chevy suddenly popped open and acted as an air brake. Luckily, there was no structural damage, and we were able to close the bonnet and drive back to San Diego[9].

compelled to make a purchase, and chose one that weighed in at an impressive 35 lbs – or close to 16 kg. The only available space in the car for this giant was on the floor, between the feet of the front passenger – me.

The rest of the trip was uneventful, until we reached the Brown County State Park in Indiana. We hit wet weather on a winding country road and our car skidded off and crashed into a small drain. Regaining composure, I found that during the accident, I had somehow managed to shove both feet right through my treasured watermelon.

The park was dark, it was raining, and in 1968, mobile phones were a long way off from invention. But we were lucky; about 300 yards (280 m) ahead was a gas station – visible under the only streetlight we had seen for the past hour.

---

9 Those encounters did not mar my impression of Mexico. Many years later, my wife Kwan and I bought a fractional ownership of a villa in the city of Cabo San Lucas, which we visited regularly.

There was, as expected, a pay-phone booth at the station but neither of us had any coins with which to call for AAA assistance. Trying my luck, I checked the coin return slot – and bingo – therein lay a shiny dime which had to have been placed there by an angel. The AAA sent a tow truck, and our car was duly pulled out of the drain, in roadworthy condition. The driver lectured us on the local road conditions: as the rain had started only recently, oil was literally floating on top of the wet road surface, making the conditions especially hazardous. Thanking him, we resumed our drive to West Lafayette which, thankfully, was without further drama. We discarded what was left of the watermelon as we were quite shaken up and in no mood to eat something that bore my footprints.

After my first two years in Purdue, I received some good news – I was awarded a foreign student scholarship, so my tuition was free for the rest of my undergraduate education.

For Christmas and the New Year, I drove with Wally to New Jersey and stayed with another brother of his. Paul worked in Wall Street but lived in the New Jersey suburbs. Conveniently, we boarded the train every other day to the Big Apple, New York City. This was the America I knew before I came here to live and study, having seen the movie *West Side Story*! We went sightseeing and hung around Greenwich Village with the hippies.

In the summer of 1969, I decided once again to head out west, this time to Seattle. For my travelling companion, I chose Sze Yin, another of my closest friends in Purdue. He was a few years older and also from Hong Kong. A biology major, Sze Yin enjoyed classical music and lived one floor above me in the dormitory.

We drove through Sioux City, Iowa; and Mount Rushmore, South Dakota; on to Yellowstone Park, Wyoming; Butte, Montana; and Coeur D'Alene, Idaho, before arriving in Seattle. Whilst travelling through

Yellowstone, the radio announced the horoscope predictions for the day. Mine? I was destined to meet with an accident, if on the road. Undaunted, and to prove them wrong, I kept driving till midnight – "So there!" I crowed.

But oops, I had forgotten about the time change from Mountain Standard Time to Pacific Standard Time – there was still another hour to go before midnight. With due care and attention, I managed that extra hour without a problem…phew.

After we arrived in Seattle, the first thing we did was to buy a newspaper to comb through the classified ads for lodging. We rented a room each on the second floor of a house from an old couple.

Both of us found summer jobs through an employment agency: I was a cook's helper in a Chinese American restaurant, responsible for grilling hamburgers and making sandwiches, while Sze Yin worked as a chef in a sandwich bar downtown.

Before the lunch rush hours, I had to wash and cut all the vegetables and prepare the *mise en place*. After the lunch service, I might be tasked to make egg drop soup for dinner or a few hundred spring-roll wrappers for the week. To be honest, I would love to have Sze Yin's job as the environment was much more pleasant, but the place served alcohol and I was underaged.

One day, we came back from work and was surprised to see that our 70-year-old landlady had dyed her grey hair blue and put on a pair of fishnet stockings under a mini-skirt. She told us she had bought tickets to a concert featuring the famous country music singer Tammy Wynette.

On weekends, we would drive north across the border to Vancouver, British Columbia, to visit Sze Yin's brother, who practised as a psychiatrist at the Coquitlam Mental Institution. Sze Ming kindly showed us all the scenic attractions of the region.

One weekend, when we tried to drive into Vancouver, the Canadian immigration officer refused to allow us entry because my US student visa had expired. This had never been a problem since I still had a valid I-20 form, which confirmed my status as a bona fide US visitor student. To solve the problem, I was told to visit the US Embassy in Vancouver, present my passport and I-20 form, and receive a student pass update.

BANK HEIST

One fine Monday morning in autumn that year, I dropped by an on-campus bank to cash a cheque. I was being attended to by a lady-teller when a man wearing oversized sunglasses suddenly appeared alongside her. Pointing a gun at her head, he told her to move away from her station. I glanced over my right shoulder and saw another man, burly and wearing similar sunglasses, waving a gun at me, indicating that I should step back from the counter.

He rounded up all of us customers and bank employees alike to a corner, told us to lie face down on the floor and clasp our hands over our heads. The manager was on the telephone at that time, and I recall vividly how he ended his conversation with "Er – er Harry – I have to go now" before he joined us on the floor.

There being insufficient space for me to lie flat out, I just sat down with my hands placed behind my head. Suddenly, a thought popped into my mind: what if the guns were not real? Having come from a country where guns were a strictly controlled item, I thought what a laughingstock I would be if it transpired that I had been held up by a man brandishing a toy gun. Out of the corner of my eye, I took a close look at the gun. It was real all right, and sufficiently heavy, because the gunman let it dangle as he kept watch over us.

Meanwhile, his partner behind the counter was scooping up several bags which apparently contained the weekend's cash takings from a few of the department stores in town. He was so absorbed with what was before his eyes that he couldn't be bothered to enter the invitingly open vault. Then two guys who were lying close to me began whispering to each other. That made me uneasy, because the gunman watching over us might get nervous and start shooting. Instead, he shouted, "Shut up!", and all was quiet again.

The whole incident lasted no more than five minutes. The robbers bolted out the rear entrance where they hopped into the waiting getaway car and high-tailed out of the parking lot.

Following the standard operating procedures, the manager locked both entrances and instructed us to jot down our personal contact details. We had to wait until the police arrived – which seemed to me to be a very long time – and we were asked to provide once again our personal particulars.

At this point, a lady entered the bank and informed the police that she had noted down the getaway car's number plate. Minutes earlier, she had driven up to the bank's drive-in service window, where she was told by a man wearing large sunglasses that the bank was closed for the day. She felt that there was something fishy; she drove off, but only around the building. Then she spotted a car with its engine running in the parking lot, and so she noted down its licence plate. A few minutes later, she saw two men running out from the rear entrance with the bags of loot. The getaway car had Illinois plates, which classified this as an interstate crime, triggering the FBI's involvement.

The following day, I was visited in my dormitory by two FBI agents. They dropped in at the reception, identified themselves and asked to see me. I was not surprised when the receptionist called me to say: "The FBI is here to see you." The agents recorded my statement and handed me more than a hundred "mugshots", hoping that I could identify the robbers among them. I could not.

Around six months later, another dorm resident told me he heard on the radio that one of the robbers had been arrested. The very next day, the FBI visited me again. This time they had just 12 mugshots for me to examine. Oddly enough, I noted that five of the shots were of the same person, and the photos were dated two days earlier. The shots were taken from the front, left, right, back and top of the same person. I mentioned to the agent that I heard on the radio that they had arrested one of the robbers and perhaps these photos were of him. Unfortunately, I couldn't verify that, as the photos were of a man who had a beard and looked as if he had not slept for weeks.

However, from the remaining seven photos, I recognised one who re-sembled the robber who had pointed his gun at the teller and scooped up the loot. Even though he had worn large sunglasses that day, I recalled that he had high cheekbones and a pointed jaw. The FBI then told me that I was the only one out of the 11 people in the bank that morning who had correctly identified the man they named as "the other robber", a.k.a. the mastermind of the heist. They would not confide in me how they knew that this was indeed the guy but admitted that their biggest problem was to navigate through the many discrepancies of the eyewitnesses' descriptions of the robbers. Apparently, the robbers' height ranged from 5'9" (1.75 m) to 6'4" (1.93 m), and they weighed anything from 150 lbs (68 kg) to 230 lbs (104 kg)!

Two weeks later, the radio news reported that the arrested robber was shot dead in a Canadian motel. Apparently, he had skipped bail. He was 22 years old, just two years older than me.

However…there was a problem: the US Embassy was closed on weekends. Stuck in no-man's land, we had to U-turn back towards the US immigration office at the Seattle–Vancouver border. Here, the officer queried our strange action – we had technically exited the US – but did not go anywhere! After hearing our explanation and the Canadian officer's concern that we might be barred from re-entering the US, the American officer responded – jokingly, I think – with "What makes you think I'll let you back in?"

But thankfully, he did. Since summer was coming to an end, and to avoid any more hassle, Sze Yin and I decided to give British Columbia a miss for the rest of our time in Seattle. The following weekend being the Labor Day holiday, we took the Pacific Coast road south to Portland, Oregon, and then drove along the Columbia River to Pendleton[10], before heading north back to Seattle.

This stretch of coastline along Highway 101 between Seattle and Portland has had to be the most scenic drive that I have ever experienced, with wide swathes of beaches, and cliffs with cottages perched atop. One could truly feel the power of the mighty, roaring Pacific Ocean, creating a mist from the ocean spray. Locals on horseback were riding up and down the beaches, and the cottages on the clifftops had smoking chimneys – the scene was right out of a fairy-tale picture book.

Sze Yin eventually settled down in Vancouver after college. We still keep in touch, and he came to Singapore to visit me in 2012; I also have a meal with him whenever I drop by Vancouver.

Although I played soccer for the school team at Menlo, I did not try out for Purdue's soccer team initially, because joining the team meant having to attend 2-hour training sessions, five times a week during soccer season. My academic results took priority. Only in my final year when I knew that my grades and credit hours were good enough for me to graduate, I decided to try out for the university soccer team. I made it on the team as the centre half. During soccer season, I

---

10 Pendleton is where the world-famous Pendleton woollen shirts originated. The American rock band the Beach Boys used to be known as the Pendletones – they took their name from the wool plaid shirts, and made the shirts a fashion trend in the 1960s.

enjoyed travelling to other universities on weekends to play against their respective teams.

Sometime later, my parents sent me a sum of money but it was remitted to a bank in Indianapolis, 66 miles (106 km) away. The bank teller in Sandakan probably didn't know any better, thinking that Indiana was not very big. The Indianapolis branch requested me to show up in person to collect the funds, so I grabbed my passport (in case the bank needed it for identification purposes), jumped on a Greyhound bus and took the 1½-hour coach ride there.

After I had collected the remittance and taken a quick meal, I was about to walk back to the bus station when I suddenly realised that my passport was no longer on me.

I had to have dropped it somewhere. The bank and bus station were both in downtown Indianapolis, so in pure panic mode, I dashed back and retraced my steps to the bank. Lo and behold! My passport was lying face down on the pavement, and yes, in downtown Indianapolis, the capital of the state of Indiana.

With the college and dormitory closed for the Christmas holidays, I holed up in a nearby apartment with my good friend Wing Kee. Before he came to study in Purdue, Wing Kee stayed in Thailand for a year. He loved to cook and eat his own meals, so after two years of dorm life, he moved out and rented an apartment with three other students because the apartment would have a kitchen.

At that time, his brother Wing To and a cousin Wing Cheung[11] were both attending universities in other American states, and they visited us for the festive break.

---

11 Wing Kee's family also followed the traditional Chinese naming convention of giving all the sons in the same generation the same middle name.

One bright December morning, someone casually asked, "So what are we going to do today?" Meant simply as a joke, I replied, "Let's go to Miami." There was a spontaneous positive reaction from the trio, and within a short span of time, having packed essentials like a change of clothes and shaving gear, we were on the road in Wing Kee's Chevrolet Corvair, heading for the state of Florida.

But first, it was a quick trip to the local Kentucky Fried Chicken restaurant to pack lunch. We bumped into a fresh-off-the-boat graduate student from China, and we told him about our lunch plans. He advised us in all seriousness that we might become quite famished as Kentucky was so many miles, and hours, away!

I drove for 16 hours straight, and tiredness began to set in at around 2 a.m. I asked for someone to take over the wheel so that I could grab a few winks. Wing Kee obliged. Within seconds, we were almost creamed by a truck as we re-entered the freeway. Wing Kee assured us that his Thai driver's licence was not bought, and he had actually passed the driving test. I explained that I would not be able to sleep with so lousy a driver at the wheel, so we pulled over and parked while I slept for an hour.

At 3 a.m., I took the driver's seat again and continued driving till we arrived in Jacksonville, three hours later. Here we sat on the beach to watch the sunrise and enjoyed, appropriately, surf-and-turf open sandwiches for breakfast before continuing on our journey, arriving in Miami at 4 p.m.

That night, we booked a motel room. Our modus operandi was to check in with just two persons at the reception counter and then sneak in the other two after we were given the room keys. Since all of my travel companions agreed that I had earned it, I was allotted a bed.

Over the next few days, we toured the region, including a trip south into the Florida Keys. Initially, we were going to drive all the way out to Key West, 160 miles (260 km) away, but having seen the same scenery of beaches for the first two hours, we camped out on the beach that night and went back to Miami the following day.

On our return trip to Indiana, we made brief stops in Alabama and Tennessee. Close to midnight, we ran into a blizzard in Kentucky. Visibility was so low that I blindly followed the taillights of a semi-container truck ahead of us. As the fuel level in the car dropped lower, all the other occupants in the car urged me to turn off the highway to take on more gasoline. I was reluctant because I was not sure if I could get another navigational aid later, such as another semi-container truck to follow. However, I was outvoted.

After refuelling, I re-entered the highway, and as I had expected, there was no other traffic on the road. I also had a lot of trouble steering the Corvair steadily on the road, for the same reason that Ralph Nader successfully campaigned to force General Motors to stop the production of the Corvair.

We gave up slipping and sliding on the icy road, and spent the night in a motel in Kentucky, using the same modus operandi as before.

Years later, Wing Kee entered politics in Hong Kong and made the big time, rising through the ranks to become one of the representatives of Hong Kong to the National People's Congress of the People's Republic of China. On my first visit to China[12] with a friend in 1982, he made arrangements for one of his factory managers to host us. We still keep in touch, always making time for each other to have a meal, when I visit Hong Kong or when he comes to Singapore.

During semester break in January 1970, I spent a week on a Native American reservation in McLoud, Oklahoma, doing social work for a tribe of indigenous American Indians. It was an opportunity for me to see how they lived and mingle with their youngsters.

Graduate School And Beyond

I graduated from Purdue in January 1970, earning a Bachelor of Science with distinction in Aeronautical Engineering. Although I was accepted by Stanford University for graduate school, I decided to stay put in Purdue for my graduate studies because I was offered a teaching assistantship where I was able to support myself financially without depending on my parents. I also wanted to be with Kwan, my then-girlfriend (and now-wife), who was still studying in Purdue.

---

12 See Chapter 6 "East Asia" for my adventures in China.

In March, I joined a few graduate students to drive around the Deep South – including visits to Gulfport and Jackson, Mississippi; and New Orleans, Louisiana. With the goal of visiting all of the 50 American states in mind and literally seeing what was on "the other side", I persuaded the group to allow me to drive over the bridge from Greenville, Mississippi into Arkansas, thus enabling me to add that state to my "visited" list.

One day, my parents decided that they had better check me out after hearing all the horror stories about the drug scene in the US. It had been three years since they last saw me; the photos I sent home disconcerted them further, because I wore my hair long. So when the summer holidays came, I took another road trip to San Francisco where I would catch a flight to Hong Kong and connect to another flight home.

After arriving in San Francisco, I met up with my old pal Wally again. At that time, he was attending graduate school at the California Institute of Technology in Pasadena. We were going to take the same charter flight to Hong Kong, so the two of us unofficially "lodged" in one of the dormitories at the University of San Francisco, which was deserted during the summer break. This covert operation was made possible via a spare dorm room key courtesy of Wally's cousin.

We brought our own pillows and crept into his cousin's old room. Before hitting the sack, we decided to shower. The bathroom had been spotless before our arrival, having been given a thorough cleaning in preparation for the arrival of students for summer school. Unfortunately, in the morning, a janitor discovered the recently soiled bathroom and immediately alerted the campus police, who started a room-to-room search for the culprits.

I awoke to a sound emanating from down the hallway, and roused Wally from his slumber. We heard the cops going into a room nearby, so the two of us grabbed our gear instinctively – with no shirts on our backs – and made a dash for the exit. They heard us when we came out of our room, and gave chase. As we were sprinting away, I asked Wally what we should do, to which he replied we should split up and head in different directions.

I ran down to the basement while Wally bolted away. Then I hid my pillow under a couch in the TV lounge and found my way out of the building. The moment that I was outside, I headed for Wally's car. I was able to break into it quickly as it was a convertible.

In the car was a U.C. Berkeley T-shirt that I had bought the day before. In a flash, I grabbed it, slipped it on and sat in the car, watching as a procession of campus police cars cruised by, presumably on a manhunt for two shirtless guys carrying pillows.

A couple of hours later, Wally returned to the car. He had been caught and the university made him pay for a new round of bathroom cleaning – and his cousin, the owner of the room key, was given a reprimand. I had avoided arrest!

I spent the summer at home in Sabah and reassured my parents that I had not turned into a hippie. Little did they know, I met a couple of American Peace Corp volunteers in Sandakan who were growing marijuana right on their porch, and I had a chance to sample some of their organic produce. When summer was over, I returned to Purdue to finish up my master's degree in aeronautical engineering. Crossing the Pacific, my flight made a technical stop in Anchorage to uplift some fuel, so I spent an hour in the airport terminal and added Alaska to my list of states visited.

In June 1971, I decided that upon graduation, I would resettle in Asia. One of my thermodynamics professors tried to convince me to stay on to do some research and write a dissertation for my doctorate. However, I was "schooled-out" by then, having attended school from the age of 3 to three months shy of 22, with no breaks in between whatsoever.

I could finally hold a can of beer in my hand legally, because out of the seven years that I spent in the US, I was under 21, the legal drinking age for six of those years. I always had to borrow an identity card from one of my older friends whenever I joined them for drinks at a bar.

Once, I was asked by a bar waitress for my identification document (I.D.) to show proof of age. She said that I was using someone else's I.D.

I decided to challenge her. "If that I.D. does not belong to me, then whose is it?"

She looked around the table of six or seven Chinese guys, and pointed to one. "It's his." Luckily, she was wrong. That guy took out his own Purdue University student card and said, "Here is mine". She accepted her mistake and dropped the matter. Truth be told, the rightful owner of the I.D. that I had borrowed was sitting just across from me! This incident goes to show that "all Chinamen look alike". Because of such surprise checks, I had to remember the birthdays of all my friends who lent me their I.D.

Taking stock of my state-visits tally, I had set foot on almost all 50 American states, apart from a few on the east coast. I still wanted to visit those states, but was not sure how I could make that happen.

Then Wally and I made plans to tour Europe[13], which involved flying out from an airport in New York. He offered to drive his convertible over from California several days before the trip to pick me up at Indiana, but he intended to leave his car in the care of his brother Joe during his absence. As Joe had moved to Florida, this meant that we would be driving from Indiana to Florida, which coincided perfectly with my dream to visit the remaining American states on my list.

So off we went. From Indiana, we drove to Baltimore, Maryland, visiting the many monuments in Washington D.C. Then we headed down to the southeastern seaboard states of Virginia, North and South Carolina, and Florida. We took the Carolinas Rural Route in the outer bank, stopping in Kitty Hawk where the first heavier-than-air powered flight took to the air, albeit for less than a minute.

Arriving in Tallahassee, Florida, we left the convertible with Joe. Then we picked up one of Joe's cars and travelled north to New England, traversing Wilmington, Delaware; Philadelphia, Pennsylvania; New Haven, Connecticut; Providence, Rhode Island; Boston, Massachusetts; Portsmouth, New Hampshire; Kittery, Maine; and finally, Killington in Vermont. And with that last stop, I had achieved my ambition of having set foot in each of the USA's fifty states – the big 50!

---

13 See Chapter 3 "Europe" for my adventures in various European countries.

To celebrate my achievement, I raised my can of beer, faced south-southwest and made a toast to the United States of America.

Ironically, after completing my graduate studies, I did not re-visit North America for the next 15 years. When I went back to the US in 1986, I really had a culture shock. In 1971, there were just three TV networks, namely NBC (Channel 4), CBS (Channel 5) and ABC (Channel 7). Turning on the TV in my hotel room in 1986, I had to figure out what all the other channels were, like ESPN (sports), CNN (news), HBO (movies), MTV (music) and other local Public Service channels. I marvelled at the remote control that allowed me to change channels without having to physically go up to the TV set and turn the dial.

New dietary (Lite) soda pop appeared on the supermarket shelves. Bacon sandwiches accompanied by lettuce and a slice of tomato were called "BLT" sandwiches. Grilled sausages served with mashed potatoes were called "Bangers and Mash". Gone were the 15-cent McDonald's hamburgers. In its place were Big Macs, Double Cheese, Quarter Pounders and endless combinations of patties.

Being a boarder during my student days in Menlo, I made some very close friends with whom I kept in touch after I had graduated. I have been going back to Menlo for our anniversary reunions: in 1991 (for the 25th anniversary), 1996 (for the 30th), 2001 (for the 35th), 2006 (for the 40th), 2011 (for the 45th) and 2016 (for the biggy, 50th). We could not meet in 2021 for the 55th anniversary because of the COVID-19 pandemic.

In 2019, I went back to Homestead High School to request for my transcript, which had the address of Auntie Laddie's house where I first stayed. I had forgotten the exact address after all these years. The house in Los Altos was only 4 km from the school. Visiting the house brought back fond memories, such as the walk home after being dropped off by the school bus. Auntie Laddie moved to a farm in southern California after living in Los Altos. I visited her several times over the years; she even made a trip to Singapore to see me.

I also spent Christmas in the Central American country Costa Rica in 1998, first in its capital San Jose, then down to Flamingo Beach on the Pacific coast. We were there with my family, and my brother-in-law and his family. We decided to hire a boat for an outing, so we drove down to a marina in our rental car and made arrangements to go out to sea the following day.

When we returned to the car park after paying a deposit for the boat, we found that someone had smashed into the front of our car. There was a note on the windscreen giving us a phone number and an address to contact. As we were in a hurry to go out for dinner and the rental car was fully insured, we did not bother to contact that person, especially since the car was still drivable.

In the morning, we went out to sea on the beautiful boat that we had rented and acquainted ourselves with the crew. The captain mentioned that the previous day had not been very good for him. Nursing a bit of a headache from a hangover, he had smashed into another car in the car park when he was backing his car out of his lot. He said that he had left a note on the windscreen of the damaged car and was waiting for the owner to contact him.

After hearing this, I quickly familiarised myself with the location of every life buoy and life jacket on board, because there was no way I could trust his piloting skills when he could not even drive a car.

CLOSE ENCOUNTERS WITH U.S. CUSTOMS & IMMIGRATION

On one of the domestic flights, my carry-on luggage was searched by a Transportation Security Administration (TSA) agent who found a 90-ml tube of toothpaste in my shaving kit. The agent only knew that passengers were allowed to bring onboard containers that were 3.4 fl oz or less, but she was not familiar with the metric equivalent. Scratching her head, she asked her supervisor standing nearby, "Hey, what is 90 ml?"

The supervisor replied, "It is less than 100 ml!" The agent said, "Are you trying to be a wise ass?" The supervisor proceeded to explain to her that *ml* is a metric measurement, and 100 ml was the carry-on limit for liquids.

* * *

On another trip, I was told to take everything out of my pockets for the full-body scanner at an airport. I did as I was told, and even performed my own little pat-down to make sure my pockets were empty. Then I stood in the machine and put my hands over my head. The TSA agent became all huffy and pulled me out of the machine, demanding to know what was in my pocket.

"Nothing is in my pocket!" I said.

"Check," the agent said. I shoved my hand in my pocket and was dismayed to find a handkerchief.

"Oops, I forgot my handkerchief," I answered with chagrin.

"Can't you follow simple instructions?" the agent huffed. He must have thought I was one of those magicians on TV who could blow up a plane with a handkerchief.

* * *

At another airport, I was about to walk through security with my passport in hand, when a TSA agent stopped me. He instructed me to place everything into the plastic bin of personal effects to go down the X-ray conveyor belt.

I calmly stated, "In my country, we were taught never to let our passports out of our sight, so I would like to keep it with me."

Irritated by my response, he asked impatiently, "What did you say?"

I repeated myself, telling him that I would not like to let my passport out of my sight. Although he was not pleased, he finally allowed me to keep my passport in my hand while I was being scanned!

* * *

My mother-in-law passed away at the Stanford Medical Centre on the eve of Chinese New Year in 1982. I was left in Singapore with my daughter Oi Leng (who was just 4 years old), while the rest of the family were in the

US. On the first day of Chinese New Year, a lot of my mother-in-law's relatives and friends – unaware of the events – telephoned in to convey their festive greetings to her. Because I was not fluent in Hokkien (my in-law's dialect), I did not know how to express her passing in an appropriate manner, such as "she passed away" or "she went west". Instead, I told them in basic Hokkien: "She died". All the relatives were shocked by my crude answer, especially on such an auspicious day. They couldn't believe their ears.

The news of her demise spread like wildfire. By early afternoon, the phone was ringing off the hook. All the callers wanted to know where my mother-in-law had died, what the cause was, when the funeral would be held, where she would be buried. I happened to have asked my sister Pat to watch over Oi Leng in her house just before Chinese New Year, so I was the only one at home, and I had no peace answering those phone calls. Finally, I decided to get out of the house, and went to a cineplex. I watched three movies one after another, stopping to catch a bite in between. I only returned home after the 9 p.m. show.

Some time later, Kwan and her sisters decided to divide their mother's cache of jewellery among themselves. When I was making a trip to the US to visit our son Pak Seng in 1989, Kwan asked me to bring her sisters' shares to them, as they were living in the US. She packed each sister's jewellery portion into separate silk pouches.

When I was going through customs search in San Francisco, the TSA agent asked me where I was from and what the purpose of my visit was.

"Singapore," I said. "And I am here to visit my son who is attending a boarding school."

He told me that he had been to Singapore and was even wearing a gold Merlion pendant bought in Singapore, which he pulled out to show me. We talked about Singapore as he searched my luggage. He found the jewellery pouches and began laying out all of the jewellery. They were nice pieces and some still had price tags on them.

"What is this all about?" the agent asked, and I told him the truth. He then said, "I shall give you the benefit of the doubt. You could have told me that these are for your son."

I laughed, and said no. "If these were for him, I'd be having bigger problems!" He laughed in return, and allowed me to pack up the jewellery and leave.

* * *

A good friend of mine told me his daughter had just graduated from college and announced that she had found a job, working for the TSA. She also told him that she would be earning the minimum wage (about US$7.25 in those days). He was infuriated and told her, "I forbid you to work there because I did not send you through college just so that you earn minimum wage".

* * *

One year, I was invited by the US Army Attaché to attend their Fourth of July reception at the Ritz-Carlton Singapore. When I arrived at the hotel's car park, I opened my briefcase and took out my Palm Pilot, leaving my passport, credit cards and other documents inside. Then I locked my briefcase in the boot of my car and went to the reception. When I reached home that night, I opened the car boot, and found – no briefcase. I reported the theft to the police and had to go about getting replacements for the stolen documents.

Over the next two years, I travelled to the US about four or five times uneventfully with the new passport. Then my passport woes struck. On that occasion, the immigration officer asked if I had lost my passport, and then led me to an office "in the back".

I waited for more than an hour before they told me that I was cleared to go. The officer also advised me to get a new passport, because my passport had been flagged as stolen. Every time I entered the United States, they would have to verify with Washington D.C. if the expiry date on my passport was different from the one that I had lost (at that time, the Singapore passport number was the same as one's National Registration Identity Card number, so the only difference between an old passport and its replacement was the expiry date). The verification process could be quick, or it could take a long time, especially since San Francisco is four hours behind Washington local time.

"But it's been two years since that theft," I said.

"Then it must have taken two years for the theft to be reported to Washington," he said, like it made perfect sense!

Sometime later, I met a man who could only be called a "tycoon" (this man was worth millions of dollars). I told him my story about the stolen passport, to which he laughed and said, "That's nothing!"

"I was busted with two Cuban cigars once," he said. "Two lousy Cuban cigars. And every time I come to the US now, I'm subjected to a thorough search because I must have been flagged as a Cuban cigar smuggler!"

I also know of a gentleman who experienced American customs and immigration troubles that started out of the blue. He finally encountered a talkative immigration officer who revealed the reason for his passport woes. Apparently, an "update" to the computerised system had changed his sex from male to female!

My takeaway from these encounters is that once you get onto their "blacklist", your record stays in the system for a long time, maybe forever.

✳ ✳ ✳

I remember flying into Los Angeles International Airport in 2001 soon after the September 11 bombings, when security was at a heightened state. I stood with my luggage at the X-ray line for over 30 minutes before my bags were finally screened and passed. A porter placed my luggage on his pushcart and rolled it over to the airline check-in counter. I was next in line, and waited for the passenger in front of me to complete his check-in.

When the agent called "NEXT!", I pushed my luggage forward (no more than five feet or 2 m) and approached the counter, only to be given a lecture that I was not supposed to touch my luggage after it had been X-rayed.

My luggage and I had to return to the X-ray station for a re-scan. I waited in line for another 30 minutes, just so that my already-screened bags could be X-rayed again.

✳ ✳ ✳

One year, I flew to San Francisco to visit my younger brother Fred. An immigration officer of Vietnamese descent looked at the address I had listed on my immigration form (Fred's home address) and asked if my brother was a US citizen.

"Yes, he is," I replied.

"Has he ever petitioned for a green card for you?" she asked.

"Uh, no, he hasn't," I replied.

She then asked, "Why not?"

I felt insulted, so I replied, "Why, does he have to?"

"No, it's not important," she said. Then she asked me where I worked.

"At a high-tech company," I said.

"Are you a mechanic?" she asked snidely.

"Uh, no, I'm on the sales side of things," I replied.

"Are you a manager?" she prodded.

"Well, yes, you could say that," I answered.

"Do you make a lot of money?" she persisted.

"I make enough so that we have a home and we're comfortable," I answered warily.

She finally let me pass, although I still have no idea to this day why she had asked me all those questions. I suspect she might have regretted going to the US as a refugee and was stuck with a low-paid job.

Whenever I experience this line of questioning from immigration officers, I remind myself of what my daughter-in-law Suzy (a Korean lawyer born in the United States) once said: "You don't argue with them or they can get mean. They will first ask if you have a connecting flight, and if you do, they will delay you purposely so that you will not make that connecting flight."

✳ ✳ ✳

Coming into the US from Canada back in the days of the old I-94 form, I had forgotten to complete the back of the sheet. This section of the form required travellers to declare any previous criminal history or convictions.

My luggage and I finally reached the immigration officer, and he began reviewing my documents. When he saw the incomplete form, he sent me to the back of the waiting area to fill it out, and insisted that I lugged all my bags with me.

I ended up back in his line, as it was the shortest.

There were no issues with my paperwork, but the man placed the entry stamp right in the middle of two pages of my passport, leaving no room for any other stamps.

When you travel as much as I do, that's just rude. When all the pages in my passport are stamped, I would have to go through the time and expense of getting a new passport.

✳ ✳ ✳

A good friend of mine worked for immigration in Singapore. He told me about the time he was issued a passport that started delaminating on the page printed with his particulars and photograph. This was a known problem with a certain batch of Singapore passports issued around that time. On a trip to the US, my friend explained this to the immigration officer, but the latter insisted on checking with the Singapore Embassy and immigration office to verify the authenticity of his passport.

My friend tried to explain that he worked for immigration in Singapore, but they still made him wait in a back room.

After some time, the officer came back and said that they had just had a group of people with Singapore passports which looked suspicious.

"Can you come look at these people and their passports, and tell us if they are genuinely from Singapore?" he asked.

"I don't need to look at their passports; I can tell without even looking at their passports," my friend said. "I can just look at their behaviour, their hairdo, and their clothes."

The immigration officer was so impressed that he brought my friend to see his supervisor, who offered my friend a job with the Immigration and Naturalization Department in San Francisco.

My friend was not interested but was polite enough to tell them that he would need to discuss the offer with his family.

By then, several hours had passed and my friend was a bit irritated at the delay. When he was finally cleared, the original officer thanked him and sent him on his way.

My friend thanked the officer in return, but added cryptically, "I know your name. I recognise your face. I'm going to give you the same treatment you gave me if you ever come to Singapore."

My friend was later posted to the Singapore Consulate in India. He rejected several visa applications and was subsequently knocked down by a truck while walking home one night.

Chapter 3
EUROPE

After spending seven years in the USA, I was looking forward to starting a new life back in Asia. However, my friend Wally suggested that we take a backpacking (cheap!) trip during summer: we would fly across the Atlantic Ocean, travel around Europe for two months and then make our way to Asia.

So, armed with the travel book *Europe on 5 Dollars a Day* by Arthur Frommer and our two-month Eurorail[1] passes costing US$150 per pass, we flew over to London from New York.

The Eurorail passes allowed us unlimited travel on the trains throughout Europe. This suited us as we *did not* have a travel plan. In those days, airlines did not impose a penalty when you change your flight bookings. Our fallback was an American Express card that Wally's mother had provided him. Frommer's guidebook directed us to hostels where, for US$1 per night, we could use the shower facilities and get a space to roll out our sleeping bags. Some of these hostels even provided breakfast consisting of bread, butter and jam plus tea and milk! A lot of the hostels were schools which had closed for the summer, and the government decided to turn the classrooms into hostels for backpackers like us.

England

Our first stop was naturally England, because at that time, both of us were holding British passports and there was no excuse for us not to

---

1 The Eurorail pass is now known as the Eurail pass.

visit England. We took off from New York City and landed at Stansted Airport on 26 June 1971, raring to start our European adventures.

We were met and hosted by Wyman and her husband Chan Sik: she was the sister of Wally's graduate schoolmate, and he was a doctor who had just finished his specialist training in geriatrics. They were kind enough to put us up in their apartment and show us around London, going to places that they did not have a chance to visit when Chan Sik was doing his post-graduate studies. We also took the train up to Manchester to visit one of Wally's cousins. I remember drinking out of an unlabelled and unchilled half-gallon can of ale because pubs had to close at the uncivilised hour of 6 p.m. at that time.

It so happened that Chan Sik and Wyman had planned to drive around Europe from July to September in a Volkswagen Kombi van with three other friends – another couple plus Kok Tai (also a doctor) – before they would all return to Hong Kong to start their practice. Because of other commitments, the other couple would cut short their road trip and leave the group at Vienna, Austria on 8 August in order to fly back to Hong Kong.

That gave us a plan. Wally and I just had to roam around Europe with our Eurorail passes, show up at the Vienna airport on 8 August at mid-day, and then we could join Chan Sik, Wyman and Kok Tai to drive through Yugoslavia[2], continue on to Athens and then drive back to England.

So the following seven weeks for Wally and me were spent travelling from one European country to another: England, France, Spain, Monaco, Italy, Switzerland, Luxembourg, Belgium, The Netherlands, Germany, Denmark, Norway, Sweden, back to Germany, and then Austria. With no plan except to arrive in Vienna on 8 August, we just zigzagged across the continent.

We slept on trains, inside railway stations, in youth hostels and once in a long while, in roadside inns where we could get a warm shower and sleep between some clean sheets. Usually, we would spend US$1

---

2 Political conflicts in the 1990s split Yugoslavia into these present-day countries: Bosnia and Herzegovina; Croatia; Kosovo; Montenegro; North Macedonia; Serbia; and Slovenia.

on lodging, US$2 on food and even had US$2 left over for museum tickets per day. Whenever we had surplus cash, Wally would spend it on the finer things in life, such as chocolate, cheese and asparagus. I would invariably spend it on beer.

France And Spain

As the Chunnel[3] had not been built yet and there was no Eurostar train, we had to take a ferry across the English Channel from Dover to Calais, France, followed by a train onwards to Paris. We spent the next few days in the French capital, taking in all the tourist sights. Neither of us spoke French, but it was easy to get around by following the guidebook's listings. We climbed the Eiffel Tower, lined up to see the Mona Lisa at the Louvre and took a cruise down the Seine River. I also discovered that in Paris, beer was actually cheaper than Coke or mineral water!!!

When we felt that we had enough of Paris, we hopped on a train to Barcelona, Spain. There, we had some ceviche accompanied by some "genuine" sangria. The spices used in the ceviche were somewhat similar to what we were used to in Asian seafood dishes – a lot of garlic, onion and some pepperoncino.

To concoct the sangria, the bartender cut up some fruits, pour in the wine, then squatted down below the bar counter to put in the finishing touch. "A little bit of mystery," he said. After we ordered a few more pitchers of sangria, he finally told us he added a shot of soda water to complete the process. We also watched a bullfight, although it was not a grand affair. The arena was small but at the very least, it gave tourists like us a chance to claim that we had seen a bullfight.

Italy And Switzerland

From Barcelona, we rode the train through the Riviera to Rome. The train chugged along the scenic French Riviera coast and passed through

---

3 The Chunnel (Channel Tunnel) is an undersea railway tunnel connecting the United Kingdom and France. It was completed in 1994, and the high-speed Eurostar train began running between London and Paris later that year.

Monaco. After Monaco, the train turned south and passed through the Italian Riviera. Border patrol officers would board the train and ask to see our valid passports, but there were no other immigration formalities.

By then, we learned that one way to save on accommodation was to find a train that left at 10 p.m. from wherever we were and rolled into another town or city around 7 a.m. the next day. It did not matter where we were going as long as we kept going. Of course, with the Eurorail pass, we were not entitled to sleepers, and so we slept by leaning forward and laying our heads on our backpacks.

We also had a debate between us, whether we should drink water during or after a meal. If we drank during the meal, the bread would expand and we would feel full for the moment, but grow hungry again in less than two hours. If we did not drink during but after a meal, the bread in our stomachs would stave off our hunger a bit longer.

When we arrived in Rome, it was after dark, so we decided to spend the night in the train station. We settled down on some benches in the passenger waiting area. In the middle of the night, there was a commotion when a petty thief tried to dip his hand into the backpack of someone sleeping in the station. The victim woke up in time and kicked the thief in the face. We also witnessed a catfight between two prostitutes tussling over a John.

Because most of the business establishments were closed at night, we could not even cash our traveller's cheques to buy food. Luckily, I saw two Asian female backpackers in the station, so I went up to them and asked if they had any spare change. They were heading to the east coast of Italy to catch a ferry to Corfu Island in Greece, so they gave us some of their leftover liras[4] which we used to buy some bread. For the first time in my life, I had to resort to begging.

The following day, after cashing our traveller's cheques, we repaid the kind deed forward by buying lunch for a Taiwanese backpacker. He was looking for a lady friend who had come to Rome to learn to sing the opera. He said he was in Switzerland earlier where hashish was in abundance, and he invited us to share some of his.

---

4 The lira was Italy's currency until 2002, when it was officially replaced by the euro.

In Rome, we did what most tourists would do, visiting the Colosseum, Vatican City and the Vatican museums. We had wanted to take the train down to Naples but were told by the lady at the train information counter that all the beaches there were closed due to pollution. Mind you, this was in 1971.

Since we could not travel south, we decided to head north to Switzerland instead. The train ride through Bologna and Milan to Geneva was quite uneventful. Many years later in the late 1990s, I went to Genoa with my wife because we wanted to visit the scenic Lake Como. We saw many beautiful villas along the shores of the lake, some of which were open to visitors. We toured the Villa del Balbianello, a beautiful complex owned by Count Guido Monzino, who led the first Italian expedition to climb Mount Everest. The villa is a popular setting for many movies, and houses a museum honouring the count, displaying artefacts, maps and other memorabilia related to his expeditions. This time, we travelled in style, staying in expensive hotels in Como and also Venice along the way.

Back to our backpacking trip – after we disembarked from the train in Geneva in 1971, I suddenly had the urge to take a dump. I walked along the station platform to the nearest train carriage where a group of people had gathered at the back of the carriage, just outside the train's toilet. From the platform, I asked if someone in the group would get me some paper. One of the guys asked, "What, to roll with?" "NO!" I laughed so hard that I almost shat in my pants.

Later on, Wally and I wandered off to the lakeside, where we saw one of Geneva's landmarks, the Jet d'Eau fountain, before heading back to the train station.

Benelux

From Geneva, we rode a train to Luxembourg, backtracking through France. Naturally, the next stop was Brussels, the capital of Belgium. In Brussels, Wally spent the surplus he had from the US$5-a-day budget on fine chocolate while I spent mine on Belgian beer. That was before Hoegaarden was popularised. It was much later that I found out the common Belgian family of beer includes Stella Artois, Leffe (Blond and Dunkel), Hoegaarden and Forbidden Fruit.

Moving north, we reached Amsterdam. A visit to the Dutch capital was not complete without a visit to the Heineken brewery. Our main purpose, of course, was to imbibe the various types of Heineken. Strangely, the brewery did not bother to serve the non-alcoholic version; maybe we did not look hard enough or maybe a non-alcoholic drink made from barley and hops was not considered beer in those days.

We also walked along the canals to admire the pretty ladies (old enough to be my mother) standing behind the glass windows in the infamous red-light district. One could not help but notice the number of used condoms floating in the canals. I did wonder when they would invent biodegradable condoms.

My takeaway from visiting Amsterdam was that there were many Chinese restaurants, presumably owned by Indonesian immigrants of Chinese descent who were driven out of Indonesia after the 30 September Movement of 1965. However, we were disappointed with the quality and authenticity of the Chinese food they served. It made us wonder, how could one possibly ruin a plate of fried rice?

Germany: Round 1

Leaving Amsterdam, we crossed over to Germany, where I had a chance to practise what I had learnt in my German classes at Purdue. Our intention was to head further north to Copenhagen, the capital of Denmark subsequently. Somewhere in Germany, we felt that we had spent too many nights on trains and that we both needed a good wash. We decided to splurge and checked into a motel, thinking we would get a good night's sleep and a hot shower. In the middle of the night, we were awoken by the rumblings of a train. Lo and behold, the motel was literally 10 m away from a railroad track, and a real train had just passed by. Wally and I sat up in our beds and laughed our heads off.

Scandinavia

When we arrived in Copenhagen, the first thing we did was to find out where the Carlsberg brewery was, so that we could sign up for the next available tour. Thinking that there was only one type of Carlsberg in a green can, we were surprised when they served up Carlsberg in blue, brown and gold cans, and other different types of Carlsberg. After we had our fill of Danish beer, we walked along the waterfront and took a picture in front of the Little Mermaid statue.

From Copenhagen, we went up to Oslo, Norway, curious to see the Nobel Prize award ceremony venue. At that time, I was not aware that although the Nobel Peace Centre was located in Oslo, the Nobel Prize award ceremony was actually held at the Stockholm Concert Hall every year. The centre turned out to be a bit of a let-down – I was disappointed to see that it was not a very grand building. Furthermore, in those days, we were not accustomed to eating raw herring and salmon, so after a very short stay we were ready to move on.

Sweden was our next destination. Our stay in the capital Stockholm was quite uneventful. The "hostel" we booked had no hot water, so we took our showers in icy cold water. The water was so cold that it made my head ached when I was washing my hair. The only reason I was able to tolerate this was because it was a communal bathroom and there was a half-naked girl showering next to me.

We had wanted to continue north to Finland, but some backpackers who had just returned from Finland told us that the mosquitoes up there could blind a buffalo. We gave up that idea and decided that Stockholm was as far north as we would go. So Wally and I took a train down to Malmö in southern Sweden, and boarded a ferry to Lübeck in northern Germany.

Germany: Round 2

Re-entering Germany gave me more opportunities to polish my German language skills. We bypassed Hamburg because we were told that being a big port, Hamburg was not a safe place for backpackers. Instead, we went to Cologne. Wally snapped a picture of me on the Deutzer Bridge. Thirty years later, my daughter Oi Leng married Thorsten, a German from Cologne, and when I showed my son-in-law that picture, he knew the exact spot on the bridge where I had stood.

Armed with two litres of wine each, a long sausage and two baguettes, Wally and I took a 14-hour cruise up the Rhine River from Cologne to Mainz. We sat ourselves down on the upper deck of the ship, soaking in the sun and admiring the scenery while we polished off the food and wine.

Forty years later, I took a river cruise down the Irrawaddy River from Mandalay to Bagan in Myanmar, and I felt that the cruise ship looked similar to the one I had taken on the Rhine in 1971. When I asked the captain where that ship had come from, I was told that it used to cruise up and down the Rhine in Germany. Although I doubt if it were the same vessel, it sure brought back memories.

Mainz was the nearest Rhine city from Frankfurt but we decided not to explore the port city because by then, we were "museumed- and gardened-out". So we just feasted ourselves on curry shashlik and more beer as we looked at train schedules to bring us over to Munich.

When we reached the Bavarian capital, we made the mistake of asking a tourist information receptionist how to get to the famous Dachau concentration camp. The beautiful *fraulein* turned very hostile and told me that there were lots of those in Vietnam and that we should go there instead.

Like Amsterdam and Copenhagen, Munich is a great beer and brewing capital in Europe, and we were told that we had to visit the Hofbräuhaus. It was a big beer hall and beer was served in two-litre steins. The servers, all ladies, were famous for being able to carry four steins in each of their hands. Even though these were crude ceramic steins, we thought that they would make a good conversation piece if we went home with them. So, Wally and I secretly took one each, rolled them in our sleeping bags and tried to walk out of there nonchalantly after finishing four litres of beer each.

There were security men at the exit and they had to have seen people like us every day. They touched the sleeping bags secured on our backpacks and questioned us, "How many steins do you have in there?" "Just one, sir," we replied. They said, "All right, go go go. Get out of here."

I remember there was a tram line that ran just in front of the Hofbräuhaus. After drinking four litres, (although I doubt if we actually had four litres because there was such a big head of foam in each stein), Wally was almost run over by a tram.

Road Tripping: Austria, Yugoslavia And Greece

As our 8 August D-day was fast approaching, we did not spend much time in Munich before we moved on to Innsbruck, Austria, just across the border. German is the national language of Austria, and I actually had an easier time understanding the Austrians than I did the Germans in Germany, probably because of all the dialects that were spoken in the latter country.

A few more days of train ride finally brought us to Vienna, one day ahead of schedule. At that point in time, I had not finished my roll of 36-shots Kodak film in my camera, so I used up the last few shots at the Vienna airport.

When our doctor friends finally showed up in their Volkswagen Kombi van at the airport, boy, were we relieved. Now we did not have to decide on where to go and what to do next, because the doctors had meticulously mapped out the rest of the drive and we knew that there would be a roof (albeit a tent) over our heads at night.

Leaving Austria and driving into Yugoslavia, we made Zagreb our first stop. It was not easy getting used to the standstill during the siesta in that country. All businesses would close after lunch and not reopen until 7 p.m. Although it was summer and the evening would still be bright, it was a problem to keep ourselves occupied when we were camping out at camp sites. Another takeaway was the abundance of apricot brandy. Every shop we went into, the shelves would be filled with the amber liquor.

Yugoslavia was still a communist state then. I remember we became totally lost when driving one night. We saw some light from a lamp post and drove up to ask for directions, only to be shooed away by a machine-gun-wielding soldier. We did not really sightsee in Yugoslavia – we left there as quickly as possible so that we could cross over into Greece.

The warm weather and intense sun were a welcome to all of us. In the capital Athens, we went to see all the old relics and even ventured out to pay a visit to the village of Olympia where the first Olympic Games was held. We saw sultanas being sun-dried along the sides of the country roads, and to this day, I can still recall their sweet and earthy scent.

Our Volkswagen Kombi van was a manual shift vehicle. I think our doctor friend Kok Tai was trained to overtake in third gear and cruise in fourth gear. In one section of a two-way country road, he was overtaking a truck in third gear when an oncoming truck barrelled towards us. Kok Tai just would not upshift to fourth gear. As the engine was near redline and van would not go any faster in third gear, I really thought "that was it". Luckily, both trucks jammed on their brakes and let us squeeze back into our side of the road.

Our plan to drive back to London was derailed when Wyman found out that she was pregnant. So preparations were made to ship the Kombi van back to London, and we would all disperse from Athens after that. The two doctors and Wyman would fly back to Hong Kong, while Wally and I would fly on to Singapore. I had invited Wally to go to Singapore so that we could make a side trip to my hometown Sandakan, in Sabah.

While we were waiting for the clearance to ship the van out, the tent in which Wyman rested during the day was also the roof over our heads at night. As a parting adventure, I was bitten by a rat on our last night in Athens. Wyman had been consuming food in the tent, and the rat was probably attracted by the food crumbs. I must have rolled over the rat in my sleep – he bit me and dragged his testicles across my face as he made a break for the tent opening. I screamed for help in the middle of the night. Luckily, our travelling companions were doctors; they looked at the bite and declared that I would live.

The following morning, we said goodbye to one another at the Athens airport, and went on our separate ways[5]. The first stop for Wally

---

5 I still keep in touch with Chan Sik via e-mail, and we would catch up over meals whenever I am in Hong Kong.

and me after Athens was the Turkish city of Istanbul, followed by the Lebanese capital of Beirut.

Who would have guessed that four years later, Lebanon would break out into civil war, leaving the country in complete shambles? At the Beirut airport, I had my first Arabic coffee espresso. Despite emptying seven sachets of sugar into it, I still could not stand its bitterness. I left that 60-ml cup of coffee unfinished, and we proceeded to catch our connecting Pan Am flight to Bangkok and Singapore.

On the flight to Bangkok, there was a bald passenger who occupied an aisle seat. He wore a suit and frequently slid down in his seat, leaning out towards the aisle. Once, the stewardess accidentally spilled some hot coffee on his head. He jumped up cursing and the stewardess apologised profusely.

Less than 15 minutes later, the aircraft hit some turbulence and the same stewardess spilled some hot coffee on this passenger's head again. From where I was sitting, I could not tell if it was on the same spot on his head. Once again, the passenger jumped up and this time, he grabbed the stewardess by the lapel and shook her violently, screaming, "You must be doing this on purpose!" The chief purser came up to him and personally apologised.

From Bangkok, Wally and I took a flight to Singapore. As it was also the summer holidays for Kwan, she travelled from America to reunite with me. The three of us then flew to Sandakan, and I brought them home to meet my parents. We also visited the Sepilok orangutan sanctuary where orphaned baby orangutans are rescued, trained and then released back into the wild, even to this day.

Revisiting England And France

After my backpacking adventures in 1971, I did not travel to Europe again until some 16 years later. During the period when I worked for Bell Helicopter (from 1987 to 2006), I would attend the Farnborough Air Show in England and the Paris Air Show in France on alternate years. Our marketing staff were there to show off the company's new products to potential and existing customers during the daytime. And of course we had to entertain them in fine dining restaurants in the evenings.

The Greek Islands

In 1992, Kwan's sister Christina and her husband Doug chartered a sailing boat to go island hopping in the Aegean Sea, and invited us to join them. The boat was on her maiden voyage and was owned by the retired musical director for *The Nana Mouskouri*[6] *Show*.

Although George had a marine license, he was not very experienced and we were almost run over by a cargo vessel even before we had left the Athens harbour. Initially, the diesel engine was used to power our island hopping mainly because of the hassle of rigging the sails. However, after meeting up with the same boats on each of the night stops, I realised that it was the routine for all the other boats, so I insisted that we hoist our sails and cross over to the eastern side of the Aegean Sea. At least we managed to do some sailing and meet new friends on the subsequent days.

The routine was to move out after breakfast, and stop in a cove for some swimming and snorkelling. We would pull into another harbour by the afternoon, visit the fish market, and maybe pick out a restaurant for dinner that night. In the market, we saw some locals slicing up a sea urchin and sucking up the raw *uni* together with its natural juice. We actually had a chef on board, and on some nights, she would cook us a typical Greek meal.

England And Germany

After her wedding[7] in 2009, my daughter Oi Leng moved to London with Thorsten. Kwan and I would visit them at least twice a year. It so happened that my son Pak Seng found a job in London, and he moved his whole family there as well in 2010, so we would divide our time between the two families during our visits. Thankfully, they live only half an hour apart by road.

I help out with their driving duties whenever I visit them. We try to visit London during Chinese New Year, so that we can have our

---

6 Nana Mouskouri is a singer from Greece who has won international acclaim and recorded songs in numerous languages. She had her own TV series in the 1960s and 1970s.
7 See Chapter 4 "Southeast Asia" for the day I walked my daughter down the aisle.

reunion dinner together. There was a year when we spent Christmas with Oi Leng's in-laws in Cologne to experience the German Christmas spirit. We were joined by Pak Seng, Suzy and their three boys.

Another year, Thorsten invited us to the Munich Oktoberfest, knowing my fondness for beer. I arrived in Munich in the early afternoon and the beer festival was already in full swing. Thorsten enjoyed himself so much that he danced on the table and fell into the lap of some other patrons sitting at our table several times. Because I was jetlagged, we staggered back to the hotel around 7 p.m.

Thorsten also told us that for his bachelor's party before his wedding in 2009, his friends took him to the Oktoberfest in Munich, where he had to dress up in a Bavarian dirndl dress. He had so many hostile stares from the other Bavarians who must have felt he was poking fun at them, that he changed out of his outfit in no time.

In some years, we visited during the UK school holidays, and our children would organise a family trip to other parts of England, such as Bath, Cornwall, Isle of Wight, and Whitstable.

Portugal

In 2012, we accompanied Oi Leng to Portugal to babysit my grandson Kai, so that she could attend a wedding and then party in Cascais, a popular coastal resort 30 km west of Lisbon.

While I was in Lisbon, I rode the tram to visit some of the tourist sights. In each of the trams, there were posters warning passengers to beware of pickpockets.

On one occasion, a man behind me kept leaning on my back as if there were many other passengers nudging and pushing him to board the tram. I did not think much of it until I felt someone trying to pull my wallet out from my back pocket. Because I had a cheap wallet made from synthetic leather which was slippery, he did not succeed. I slapped his hand away, and the culprit immediately mingled with the other passengers so as to get to the rear exit of the tram.

I suspected that the tram driver and conductor were in cahoots with the culprit, because they could see these gangs of pickpockets getting on the tram at the same station and invariably getting off at the next.

Croatia

The following year, we spent a few days in Dubrovnik, Croatia to babysit my granddaughter Lena so that Oi Leng could attend another wedding and join the after-party.

One day, we were strolling along the waterfront in the old town, looking for a café to have lunch. The squid ink risotto was a godsent for our daughter's Filipino helper who had accompanied us on the trip. It just reminded her so much of the food back in the Philippines: rice with seafood.

The whole setting of the old town and the city wall bore a resemblance to a scene straight out of the American fantasy TV series *Game of Thrones*. High above us, on the wall itself was a crowd of spectators obviously watching some filming. As we went closer to the base of the wall, we saw containers of lighting equipment and boxes of props with the words "Game of Thrones" stencilled on the side. We had stumbled upon their on-location shoot!

That night, when Oi Leng came back from the wedding reception, she told us that it was held in the same hotel that the *Game of Thrones* cast members were staying. Cersei Lannister, Tyrion Lannister, Lord Varys the eunuch and Gregor "The Mountain" Clegane were seen having drinks in the bar after a hard day's work under the bright sun of Dubrovnik.

Norway And Ireland

In 2014, I made a trip to Stavanger, Norway, to attend a World Association of Chefs' Societies (Worldchefs) Congress[8]. I was simply "herringed out" after a few days, because breakfast at the hotel invariably served up (among other things) glazier's herring, herring in tomato sauce, herring in sour cream, and herring in mustard sauce.

In that same year, I took a road-trip vacation in Ireland with Kwan, her sister Christina and her husband Doug. What impressed me most about Ireland was the abundance of fresh seafood. Although I thought I

---

8 Worldchefs was founded in 1928 at the Sorbonne in Paris, with the goals of maintaining and improving culinary standards. It is a global network of chef associations, and it organises a congress biennially for its members.

would be drinking mostly Guinness stout, I found a local lager that really suited my taste.

Kwan and I landed in Dublin, and we drove over to Shannon Airport to pick up the other couple. We spent a few nights in Ashford Castle which was established in the year 1228. This was once home to the famous Guinness family, and was turned into a five-star hotel in 1939.

Using Ashford as our base, we drove around the area, visiting old castles and seaside villages. After that, we drove south to the Dingle Peninsula where the 1970 movie *Ryan's Daughter*, which won the Best Cinematography and Best Supporting Actor Oscars, was filmed. The scenery was simply magnificent. We drove around southwestern Ireland and headed back to Dublin to spend the night before we flew home.

Greece And The Czech Republic

Two years later, in September 2016, we attended another Worldchefs Congress, this time in Thessaloniki, Greece. During the event, it was near impossible to hold any function outdoors because of the bugs humming in the air.

After the conference, we dropped in on Prague, the capital of the Czech Republic. We learned that Budweiser beer originated in Prague and the brewery there had sued the American brewing company Anheuser-Busch for trademark infringement. Naturally they lost. We also drove by the house in which the famous Czech composer Antonin Dvorak lived when he composed the New World Symphony.

The Czechs are proud of their Skoda cars. Our tour guide coined it "German technology at Czech labour price". The Germans are known for their fine technology and car marques, and ever since Volkswagen bought over Skoda, Volkswagen has been incorporating its technology into these cars. Yet the cars are still affordable because they are built using lower-cost Czech labour.

The French Wine Region And Poland

In April 2019, we had an opportunity to visit the wine road of Alsace. We spent a night in the French city of Strasbourg located right on the border between France and Germany. One could simply walk across a bridge from Strasbourg to the German town of Kehl.

We visited all of Strasbourg's historical sites. Although the city is decidedly French, it is characterised by German architecture especially around the centre. Geographically strategic, it was fought over for centuries between the French and the Germans.

The following morning, we boarded a train, heading south through Matzenheim, Selestat, and Colmar. Vineyards lined the sides of the railroad. This is the wine-producing country of Alsace, also known as the Alsace Wine Road.

We spent the night in the charming wine village of Ammerschwihr, only 12 minutes away from Colmar. We treated ourselves to a sumptuous dinner at the Michelin-starred restaurant Julien Binz. The following morning, we caught the train back to Strasbourg and onwards to Paris.

After spending the night in the French capital, we took a flight to Warsaw, Poland, where the world's only Note by Note restaurant, Senses, was located. Note by Note cuisine is a style of cooking that replaces traditional ingredients such as meat and vegetables with their composite compounds. This process can feed more people, prevent food spoilage and save energy. The restaurant, owned and run by Chef Andrea Camastra, gained its Michelin star in 2016. Chef Andrea showed us his lab where he developed the recipe for his various Note by Note dishes.

Scandinavia And Hungary

In September 2019, I revisited Stockholm and Copenhagen. This time round, on the invitation of Doug and Christina, Kwan and I did it in style, staying at two 5-star hotels: the Grand Hotel in Stockholm and Hotel d'Angleterre in Copenhagen. Pak Seng and Oi Leng joined us in Copenhagen for my seventieth birthday celebrations.

From Copenhagen, Kwan and I hopped over to Budapest, Hungary where we spent four nights. We were fortunate to have P.J. Moccand, the son of one of our ex-neighbours, as our tour guide. He seemed to know every restaurant there was in Budapest, having lived there for 17 years.

We stayed in a boutique hotel on the east side of the Danube River, very near to the main market hall where we could sample all kinds of

Hungarian food as well as herbs and spices. The subway and tram systems in the city were very convenient, so we were able to visit all the famous sights such as the Hungarian Parliament Building, Heroes' Square, and the Basilica. We even spent an afternoon walking all the way around Margaret Island, capping off a memorable birthday vacation.

Chapter 4
SOUTHEAST ASIA

I first lived in Southeast Asia in 1956 and spent a good proportion of my childhood here. It is a region in Asia that lies within the warm, humid tropics, and is ethnically and culturally diverse. It also exhibits great biodiversity, in plant life and wildlife, including marine wildlife.

The Association of Southeast Asian Nations (ASEAN) was formed in 1967 initially with just five member countries (Indonesia, Malaysia, the Philippines, Singapore and Thailand) in an effort to prevent the spread of communism in the region and to promote economic cooperation. ASEAN later expanded to include Brunei, Vietnam, Laos, Myanmar and Cambodia.

As a citizen of Singapore, it has been a breeze for me to visit the other member states in ASEAN over the years. The only exception was Myanmar, which required the citizens of other member countries to apply for entry visas even after it joined ASEAN in 1997. However, since December 2016, it has waived the visa requirements for Singaporeans on tourist visits for up to 30 days.

I have visited all the other nine member countries, some for business, some for scuba diving, and some for family vacations. Compared to Singapore, they are considered cheap holiday destinations, even to this day.

Indonesia

Indonesia was a former Dutch colony which proclaimed independence in 1945. Part of Indonesia is only a mere kilometre from Singapore, so it is less than an hour's ferry ride away. However, the chain of islands that make up Indonesia measures 5,000 km from the western tip to the eastern front. Two of its largest islands are Sumatra and Java.

In the late 1970s, I spent nine months in Medan, Sumatra, exploring the prospect of setting up a vegetable oil refinery in Belawan. The raw material for our refinery was palm oil, extracted from the fruit of the oil palm tree, and Sumatra was the biggest oil-palm growing region in Indonesia at that time. The project involved building the refinery, and we had counted on securing crude palm oil from the government-owned plantations.

We chose to build the refinery in Belawan because that was the main port in North Sumatra. The company obtained in-principle approval from the Indonesian Investment Coordinating Board (BKBM) and was later issued a licence. I travelled back and forth between Singapore and Medan, looking to acquire the land to construct the refinery, meeting with equipment vendors, local construction companies and most importantly, government officials to secure the allocation of crude palm oil for our refinery.

Unfortunately, BKBM changed their policy and directed us to invest in our own oil palm plantation so that eventually, we would not have to rely on the government plantations for our crude palm oil. I flew down to Riau province to look for land to cultivate the plantation, and spent a few days in its state capital Pekanbaru. We drove out to the deep water port of Dumai, slip sliding on an unpaved road covered with diesel just to keep the dust down. However, the implication of this new policy was, from a US$5-million project, we now had to invest US$50 million. Our consortium decided to walk away from the project and sell the licence to a local conglomerate, so I came back to Singapore.

During my nine months in Medan, I picked up Bahasa Indonesia because most of the Indonesians I met at that time did not speak English. As a matter of fact, I am more familiar with Bahasa Indonesia than Bahasa Melayu (the Malay language).

I explored different parts of Indonesia during my stay in Medan. On one trip, I obtained permission through the Singapore consulate to visit the massive Asahan Dam, which was built to provide hydroelectric power to the aluminium smelter nearby.

HIGHWAY CODE: MEDAN STYLE

I was driving with a friend in Medan and came up to a red traffic light. As I stopped and waited for the light to turn green, my friend told me to go ahead and run the red light. I pointed to the policeman standing under the traffic lights and said, "I can't do that". This friend said, "If you dare to run this red light, he would not dare to stop you because he would probably think that you are an influential person and he had better not cause you trouble".

The drive from Medan to the dam was five hours, taking us through some country roads. On our way back to Medan, we encountered heavy rain and one of the bridges we had crossed earlier was washed away. We had to divert to an unpaved road that cut through some oil palm plantations. The condition of the plantation road was so bad and bumpy, that when I sent the car for washing the following day, the workshop mechanic told me that the battery had actually fallen off the battery tray and was dangling by the earth lead.

I also went up to the hill station of Brastagi (Berastagi) several times, including overnight stays in Lake Toba. I took a charter flight that flew over Lake Toba to Sibolga, a port on the western coast of Sumatra. I visited Tanjung Balai, a major fishing port in North Sumatra, to look at buying over an ice factory for a different project. I also spent a few days in Padang, famous for their popular cuisine which is served all over Indonesia.

In Medan, mud crabs were plentiful. The Singapore Airlines station manager told me that the airline used to transport about 5 tons of mud crabs to Singapore daily. Once, I bought about 20 kg of mud crabs from Medan to take home to Singapore. After check-in, a customs officer hassled me and said that I was not allowed to bring crabs out of the country unless, of course, I paid him a certain amount of "fine".

The crabs were packed in two paper cartons. I didn't anticipate this, but one carton became wet during the flight and started to disintegrate, releasing about 10 kg of live mud crabs onto the conveyor belt in the

STAYING IN TOUCH WITH MY FAMILY

Once, I made a long-distance call to my family in Singapore from Indonesia. In those days, there was no International Direct Dialling in Indonesia. I had to call the hotel switchboard and ask them to place the call to Singapore. About an hour later, my call was connected. I had barely spoken to Kwan for a minute when the call was dropped. We would have had to go through the lengthy process again, if we hadn't discovered a simple trick to overcome the telecommunication problem – she simply called me back by Direct Dialling from Singapore and we were instantaneously reconnected. On another occasion, my friend brought me down to the telecoms office after hours, when I could call Singapore at a much reduced rate arranged by the technician on duty.

Paya Lebar airport in Singapore! When I went to claim my baggage, there they were, little mud crabs scuttling all over the conveyor belt. I noticed that my other box of crabs was intact as it circled the belt. I grabbed that box and left quickly, before anyone realised that I had two boxes to begin with!

I have also been to Java, which is another large island of Indonesia. I made numerous trips to the capital Jakarta in the late 1970s to meet with the central government officials regarding the palm-oil project. When I switched to a new career in aerospace later, I went up to Bandung many times to visit Industri Pesawat Terbang Nusantara (IPTN), the national aerospace company that manufactured helicopters and utility aeroplanes under licence. In 2012, as part of a "Hash House" gathering[1] in Jogjakarta,

---

1   See Chapter 13 "Hash House Harriers" for the hobby that I have taken up since I was a teenager.

I had the chance to visit Borobudur, a 9th-century Mahayana Buddhist temple complex.

It takes less than two hours to fly directly between Jakarta and Singapore. I remember a particular flight back to Singapore from Jakarta very well. As the plane started its descent into Changi Airport, we were told by the captain over the PA system that Changi was closed to traffic because of a storm. The aircraft had to be diverted to Senai Airport in Johor, Malaysia. When we landed in Senai, I saw that there were more than ten other airliners parked on the tarmac to wait out the storm.

We were served some drinks and snacks while we waited for Changi to reopen. About half an hour later, the captain announced that the storm had blown over and Changi Airport had reopened. Even though we were one of the last aircraft that had landed in Senai, we were the first aircraft that started up and taxied out for take-off.

The only trouble was, by then, the storm had been blown north and was now approaching Senai. The rain picked up as we sped down the runway. As we lifted off, we flew right into the storm. The aircraft was tossed around violently; we could see heavy streams of water running down the outside of the windows. Every now and then, there were flashes of lightning. The ladies in the aircraft screamed and many of them started wailing, expecting to meet their end. Very soon, the men were chanting the Koran at the top of their voices. As it was supposed to be a very short flight and there was so much turbulence, none of the cabin attendants left their crew seats. I noticed that my seatmate Dave – a pilot with more than 15,000 flight hours of experience – had disappeared.

In no more than 10 minutes, we were on our final approach into Changi. The aircraft suddenly broke out of the clouds when we were on short final. The sky had cleared, the wind was calm, and there were a lot of ground activities in the airfield. We had a very smooth touchdown.

After we disembarked from the aircraft, I saw Dave in the terminal and asked him where he had gone. He said that when we taxied out to take off in Senai, he saw the storm out of the window, so he moved to the last row of the aircraft next to the emergency exit, "just in case".

My wife Kwan, having been a competitive swimmer when she was growing up, was keen to take up scuba diving. She signed up for an open water scuba diving course in Singapore and received her certification in 1978. When I finished my military service, I also went through the course and was certified in 1979.

Our scuba-diving adventures have taken us to various popular dive spots around Indonesia. We have been on several memorable live-aboard dive trips, including one in 2009 to the Banda Islands[2], also known as the Spice Islands. On these dive trips, we lived on a boat throughout the duration of the trip, with meals and accommodation included. Every day, the boat moved to a different part of the sea for the divers to explore.

One other dive spot is the Komodo National Park, where the underwater visibility goes for miles, but the currents are very strong. Large reptiles known as Komodo dragons roam freely on this island. During one of my trips there, the crew on our boat baited a Komodo dragon onto a sampan, then towed the sampan out to the middle of the bay, where all the divers were waiting with their cameras underwater for the dragon to swim back to the shore.

On another trip, we flew to Manado, another popular diving site in Indonesia, but it was the wrong time of the year and there was a storm, so visibility was very poor.

As for the northern part of the Indonesian archipelago, we did a liveaboard trip exploring the infamous 97,750-dwt MV *Seven Skies* tanker[3] which sank in October 1969 near the Anambas Island. The wreck sat upright, resting on a sandy bottom. The top of the funnel was

---

2 See Chapter 11 "The Hardship Group" for my marine explorations in the Banda Sea with Kwan and our group of close friends.

3 Unfortunately, the tanker was salvaged illegally in 2015 and what was left of the wreck is no longer suitable for diving.

22 m from the surface, but the bottom was 62 m to the surface. We were very lucky as it was a sunny day, and the current was minimal. It was here that we swam with a whale shark that came to check us out.

Bali is an internationally renowned island that is very popular with tourists. I have visited it numerous times, staying in five-star hotels as well as bed and breakfast places by the beach, drinking toddy in those bamboo huts facing the sea, savouring the relaxed atmosphere.

On New Year's Eve in 2009, my daughter Oi Leng held her wedding at the Morabito Art Cliff villa on Canggu Beach, Bali. Her husband-to-be, Thorsten, was born in Germany and her in-laws' family came over from Cologne for the wedding. Many of her university mates flew over from the US, and so did her friends from Singapore. Kwan's relatives came from the US and Thailand. Oi Leng engaged a wedding planner to set up the whole wedding. Kwan brought the groom's parents over to the Chinese Emporium in Singapore and suited them up in some traditional Chinese outfits for the Chinese wedding tea ceremony.

We held the tea ceremony in another hotel earlier in the day. The wedding couple served tea to all the relatives who, in turn, gave the couple their blessings and handed over their wedding gifts.

In the afternoon, as the guests arrived for the wedding ceremony, the German side of the family arranged for the Polterabend, a German wedding custom in which each guest was invited to break a plate into a barrel to bring luck to the couple's marriage. The solemnisation was administered by Thorsten's uncle. Afterwards, the broken plates were laid out onto a tarpaulin and the newlyweds put on aprons and took brooms to sweep up these pieces to denote the sharing of housework in their marriage.

After all the photo taking and cocktails, dinner was served. At the stroke of midnight, Oi Leng arranged for an Ogoh-Ogoh (big bull)

My grandfather Lui Yum Suen (second from right) and his three younger brothers.
(Picture courtesy of Katherine)

My grandmother's photo on the ancestral altar in our house in Sandakan. The calligraphic tribute at the top of the portrait was written by my grandfather.

My grandfather's law certificate bears his professional name 雷祖根.
(Picture courtesy of Katherine)

My grandfather Lui Yum Suen (right) had seven sons and three daughters. My father Lui Chak To (left) was his sixth child.

My parents' wedding dinner invitation card. After finding the card among some old family records, I decided to track down the restaurant in India.

The gold pendant gift from my grandfather. In the middle of the pendant is my name 元亮. At the top is the phrase 三桂競秀 (*Three outstanding descendants compete for excellence*).

I must have been about three years old when this photo with my grandfather was taken at his villa (the "Lychee Villa") in the New Territories.

All dressed up and ready to go on a car ride. From left: My mother, Pat, my father, Shuk Tak, Fred and me.

嚴 八秩 開六 壽辰 聯慶紀念 壬辰年九月二十五日 攝於香江
并隹 游重 津水 一九五二年十一月十二日

This was my grandfather's 76th birthday celebrations in November 1952, with many of the Lui clan members present. I was seated on the floor (first from left); my elder sister Shuk Tak was beside me. My mother was carrying my younger sister Pat on her lap (second row, first from right), while my father was wearing a white jacket (back row, seventh from right).

Beach boys and bunnies, South Bay, Hong Kong, early 1950s. My fifth maternal aunt Frances lived in a villa by the sea. My siblings and I spent many happy weekends there playing with her children. From left: Pat, me, Cecil, Inez, Shuk Tak and Cynthia.

Conducting the percussion band in a competition, Hong Kong, early 1950s.

The Fabulous Four: look how we have grown!
Both pages, clockwise from left: Shuk Tak, me, Pat and Fred.

1982

Over the years, Pat took very good care of Woo Woo, an orphaned baby gibbon which grew up well and became our beloved family pet.

Working with a friend (right) as labourers in my father's construction company during the school holidays in Sandakan, 1964.

At the airport, before I set off on my journey to America. From left: Our domestic helper and cook Yue Jie, me, my parents, Pat, Shuk Tak and Fred.

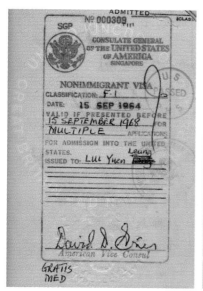

The first American visa issued to me, 1964.

The view from my window seat on the PanAm Boeing 707 during my flight from Hong Kong to San Francisco in 1964.

Fresh off the boat, going to a county fair with my guardian Auntie Laddie, the day after I arrived in San Francisco.

Ted Thoman – the first American friend I made after my arrival. Ted tragically died in a helicopter crash during the Vietnam War. (Souvenir picture from Ted)

Auntie Laddie's house in Los Altos, California – the first house I lived in after arriving in the United States. It was here that I experienced fresh milk being delivered to the doorstep in glass bottles.

On the lawn of Menlo School with Wing Ning (right) during our school graduation ceremony in June 1966.

Visiting my paternal relatives in Vancouver in 1966. I spent summer there after graduating from Menlo, staying with my father's older brother Uncle Chak, Auntie Irene and their two sons, David and Philip. Front row from left: Auntie Irene, Philip and Raphael (a son of my third uncle). Back row from left: Me, David, Uncle Richard (my fifth uncle) and Uncle Chak.

Relaxing in my dorm room, Purdue University. We had to wear a green beanie during freshmen orientation week.

I was given these pins after my induction into honour societies: (from left) Phi Eta Sigma; Sigma Gamma Tau; and Tau Beta Pi.

Getting ready for my 500-mile drive after just 15 minutes of driving experience taught by my maternal cousin John (left), in 1966.

At Mount Rushmore, 1969, with four American presidents watching my back.

Under the blazing sun with Wally (right) at the Acropolis, Athens in 1971. Greece was one of the stops on our two-month Europe backpacking trip.

With my backpack on the Deutzer Bridge, Cologne, 1971.

The 25th anniversary reunion with my Menlo School classmates in October 1991. 31 out of the class of 50 met up for the first time after 25 years. The gentleman in the front row, sporting white slacks and a dark jacket was Mr Fred Halverson, our assistant headmaster during my two years at Menlo.

Ngrupuk (ceremony). An effigy of a bull was carried down to the beach where it was lit up and burnt. The torching of the ogoh-ogoh symbolises the cleansing of all evil influences in life.

Malaysia

In 1963, the Federation of Malaya, British North Borneo (Sabah), Sarawak and Singapore entered into a merger to form the Federation of Malaysia. Due to ideological and economic disagreements, Singapore was expelled in 1965 and became an independent republic – this happened about a year after I left Sabah for further studies in the US.

Malaysia is a federation of 13 states and 3 federal territories. It comprises two regions separated by the South China Sea: Peninsular (West) Malaysia and East Malaysia. Nine of the states have royal families and are constitutionally headed by traditional Malay rulers[4].

I spent part of my childhood and early teenage years in Sabah. My hometown in the port city of Sandakan has undergone moderate development since the days when there was no telephone land line connecting it to the world. After settling down with Kwan in Singapore in the 1970s, I visited my parents in Sandakan at least once a year, usually during Chinese New Year. My elder sister Shuk Tak still lives there with her husband Yun Yaw in my parents' house on the hill.

Over the years, I have made numerous road trips across the kilometre-long Johor–Singapore Causeway into Peninsular Malaysia. Because Singapore is such a small city state, Malaysia became a vital escapade for Singaporeans. Back in the early days, I had a blue passport known as the

---

4 The royal rulers in these states are given the title of "Sultans", with the exception of Perlis ("Raja") and Negri Sembilan ("Yang di-Pertuan Besar").

Restricted Passport[5] specifically for travelling to Peninsular Malaysia; my red Singapore Passport was used for international travel.

When I first settled down in Singapore in the 1970s, I found out that many Singaporeans drove across the Causeway to Johor Bahru (commonly referred to as "JB"), the capital of the state of Johor, to fill up their cars with cheap petrol (gasoline) and diesel that was subsidised by the Malaysian government. They also enjoyed the cheap seafood and alcoholic drinks there. Due to the lower standard of living, consumer goods were generally cheaper in JB. However, because of the import duty levied on electronic goods and even imported fruits, these became common items that were "smuggled" from Singapore into Malaysia. Another commonly known reason for making trips to JB was to watch X-rated movies which were banned in Singapore. One particular X-rated movie was a big hit in JB because the main actress came from a prominent family in Singapore.

Traffic on the Causeway would build up during the evening rush hour as many Malaysians working in Singapore would return home for dinner, just as many Singaporeans would be crossing the Causeway for cheap food, drinks and evening entertainment.

The Singapore government knew that they were losing a lot of tax revenue from the petrol and diesel that Singaporean drivers were buying from Johor. So a law was passed in 1991 such that all Singapore cars leaving the country must have at least a three-quarter tank of petrol. This was known as the three-quarter tank rule. In 2012, the law was expanded to include vehicles running on compressed natural gas or CNG. In 2019, even diesel cars and trucks were not spared. At the Singapore Customs Complex, police officers would randomly pop their heads into the Singapore registered cars that are heading for Johor, with a flashlight to check the fuel gauge.

Food remains one of the main attractions for Singaporeans going to JB, even to this day. I know of a neighbourhood in JB with restaurants

---

5 The Restricted Passport had a blue cover and was issued to Singapore citizens between 1967 and 1999 for travel to only West Malaysia. In 2000, the red Singapore Passport became the only valid passport for all international travel.

serving game meats such as wild boar, civet cat, flying fox, mouse deer, crocodile, snake, turtle, monitor lizard (iguana) and pangolin. Meat from dogs and cats are illegal, but you could still order them on the side.

Singaporeans also know where they can find the best fish balls, beef balls and mutton soup. Seafood would be selling for less than half the price of what one can get in Singapore. Hence, we would drive up to JB just to have dinner, drinks and take in a show in the evening. When golf became a craze in Singapore, golf courses mushroomed in Johor because the green fees and caddies were also much cheaper there.

When our children were young, Kwan and I often brought them on weekend road trips, venturing further north into the peninsula. A 2½-hour drive would take us to Melaka (formerly Malacca), where we could enjoy authentic Portuguese[6] and Peranakan[7] meals and spend the evening walking around the night market (*pasar malam*) located downtown.

A 4½-hour drive would take us up to Kuala Lumpur, the capital city of Malaysia. To keep the children engaged, Kwan would play spelling or word games with them, like naming a fruit or an animal. Before the North–South Expressway was built in 1994, the first stop for motorists after clearing immigration and customs in JB was customarily Ayer Hitam, where one would stop for a cup of coffee or tea and use the toilets. After that, one could choose to head either west (the coastal route) or east (the inland route) to get to Kuala Lumpur.

The coastal route is straight and flat, and runs along the west coast of Malaysia, facing the Strait of Malacca. It passes through the towns of

---

6 Various European powers ruled Melaka during its colonial history – the Portuguese were the first to occupy it in 1511.
7 Melaka drew traders from all over the world, including China. Some Chinese settlers married local Malay women, and their descendants are known as Peranakans or Straits-born Chinese. Peranakan cuisine is noted for its distinctive fusion of Chinese and Malay/Indonesian culinary influences.

Batu Pahat, Muar and Melaka. However, during the monsoon season, the route would be flooded so we would be forced to take the inland road. This second route passes through Yong Peng, Segamat and Tampin. Both routes would end up in Seremban, an hour's drive to Kuala Lumpur.

From Kuala Lumpur, we had many options. We could drive out to Port Klang for seafood, or visit the Batu Caves, a pilgrimage site dedicated to the Hindu deity Lord Murugan. The caves are part of a limestone hill complex consisting of three big caves and several smaller ones, with shrines located within them.

To enjoy some cooler climate, we would drive up to Cameron Highlands (1,600 m), a hill station that was originally developed for expatriates to escape the heat in Kuala Lumpur. Since then, it has been well visited by locals and tourists alike, and is known for its tea plantations and strawberry farms. Fraser's Hill (1,450 m) is another popular hill resort. We have also brought the children up to Genting Highlands (1,865 m), where there was a theme park, casino and restaurants with variety show performances. Today, Genting Highlands is home to an integrated resort with multiple hotels, casinos, theme parks, shopping malls, restaurants and entertainment venues.

For a long weekend of three to four days, we would drive even further north, to Ipoh for some excellent food and their famous *hor fun* (flat rice noodles). After that, another two more hours or so would take us to Butterworth. Before the Penang Bridge was built in 1985, we would catch a 10- to 20-minute car ferry from Butterworth over to Georgetown, the capital of the state of Penang.

Penang used to be a free port, but the free port status was revoked by the federal government in 1969. Until then, many Malaysians travelled to Penang for shopping. Being predominantly populated by Malaysian Chinese, Penang attracted a lot of foreign investment, particularly in real estate. Ethnic Chinese from Hong Kong and ASEAN nations made Penang their second home. There are some beaches in the northern part of the island popular with visitors from the Middle-Eastern countries. It was quite a sight witnessing girls in niqab and burqa riding horses on the beach. I even saw some of them parasailing in their niqab and burqa.

Further north, one could drive to Alor Star (now Alor Setar), the capital of the state of Kedah and eventually come to the northernmost state of Perlis. From Kuala Perlis on the coast, one could take a ferry over to the island of Langkawi, which is the size of Singapore. This island has been awarded duty-free status since 1987.

I have always liked to visit border crossings. It is my "other side of the mountain" obsession. In the 1970s, on a road trip to Penang, we drove up to the southern Thailand border from Alor Star. In the mid-2000s, I flew up to Kangar, the capital of Perlis, in a four-seater aircraft. I purposely took a taxi up to Padang Besar, just to see the border post managing immigration clearance and customs to Thailand.

There was a link wire fence separating the two countries, topped by barbed wire. About 100 m from the "official" border crossing was an "unofficial" crossing. On the Malaysian side of the fence, someone had built a set of steps right up to the top of the fence. The Thais had built a similar set of steps on the other side. The people didn't cross the fence because it was illegal, but they were trading contraband like rice, cooking oil, and other dutiable/controlled goods with each other by simply handing them over the fence aided by the steps they had set up. This was done in broad daylight!

Another of my favourite drives up Peninsular Malaysia is via the east coast road. From the JB checkpoint, one could drive up to the Kota Tinggi waterfalls. Then, it is a 1½-hour drive to the fishing village Mersing, which is the launching pad for ferries to the island resorts off the eastern coast of Malaysia. The largest island is Pulau Tioman where parts of the movie *South Pacific*[8] was filmed.

---

8   The romantic musical film was a box office success and won the Oscar for Best Sound in 1959.

Tioman is very popular with divers and anglers alike. On my first trip to Tioman in the mid-1970s, we could still see an abundance of crayfish and sharks when we snorkelled. Nowadays, sea life has mostly been depleted from overdiving and overfishing.

During the boat ride from Mersing out to Tioman, our boat would pass by another island, Pulau Tengah, where the United Nations High Commissioner for Refugees (UNHCR) had set up a transit camp for the Vietnamese boat people[9] after the fall of Saigon (now Ho Chi Minh City) while their case for resettlement to other countries were being processed. The Pulau Tengah refugee camp operated from the mid-1970s to the early 1980s.

As more and more boat people arrived, we noticed the deforestation creeping up the hill on the island. In the beginning, the settlers were allowed to roam around freely. They went ashore in Mersing for meals and hassled Singaporean divers like us to buy watches and cameras for them in Singapore. Many of them were ethnic Chinese, so communicating with them was quite easy.

Some of the other islands worth mentioning are Pulau Rawa, Pulau Babi Besar, Pulau Pemanggil and Pulau Aur. Pulau Rawa belongs to the Johor royal family. In the 1970s, there were no lodgings on these islands – we bunked in with the villagers and they cooked for us. Sometimes, we would even pitch our own tents on the beach. Today, proper resorts with electricity and water have been set up on most of these islands.

After Mersing, the next city further north is Kuantan, home to the Deep Water Terminal on the east coast of Peninsular Malaysia and also the Royal Malaysian Air Force base. The strategic location of the seaport meant that goods coming from Japan, China, Korea and the USA can be offloaded here instead of having ships go around the southern tip of the Malayan peninsula to reach the west coast.

Kuantan is also the largest Malaysian city nearest to South Vietnam. At the height of the exodus of the boat people after the fall of the South Vietnamese government, the beach along the east coast of the Malayan

---

9 See the section on Vietnam in the later part of this chapter for more on the boat people.

peninsula was regarded as the promised land for the boat people after one to two weeks at sea.

I remember staying at the Kuantan Hyatt and having breakfast at the patio overlooking the beach. There were rows of Vietnamese boats, tied to one another less than 50 m off the beach. The refugees were not permitted to come ashore, so they were just staring at us while we ate our breakfast. Also, at the Mersing jetty, when we went on our dive trips in 1978 and 1979, we saw bodies being unloaded by some of the fishing boats. Those were boat people who had died of drowning, disease or starvation; some might have been murdered by pirates after they were robbed.

Leaving Kuantan and heading north for about 100 km, we would pass by Kerteh, the major petroleum offshore support base for Malaysia. After that lay miles and miles of beautiful white sandy beaches as we came up to Kuala Terengganu, the capital of the state of Terengganu. Another 150 km of coastal road along this sandy beach took us to Kelantan, the northeastern corner of Malaysia. Along the way, we would pass by another two beautiful dive sites, Pulau Redang and the Perhentian Islands (Perhentian Besar and Perhentian Kecil).

In keeping with my obsession with border crossings, we drove up to the Thai border from Kelantan. About a kilometre from the border, I noticed many tents on each side of the road. I asked someone about the tents and was told that they were all paint shops. "Paint shops?" I asked. "In tents?" I wondered how anybody could paint anything in a tent with dust and bugs!

It seemed that cars stolen in Malaysia were driven into these tents where they would get a face lift with a new paint job. They were then driven into Thailand with false licence plates and would never be seen again! It was done so blatantly, and so close to the border.

I took flying lessons while I was serving National Service in Singapore. At that time, the Ministry of Defence started the Armed Forces

Flying Club to generate interest in flying amongst active servicemen. We could learn to fly for just $10 an hour because the instructors were all volunteers from the air force. Through the Armed Forces Flying Club, I compiled a little more than 100 flying hours in 1½ years and gained my first pilot's license, albeit a restricted one because I did not fulfil the necessary navigation exercise. Later, I joined the Singapore Flying Club and obtained my full-fledged private pilot licence.

Members of the flying club were periodically invited by the Malaysian Department of Civil Aviation (DCA) for fly-ins to the more remote airports around the peninsula. These included the Taman Negara airstrip, which had a grass strip that made taking off difficult after heavy rainfall; the Pangkor airstrip where we had to avoid a small hill on an island right in the flight path during short finals; and the Kangar airstrip near the Thai border. This airstrip is short, and only the first 200 feet is paved while the rest of the runway surface is gravel.

In Kangar, we were greeted by the Raja of Perlis. Wearing an aviator shirt, he came out to shake our hands, accompanied by his wife, the Raja Perempuan. I hesitated to shake her hand when she held it out to me, as Muslim women were not supposed to make physical contact with another man who is not her husband. But then, not shaking her outstretched hand would have been a big insult to her majesty.

Shortly after I qualified for my private pilot licence, I flew to Pulau Tioman with three other friends. There is an airstrip on the island built by the Japanese army during the Second World War. The airstrip is well hidden among some coconut trees, so it is not visible when one approaches the island from the sea. I have personally made many flights into this challenging airstrip.

On that day, the flight into Tioman was smooth. We enjoyed the beach and some local food at the village next to the airstrip. When it was time to go home, I took off from the airstrip and turned south to head for the mainland (Mersing). What I saw in front of me almost made me wet my pants. The whole state of Johor was covered by storm clouds. Not wanting to turn back and land in Tioman again since it was getting dark, I proceeded to head for the mainland. As I flew close to the coastline, I saw another aircraft descending rapidly, and heard the pilot over the radio, informing the Johor air traffic control tower that he was going to land in Mersing to wait out the storm.

My passengers asked me how far we were from the Johor airport, and I said that it was less than 20 minutes. The consensus was to bash through the storm clouds and head for the Johor airfield. As I was being tossed around by the turbulent winds and heavy rain, a lightning bolt flashed no more than 30 m from our plane. I shouted out "Jesus Christ!", but was promptly reminded by my passengers that, as the pilot, I was not allowed to say that. However, as my passengers, they were entitled to do just that.

At that point, I understood what was meant by the maxim "Always respect the weather". So I turned the aircraft around and headed straight out to sea again. When I saw a hole among the clouds below me, I dove through it and came out 500 feet above the sea but below all the clouds. I followed the coastline and landed at Mersing as well, to wait out the storm.

It turned out that the other aircraft waiting out the storm was flown by our Chief Flying Instructor. I was so shaken up at that time, that I asked if someone else from his aircraft would be kind enough to fly us back to Singapore. He said, "No. If you don't fly now, you will probably not fly again". However, he offered to make all the radio calls on my behalf as we headed south along the coast. All I had to do was to fly the aircraft and follow him.

On another flight to Pulau Tioman, after I had made a perfect landing, I was approached by a villager with an emergency. He told me that there was a baby born three months premature on the island. His body was all blue and they were quite sure he would not survive the bumboat ride to the mainland to get to a hospital, which took more than four hours[10]. He asked if I would be kind enough to fly the baby and his mother to Mersing on the mainland.

Of course, I would not expect to be paid for the trip. I agreed to help them, and so the father, the mother, a male nurse plus the baby showed up at the airstrip. Because we now had five souls on board an aircraft that

---

10 This happened before there were regular flights between Tioman and the mainland.

was certified for only four, I did not bother to fill up a passenger manifest and file a flight plan. Besides, mine was not a commercial pilot's licence, but a private pilot's licence. Twenty minutes later, I arrived overhead the Mersing airstrip. Just like in the movies, there was an ambulance waiting for me. After I landed, the party climbed into the ambulance in a hurry and left for the hospital.

I flew back to Tioman uneventfully, with an elated feeling in my heart. Until today, I have not heard from the parents. There might be someone walking around in Tioman who owes me his life!

On another trip, we flew across the South China Sea in a single engine Cessna 182. Midway over the sea, a sharp whining noise came from somewhere within the aircraft. The noise persisted even after we had switched off all the radios. The engine instruments indicated a normal operating engine. We finally narrowed it down to an air vent louvre at the back of the cabin. By adjusting the louvre's airflow direction, the noise went away. I was sure that there were many disappointed sharks in the sea below us.

Sabah and Sarawak are located on East Malaysia. Among the states that joined the Federation in 1963, they were relatively less developed, but were a major source of natural resources such as timber, oil and natural gas. They did not want to be swamped with residents of West Malaysia, so they retained full control of immigration matters. West Malaysians need a permit to stay and work in East Malaysia, while East Malaysians can freely choose to live and work in West Malaysia.

Sarawak is a long state geographically, measuring 750 km from tip to tip. Many of the inhabitants live in longhouses in the interior of the land, accessible only by riding in a bumboat up the river, passing by miles and miles of tropical forest. I once met a police chief over a drink in Kuching, the capital of Sarawak. He told me, "You are here to sell helicopters? I don't like you, because in the old days, when my boss wanted to visit my police post, I get a pre-warning that he is coming up the river and he'll be here, maybe the next day. Now, if he comes by helicopter, he will catch me playing truant, during official duty hours."

To drive from Kuching to the northern tip of the state on what is called the Pan Borneo Highway takes more than 15 hours, crossing rivers by ferries and travelling on stretches of sometimes unpaved road. It even passes through the country of Brunei. The first town is Sibu, home to some timber tycoons. Then comes Bintulu, which is the centre of petroleum offshore industries. Because Bintulu is the busiest seaport in Sarawak, the economy also expanded into palm oil production and processing; timber and plywood yards; and even cement manufacturing.

Continuing north, the highway passes through the coastal city of Miri, where the first oil well was drilled by Royal Dutch Shell in 1910. Today, the petroleum industry remains a major player in the city's economy. Miri used to be the gateway to the Mulu Caves, a UNESCO World Heritage Site. In the old days, the trip from Miri to the Gunung Mulu National Park entrance took days because of the boat ride from Marudi. Today, there is a Mulu airfield just minutes away from the park entrance, accessible by foot.

When I was there in 2017, it was drizzling and everyone hung around, waiting to witness the hundreds of thousands of bats flying out of one of the largest caves before nightfall. Then, it happened. First, there were just a few, then the whole lot covered the entire sky above us. Some of the caves in the park run for kilometres, the longest one being the Clearwater Cave measuring more than 100 km.

After Miri, the highway crosses into Brunei and then out again eventually at the Serasa Ferry Terminal where one can catch a ferry to either Labuan, a federal territory of East Malaysia, or Kota Kinabalu (KK), the capital of the state of Sabah. From KK, one can drive up to the northern tip of the state, or cross over to the eastern shores of the state.

There are two world-renowned dive sites in Sabah: Layang Layang and Pulau Sipadan. Layang Layang is 300 km northwest of KK, while Sipadan is just 40 km from Semporna, a fishing town on the east coast. Layang Layang has some 6,000 feet (1,800 m) vertical drop offs, while Sipadan is known for its 2,000 feet (600 m) drop offs.

AIRBUS OR SCHOOL BUS?

Many Malaysians want their children to achieve a higher standard in English, so they send their children to study in Singapore where the medium of instruction is English. Every year, when the Chinese New Year holiday comes around, flights to East Malaysia would be filled with school kids going home to Sabah and Sarawak to spend the festival with their parents. I would be among the passengers too, making my way to see my parents and sister in Sandakan. Someone once stepped into an Airbus aircraft and made a comment: "This is not an Airbus. This is a school bus."

The Philippines

The Philippines is an archipelago consisting of more than 7,000 islands. A former Spanish colony that was ceded to the United States in the 19th century, it became independent in 1946.

In the mid-1970s, I visited Manila, the capital of the Philippines, for the first time. Like all tourists, we did the 5-hour car ride up to the mountain town of Baguio and also shot the rapids at the Pagsanjan Falls.

In 1980, I went back to the Philippines for a dive trip to the Apo Reef, the second largest connecting reef in the world. It is located in the Mindoro Strait, south-southwest of Manila. On arrival at the Manila International Airport, we were greeted by guitar-strumming bands inside the airport terminal singing all the popular pop songs to create a holiday mood for arriving tourists.

After clearing immigration and customs, we climbed onto a minibus for the 100-km ride to Batangas, where our liveaboard dive boat was waiting for us. A few members of our group discovered a local rum that sold for 7 pesos (a little over US$1) a 70-cl bottle. It was labelled "E.S.Q." which stood for "Extra Smooth Quality". I gathered from them that diving headaches from their hangover at 100 feet (30 m) below the surface were nothing to laugh about. The boat ride from Batangas to Apo Reef was supposed to be 12 hours, but because of strong headwinds, we could only make it there in 18 hours.

The diving there was just fabulous. Some members of the group did a pre-dawn dive, mid-morning dive, early afternoon dive, sunset dive and then wrapped up the day with a night dive. One day, while we were diving, two locals on the boat decided to practise shooting at some empty beer cans floating on the surface of the sea. The way those bullets pierced the water was just like in the movies!

When our boat was anchored off Apo Island one night, the swells from the ocean were quite big. In the middle of the night, there was a loud crashing sound. The following morning, we discovered that the anchor chain had chewed off a big chunk of the bow of the boat.

On another night, one of the divers surfaced from the sea, took off his diving mask and put on his glasses, which he then accidentally dropped into the sea. Miraculously, someone diving in the same area the following night found and retrieved his glasses on the 40-foot-deep seabed.

Our trip soon came to an end, and some of us were booked on different flights out of Manila. After check-in, for security reasons, we had to identify our own luggage from a holding area to make sure that we would be on the same flight as our luggage. There, I noticed a diving equipment bag belonging to a fellow diver who had left for Singapore on an earlier flight. I explained to the customs officer that the bag needed to go to Singapore. The officer wanted to write down my particulars in his notebook before he would release the bag to me. However, he didn't have a pen.

"Can I borrow your pen?" he asked. I handed him my pen and he wrote down all the particulars in a logbook. Then he put my pen in his shirt pocket.

"Uh, excuse me, Sir, may I have my pen back?" I asked.

"Oh, a few more questions," he said. He added a few more notes and then put my pen back in his pocket, again.

"Uh, I am going to need my pen to fill in immigration forms at my next destination," I told him.

"Oh, yes, your pen, ha ha, so sorry," he said as he finally returned it to me.

Since that trip, we have returned to the Philippines to dive in Cebu, Puerto Princessa and Boracay. Sad to say, the sea has been depleted of fish and other sea life. According to the dive guide, they have been either fished out or dynamited out. In Cebu waters, the visibility was very, very good, but there was not much sea life. There was a storm in Puerto Princessa when we were there, and the dive boats could not even get out of the harbour. Boracay was just filled with tourists and was utterly polluted.

I have been to some fabulous restaurants and bars in Manila, many of which held live band performances. I enjoy watching the performances of local Filipino bands because they are usually made up of more than 10 members, so they bring out an exceptionally rich sound.

One unusual observation I made in the 1990s was the presence of large cages on the roads in Manila. The police had decided to act against the number of jaywalkers in the city by locking them up in big cages placed on the middle island of major roads. Any jaywalker caught would be put into these cages under the blazing sun for a couple of hours so as to warn others not to do the same. Each cage could probably hold 20 people.

On another trip to the Philippines, I decided to put all of my Singapore currency into my passport after I had cleared immigration and customs, since I would not be spending them yet. On the way out of the Philippines, I handed the immigration officer my passport. I noticed that he really scrutinised my passport, and wondered why. He was flipping through every page, turning it upside down and shaking it. Then he handed back my passport with the Singapore currency notes, and said, "Next time, do not put any cash in your passport because I might think that you were trying to offer me a bribe." Lesson learned.

Singapore

My first trip to Singapore was in 1959. Since I was only 10 years old at the time, I did not have much recollection of the trip, other than the 8-hour flight from Singapore to Hong Kong in an unpressurised DC-4 powered by four radial reciprocating engines. Other airlines were flying Turboprops such as Lockheed Electra, and Turbojets such as Comet 4 and Boeing 707, which could do the same trip in less than four hours.

On my next trip to Singapore in 1963, Malaysian Airways had leased two Comet 4s to fly that same route in less than four hours. However, on the Singapore–Hong Kong sector, one of the four jet engines was shut down in flight, so we returned to Singapore for an engine change which took more than four hours. During those two trips, I never would have guessed that I would one day make Singapore my home for the most part of my life thereafter.

In the 1970s, I became a Singapore citizen, after working for Lockheed Aircraft and serving National Service. Singapore in that era was very different from the Singapore we know today. My soon-to-be wife's family was based here and had a diesel car, so I would drive it around on weekends to explore the island.

Of special interest to me were the fishing villages (*kampongs*). On Sunday mornings, I would drive out to the *kampongs* at the end of Tuas Road, Lim Chu Kang Road, Punggol Road or Serangoon Road. These were small villages with a jetty where fishermen would come ashore with their catch and sell them to locals who came out for their breakfast in the coffee shops (*kopitiams*) near the jetties. I could still remember the big bowl of noodles from the *kopitiam* in Tuas village, all for 70 cents.

At the end of Punggol Road was the Punggol jetty and village. Choon Seng *kopitiam* was famous for their chilli crab, and water-skiers would all come up for lunch after a hard day of skiing for some cold beer and chilli crab. Just up the road was a wholesale stall selling the savoury fish cake snack *otak-otak*[11]. I could not believe my ears when he asked me how many hundred sticks of *otak-otak* I was interested to buy.

If I were set to spend a whole day out, I would also catch a bumboat out to the northeastern islands of Pulau Ubin and Pulau Tekong. The latter was converted to a military training base in the 1990s, and is no longer open to the public.

---

11 *Otak-otak* (also known as *otah*) is made of ground fish meat mixed with starch and spices to form a paste, which is then wrapped in attap or banana leaves and grilled over charcoal fire.

Within Singapore waters, I could also take a ferry out to the southern islands of Sisters' Islands, St John's Island, or Kusu Island where there is a beautiful Chinese temple and three Malay holy shrines (*keramats*). The temple houses two main deities (Da Bo Gong and Guan Yin), and thousands of devotees flock to Kusu Island during the annual pilgrimage in the ninth month of the lunar calendar, even to this day.

Around town, there were some popular and (in)famous hotspots. One such place was Bugis Street. It was an area where transvestites and foreigners hung out till the wee hours. The former would offer their services to the latter. By 1 or 2 a.m., fights would break out practically every night between intoxicated foreigners. The policemen were often completely outnumbered, so they would run to the side and blow their whistles, but do nothing to break up the fights. In the 1980s, the government redeveloped the area, and Bugis Street became part of a shopping and dining complex.

Hawkers and the food they serve are a big part of the local culture. We can usually get cheaper food from the hawkers than cooking it ourselves. All Singaporeans have their own favourite hawker for their favourite dish. The popular hawkers have their own cult following. If they move from their usual hawker centre, all their loyal customers will try to find out where they have moved to. When I asked a certain friend of mine where I could get the best chicken rice in Singapore, he would ask if I were interested in the best chicken, the best rice or the best chilli sauce.

The hawkers here have come a long way, from their itinerant days on the street to getting Michelin stars today. Hawker Chan who serves chicken rice was one of the first two street-food hawkers[12] in Singapore and the world to earn a Michelin star. The other Michelin-starred hawker serves a noodle dish. In 2020, hawker culture in Singapore was officially added to the UNESCO list of intangible cultural heritage.

---

12 In 2016, two hawker stalls in Singapore – Chef Chan Hon Meng's Hawker Chan Soya Sauce Chicken Rice and Noodle Stall, and Hill Street Tai Hwa Pork Noodle Stall – became the world's first street-food hawkers to get a Michelin star.

Thailand

The kingdom of Thailand is also known as the Land of Smiles. The Thais supposedly use their smiles to avoid confrontation, but I think there is a tendency to leave the real issue unresolved. Everything to them is "Mai pen rai" or "No problem". The "Land of Smiles" phrase actually came from a slogan used by the Thai tourism board since the mid-1980s.

However, the first thing that wiped the smile off my face on my arrival in its capital Bangkok was the long immigration queues at the airport. There just seemed to be so much checking that the immigration officers had to do before they would stamp my passport. I couldn't help but ask myself, why can't they improve their system if they really want to attract more visitors? One trick I learned was to find an immigration counter manned by a female officer. At least, they type faster on the keyboard, according to my observations. The long wait to clear Thai immigration is a persistent problem, but in recent years, the Thai immigration bureau set up special automated clearance lanes in the Bangkok airport just for Singaporean passport holders to handle the high volume of Singaporean visitors.

I first toured Bangkok in the 1970s. In those days, visiting the floating market, taking a two-day, one-night excursion down to Pattaya, having a beer in Patpong, and watching a transvestite cabaret show were some of the standard touristy things to do. I also had the privilege of a ringside seat at a Thai boxing (*muay thai*) stadium, where spectators can get sprayed by the sweat and/or blood from the boxers.

Over the years, I have explored other parts of Thailand. I have visited the beaches in Sattahip district near Rayong, and the U-Tapao Royal Thai Navy Airfield. I have also been to the Khao Yai National Park which has a cool climate because of its high altitude.

In 2003, I attended a relative's wedding on a floating hotel on River Kwai, near Kanchanaburi, the western part of Thailand. The guest rooms of the hotel were actually bamboo huts built on bamboo rafts, tied end to end like a chain. At the middle of the chain was the reception and dining area where the wedding ceremony and dinner were being held. Early next morning, the mist over the River Kwai was just like a scene out of fairyland.

In fact, I was so impressed with the setting that I revisited the area in 2018 with an ex-neighbour who is an architect by profession. However, the floating hotels were no longer built on bamboo rafts. Instead, they were built on steel pontoons.

When I found out that we were only 70 km from the Thai–Myanmar Ban Phu Nam Ron border, I made a detour to visit the border crossing the following day. My interest in border crossings came from my curiosity as to how the crossing is fortified, and what type of activities I can observe there. For example, at this particular crossing, I saw the types of produce that were being brought over from Myanmar such as banana tree trunks, fresh bamboo shoots, betel nuts and even duck eggs. Similarly, the Myanmarese would pick up some good quality batik fabric for their longyi[13], superior cooking oil and fine Thai whisky to bring back with them at the last stop, plus the money from selling the produce that they had brought into Thailand.

There used to be some fabulous dive sites in southern Thailand, around Phuket, Koh Phi Phi and Koh Similan. We did our first dive in Phuket in 1979 when there was just one dive shop on the island. The Hollywood movie *The Beach* was shot on one of the islands south of Phuket. North of Phuket is a group of islands known as Koh Similan, which is fabulous for diving. We used to have to take an overnight boat ride from Phuket to get to Similan. Nowadays, one can take a 2-hour car ride to Thap Lamu Pier, followed by a 70-minute speedboat ride to get to the dive sites in Similan. On the Gulf of Thailand is a laid-back resort island named Koh Samui. In those days, we had to drive to Surat Thani and take a ferry across to Koh Samui. Nowadays, you can fly there directly. However, all these places are now overdived with the influx of divers from China, Hong Kong and Singapore.

On the Thai-Malaysian border is the notorious sin city of Hat Yai, not very different from Tijuana, across the Mexican border from San Diego.

---

13 The longyi is the traditional and national attire in Myanmar. It is a long piece of cloth that is sewn into a cylindrical shape, and wrapped or knotted around the waist. The longyi worn by men and women differ in terms of fabric pattern and wrapping method.

Further north, there is Chiang Mai, a city that I have been to numerous times. Thais visit Chiang Mai because of the ancient temples and mountainous scenery. However, the city is getting overcrowded, and the local citizens are moving out. With the change in climate, there have been some damaging floods that brought down the price of real estate. Another popular tourist destination in the north which I have visited is the ruins of Sukhothai, the first capital of the Kingdom of Siam and birthplace of Thai art, architecture and language. Remains of the ancient palace and temples within the city walls still stand.

Four-and-a-half-hours' drive from Chiang Mai is the Golden Triangle Park within Chiang Rai, which is the northernmost province in Thailand. The park overlooks the spot where the Ruak River from Myanmar flows into the Mekong River. This spot is also known as the "Golden Triangle", because it is where the Thailand–Myanmar border meets Laos, and is one of the busiest drug-producing and trafficking regions in the world. Some tourists would take a speedboat to dash across the Mekong River just to get a Laotian immigration stamp on their passports. When we were there in 1998, Myanmar was building a casino upstream along the Mekong. Going further upstream on the Mekong for 200 km would lead you to China.

Brunei

The sultanate of Brunei is a very small independent nation on the northern coast of the island of Borneo. A former British protectorate, it declared independence in 1984. Brunei is separated into two parts by the Sarawak district of Limbang, East Malaysia. The total population is less than half a million, and its capital is Bandar Seri Begawan. Other than taking some pictures in front of the national mosque, I did not find much to do in Brunei.

On my first trip to Brunei in the mid-1980s, I stayed at the Sheraton Hotel where I could go into the bar on the ground floor and order a drink. On subsequent visits, the bar was still open, but the liquor bottles were all covered up by white bedsheets. Later, the bar would not serve alcohol, but we still managed to get a beer by going down to the sailing club. By the 1990s, we could only order beer in Chinese restaurants, which tried to beat the rap by serving it in a porcelain teapot. I remember drinking beer out of small china teacups.

There were four overland border crossings from Brunei into Sarawak: two of them from the western part of Brunei, and the other two from the eastern part. The Jalan Kuala Lurah crossing into the Tedungan Immigration checkpoint on the Malaysian side actually takes less than half an hour from the city centre of Bandar Seri Begawan. However, in the afternoon leading to the evening rush hour, there would be long lines of vehicles crossing over to East Malaysia for shopping as well as for a few pints. There were restaurants, liquor stores and supermarkets just 100 m after getting through the checkpoint.

The heavy rush hour traffic in the evening reminded me very much of the scenario[14] on the road leading up to the border between Saudi Arabia and Bahrain, because the Saudis, I was told, were also going over to Bahrain for their pint.

Vietnam

No one in Sabah cared much about what was going on in Vietnam during the Vietnamese people's struggle for independence against the French. In the early 1960s, "guerrilla warfare" was a new term we learned in our English class.

Then reality hit. During my seven years of schooling in the US, I lived through the anti-war demonstrations and riots in Chicago during the Democratic National Convention (DNC) in 1968; Woodstock music festival in 1969; the introduction of the Vietnam War draft lottery that same year; and the shooting of unarmed students in Kent State University in 1970.

I went to a talk given by Rennie Davis, one of the Chicago Seven[15]. The opening line in his speech was: "The last thing that Samson did was to tear the temple down". The audience went wild, waving Viet Cong flags and chanting: "Ho Ho Ho, Ho Chi Minh". When I was back in

---

14 See Chapter 5 "West Asia" for my adventures in the Middle East.
15 The Chicago Seven were seven men charged with conspiracy and anti-Vietnam-War protests in Chicago during the 1968 DNC. They were convicted on various charges, but were eventually acquitted.

Sabah during the summer of 1970, a Peace Corps volunteer there told me he was on the cover of LIFE magazine for climbing onto the equestrian statue of General John Logan in Chicago during the riots in 1968. These Peace Corps volunteers were growing cannabis on their front porch in Sandakan, but smoking of marijuana was not widespread in Sabah then, so they were not bothered by the local police. I also found out that the first friend I made in the US was killed in Vietnam.

After the South Vietnam regime fell in the mid-1970s, many South Vietnamese fled by boat, heading south and eventually coming ashore in the east coast of Peninsular Malaysia. The earliest batch of Vietnamese boat people came out by steamers and they brought with them antique Chinese wooden furniture which they sold for cash. I managed to buy some pieces of furniture from them.

Although the boat people might have suffered together during the journey across the South China Sea, it was every man for himself when they reached the shores of Malaysia. The men would scuttle their boats so that they could not be towed back out to sea again. The women and children who could not swim would simply be left to drown.

My business trips to Vietnam had been routine visits to Hanoi and Ho Chi Minh City. However, in 2017, I had the opportunity to see other parts of Vietnam as I joined a team from my wife's chef training academy that was making an exploratory trip of the country. Flying into Danang, we were brought to Hoi An, the ancient town which is a UNESCO World Heritage Site. Next, we flew up to Hanoi. Not to be missed is the museum with all the captured American hardware during the war and the notorious "Hanoi Hilton". The latter was a nickname given by American prisoners-of-war to the Hoa Lo Prison, where the North Vietnam government held American soldiers captive.

We also went out to Ha Long Bay, another UNESCO World Heritage Site, for a cruise around its islets. After Ha Long, we took a flight down to Quy Nhon, a coastal city in Central Vietnam, before finishing the tour in Ho Chi Minh City. Something to keep in our memory before we left the country: we had drinks at the rooftop bar of the Rex Hotel, where the infamous American military command's afternoon press conferences took place during the Vietnam War.

Laos

Like Vietnam and Cambodia, Laos was a colony in French Indochina. The landlocked country gained independence in 1953, and its monarchy was abolished in 1975.

I have only been to Laos once, and that was in the early 1990s. Its capital Vientiane was then a sleepy little city. In those days, the tallest building in town was a 6-storey hotel. The favourite pastime of the locals was to sit on the bank of the Mekong River under the Thai–Lao Friendship Bridge, sipping a cup of tea or a glass of coconut water. I also remember that our host had a panther in his house. The panther had lost its sense of balance so it could not stand straight and kept bumping into the furniture in the house. There were many French pastry shops in Vientiane, selling wonderful freshly baked baguettes.

Myanmar (Burma)

My wife Kwan was born and raised in Burma. The country was a former British colony that became independent in 1948. According to my father-in-law, Burma was such a bountiful country that one could get rich there just by breathing the air. However, in 1962, General Ne Win staged a coup and took complete control of the government. All the industries and financial institutions were nationalised. He also issued a decree that anyone taking loans from banks would be jailed. That, of course, was directed at the Chinese community who held most of the wealth in the country. When my father-in-law caught wind of this, he moved the whole family to Hong Kong in 1963, and simply left all his assets behind.

One night in 1970, General Ne Win had a dream that cars in Burma were driving on the right side of the road instead of the left, which was how the British had left it after Burma was granted independence in 1948. The following day, all the roads had to follow the Right-Hand Traffic system even though the steering wheel of all the existing cars were located on the right.

In 1985, he declared that all 50 and 100 kyat notes were no longer legal tender. They were replaced by 45 and 90 kyat notes. Henceforth, all the children growing up in Burma were required to think in multiples of 9.

In 1989, the country's official English name, which it had held since 1885, was changed from the Union of Burma to the Union of Myanmar. In 2020, new currency notes were issued, but in more useful and practical denominations of fives, tens and hundreds. In the early 1990s, we travelled to Myanmar for the first time since Kwan left in 1963[16].

On another trip, we took a three-day Orient Express luxurious river boat cruise from Mandalay to Bagan. On one of the stops, we rode a bullock cart to a picnic spot for lunch. Along the way, the cart driver stopped the cart when he saw a beehive in the shrub next to the road. Without any protective gear, he simply reached in and plucked it off the branch. It turned out to be an empty hive, but there was honey inside, so he sold it to us for US$5. For him to take the risk of getting stung, his skin had to have been as thick as cow hide.

Cambodia

The kingdom of Cambodia is a former French colony which declared independence in 1953. Unfortunately, it is also another country that was torn apart by civil war in the mid-1970s. After being badly scarred by the Khmer Rouge and the mass killings orchestrated by the radical communist regime, Cambodia managed to stabilise over the years, as political reform and reconstruction efforts led to economic growth.

I made a few trips to Cambodia when I was working for Bell Helicopter; I have also visited the country for short holidays. I remember being on a flight to the Cambodian capital of Phnom Penh, when we encountered an emergency situation aboard the plane. During landing, the pilot announced that there was a problem with the landing gear. From our seats, we saw an emergency formation of fire trucks lining the runway as our plane approached terra firma. Fortunately, we landed without incident. Phew!

One day, our Bell Helicopter representative in Phnom Penh called our office in Singapore and told us that if we could make our way to Phnom Penh before 4 p.m. the following day, he could get us a meeting

---

16 See Chapter 11 "The Hardship Group" for our visit to Kwan's birth country.

with the Prime Minister. We quickly checked with all the airlines that flew to Phnom Penh and found that we could get there early next afternoon by flying up to Bangkok in the early morning, then catching a connecting flight to Phnom Penh immediately. So, off we went.

Usually, when you seek an audience with the head of state of a nation, you will be brought into a staging area and wait to be called. However, in this case, we were taken by our representative directly to the Prime Minister's residence. Instead of sitting in a room adjacent to the Prime Minister's office, we were brought upstairs where the Prime Minister was waiting for us at the top of the stairs. We had some very frank and open discussions about his priorities and why he could not be seen spending state funds on a luxury item like a helicopter.

On the way back to our hotel after the meeting, we asked our representative how he had managed to set up that meeting. He told us that he had dinner with the Prime Minister once or twice a week, because he was dating the PM's daughter.

Chapter 5
WEST ASIA

Rich in resources such as oil, natural gas and minerals, West Asia is often referred to as the Middle East. The criteria used to define the area it covers are somewhat fluid and have changed over time. Neighbouring countries are sometimes considered to be part of the region, such as Egypt, Turkey and Afghanistan. Different faiths are prac-tised in the region, with Islam as the most widely followed religion.

My first trip to the Middle East took place in 1981 on a palm oil trade mission organised by the Malaysian government. In the 1980s, Malaysia was the biggest palm oil producer in the world. The trade mission explored business opportunities in Saudi Arabia, North Yemen, Egypt, Jordan, Kuwait, and the United Arab Emirates (Dubai, Sharjah and Abu Dhabi).

As part of a government delegation, we were very well taken care of. The Malaysian Embassy in each of the Middle Eastern countries made all the necessary accommodation and transport arrangements for us. At every trade mission stop, we had the chance to meet and network with potential local importers at a reception. An additional benefit of these receptions was that we could sample all the local cuisines of the Middle East.

Saudi Arabia

There were about twenty of us participating in the 1981 trade mission, representing Malaysian palm oil refining and packaging companies. We met in Bangkok to catch a Saudi Arabian Airlines flight heading for Riyadh. As was the common practice among Middle Eastern airlines in those days, the female cabin attendants stayed in the galley to prepare meals while the male attendants served the passengers.

It was a strange scene within the cabin when the pilot announced the imminent descent of the aircraft into the kingdom of Saudi Arabia. Many young Arab female passengers would take turns to go into the toilets to change out of their jeans and T-shirts, and emerge wearing their abaya (full-length robes) and headscarves. These were the same ladies who probably went bar-hopping in Patpong the night before.

We were warmly welcomed by the Malaysian Embassy staff in Riyadh. Our ice-breaking session was a dinner party at the ambassador's residence where we were given the programme for the next few days. We were urged to read up on the dos and don'ts for visitors to Saudi Arabia.

In addition to visiting Riyadh, we also flew over to Jeddah, where most of our consumer packaged oil was being imported by the Saudis. We realised that we were actually very close to Mecca, the holiest of Muslim cities, but we were told that non-Muslims like us would never get pass the police roadblocks on the Mecca-Jeddah Highway. However, a few Malay members of the delegation took the opportunity to go to Mecca for an Umrah (mini-haj).

I had an interesting meeting with one of the sheikhs. First, I was invited to join him in a big tent. Then I was asked if I wanted tea or coffee. I chose tea, and the servant boy brought me a cup of very light-coloured liquid. One sip told me that I was being served ginseng tea. All the delegates of the trade mission sat in the tent and all could hear the discussions that were going on.

If the sheikh was haggling with a guest over the price of cooking oil, we could all hear what was being offered and also what the sheikh's counter-offer was. Invariably, sitting next to the sheikh was either an Indian or a Pakistani, who was the sheikh's financial adviser. He was the one who did most of the bargaining; all we were seeking was a nod from the sheikh if we wanted to close the deal.

After a week in Saudi Arabia during which we visited the cities of Riyadh, Dammam and Jeddah, the Malaysian Embassy assisted us to obtain our visas from the consulate of the Yemen Arab Republic (it was known as North Yemen[1] then), so that we could fly down to the port city of Al Hudaydah.

North Yemen

Our flight landed in Hudaydah International Airport. Because we were travelling in such a big group, the hotel agreed to send a bus to the airport to fetch us. Unfortunately, our flight was 1½ hours late, and we thought that we had missed our transport. Surprisingly, the bus was there waiting for us, so we rode it to the hotel with no issues.

As usual, we had a reception at the hotel where local importers met and networked with us. Although Sana'a was the capital city of North Yemen, Al Hudaydah was the commercial centre. The following day, we visited the massive port and then we checked out of the hotel. Each of us was billed for two bus pick-ups from the airport! The manager explained that the bus had to make two trips to pick us up from the airport because we were not there at the appointed time.

Egypt

Our next stop, Cairo. Egypt is a country that is in both the Middle East and Africa. Before the trip, I was able to get an Egyptian visa from the Egyptian Embassy in Singapore. Although I did not notice it then, on closer inspection, I found out that it was issued on 30 January 1981 and would expire on 30 February 1981. Since 30 February does not exist, I wonder whether that means the visa has no expiry date.

The flight over to Cairo was uneventful. After the receptions and networking sessions, we had some free time. Like all tourists, we visited all the famous monuments such as the Sphinx and the Pyramids. It is amazing how close to the main strip of Cairo these monuments are, even to this day. The largest of the pyramids towers over the main tourist hotels and cafés, and is the only remaining wonder of the ancient world, from the original seven. We even did the camel ride and took a whole lot of photographs. However, when I returned home, I found that there was

---

1 North and South Yemen united to form the Republic of Yemen in 1990.

something wrong with my camera. All the photographs turned out with double images. So much for proof that "I was there".

That evening we went to a big tourist trap of an outdoor café to watch a belly dancing performance. The ticket included dinner with a half carafe of local wine.

Every visitor who came to Cairo wanted to drop by the Egyptian Museum to see the treasures of King Tutankhamun. So did we. But on our visit, we were disappointed to see a sign saying that the section of the museum was "closed for renovation".

As we wandered around the museum, we heard a voice whispering "Psst, do you want to see King Tut's treasures?"

"How much?"

"Cheap, $20."

When you go all the way to Cairo, what is US$20? So we gladly paid the amount and the curator led us away, parted some curtains and wow, we managed to get into the Mummy Room.

While we were in Cairo, we experienced one of its violent sand-storms. We had to hole up in our hotel for a day. When the sandstorm subsided and we were ready to leave Cairo, our travel agent called Egypt Air to arrange for our departure flights.

"I'm sorry, but all flights have been cancelled because of the sand-storm," we were told.

"That's fine, but when is the next flight out?" we asked.

"All later flights are full, sir. The earliest flight available is in 30 days," the agent said.

Thirty days? We were very lucky that we were on a trade mission; the Malaysian Embassy staff managed to arrange an earlier departure for all of us.

Jordan

Amman, the Jordanian capital, was our next stop. Malaysia and Jordan have always had a strong cooperative relationship. The local government treated us very well and hosted a reception outdoors, on a hill over-looking the city. All kinds of local dishes were laid out on long tables for our enjoyment.

Since most of our cooking oil was imported through the port of Aqaba, we were brought there as well. Just across the border is Eilat, an Israeli beach resort. I have always wondered how two warring states could share a border which is heavily inhabited on both sides: a major seaport on one side and a beach resort on the other. As we travelled along the South Beach Highway, the beach was so inviting that a couple of us just took off our clothes and jumped into the crystal-clear waters of the Gulf of Aqaba.

While we were in Amman, we had dinner at the one and only Chinese restaurant. It was converted from a big mansion, and was owned by a retired Taiwanese military attaché. Because of his connections with the Jordanian government, his restaurant was always patronised by high-ranking government officials, I was told.

Kuwait

Since we were already in the neighbourhood, we slotted in a stopover in Kuwait next. My impression was that it was a very small and strict Muslim nation. We spent only an evening there, hosting a reception for the local traders who were buying some of our refined palm oil.

United Arab Emirates

The United Arab Emirates (UAE) consist of seven emirates. Most of the Malaysian cooking oil was bought by traders in three emirates: Dubai, Abu Dhabi and Sharjah, where they were then loaded onto dhows and smuggled over to southern Iran. Hence, these three cities were important stops for our delegation.

While the UAE are Islamic states, alcohol was easily available in the international hotels. I was able to order a pint of Woodpecker alcoholic cider on tap in Dubai, something unheard of in Singapore in those days.

The queue to enter a disco in Abu Dhabi could stretch to 100 m long. The situation was similar in Dubai. At that time, as most of the flights from Asia to Europe had to transit in Dubai to pick up fuel, the disco in the Dubai Intercontinental Hotel became the hottest partying place in town because the cabin crew from Singapore Airlines, Malaysian

Airline System, British Airways, and Cathay Pacific all congregated there after their flights landed at around 2 a.m. The DJs even played some Cantopop music brought in by the Cathay Pacific crew. One floor below the disco was a casino, even though gambling is considered strictly haram.

Seafood was in such abundance in the UAE. The owner of a Chinese restaurant showed us pictures of his catch from his weekend fishing trips.

Three days later, the trade mission came to a successful completion, and our delegation flew home.

Iran

Later that year, I visited the Islamic Republic of Iran for the first time. It was still at war[2] with its next-door-neighbour Iraq then. Iran was a major oil-producing country and yet I was heading there with two objectives in mind: to avoid being killed and to sell a few thousand tons of oil – cooking oil.

First, I had to travel to the nearest place to obtain a visa to enter Iran, which was the Iranian Embassy in Jakarta, Indonesia. Then I called up Iran Air's general sales agent based in Singapore and asked about their flight schedules.

The agent apologised and said that flight schedules were not published – for security reasons viz. Iran Air was concerned that such published information "could be used by the enemy Iraq, to target and shoot down their planes". The only option was for me to fly to Dubai with Singapore Airlines and bide my time there until Iran Air advised me when to show up at the airport.

And so, I did just that. After a long, boring wait, I eventually boarded the 2½-hour Iran Air flight to Tehran. Apart from the wait, there were no issues; it was a smooth process especially since beer was aplenty in Dubai.

When I boarded the plane, I was greeted by both male and female flight attendants, the latter wearing hijab-style uniforms. Once airborne,

---

2 The Iran-Iraq War started in 1980, due to long-standing disputes over issues such as territory and religion. More than half a million people were killed in the armed conflict, which ended with a ceasefire in 1988.

the stewardesses were confined to the curtained galley where they prepared meals which were passed to their male counterparts who then served the passengers.

After mealtime, the stewardesses stayed inside the galley, out-of-sight of passengers. Later, en route to the toilet, I had a sneaky peek into the galley and saw the ladies, having shed their hijabs, relaxing and enjoying a smoke. At that time, smoking on board commercial flights had yet to be banned.

Due to the war, gasoline rationing had been imposed, limiting each car owner to 30 litres a week. My local agent arrived at the airport in a huge Buick with a 6,000 cc capacity engine, capable of consuming an entire month's ration in that one trip. But, I was informed, thanks to a thriving black market, he and others could "get around" quite well.

I was put up at the Tehran Hyatt Hotel[3]. Just before sunset, their housekeeping staff came into my room to pull the curtains closed because there was a blackout in the city as Iraqi fighter planes were known to buzz the city after dark. In the early evening, I went down for dinner at the main dining room. The waiter gave me the full Hyatt dinner menu and returned a few minutes later to take my order. I lost count of how many times he replied to my orders with "I'm sorry, we are out of that".

Frustrated and hungry, I finally asked him what they did have. The waiter replied that they *did* have cream of tomato soup and grilled chicken. So no prizes for figuring out what I had for dinner. The waiter might as well have said "You can have anything you want as long as it's tomato soup and grilled chicken".

Over the next few days, my agent drove me around town to all the tourist spots. Cruising around Tehran, my agent lamented the passing of the good old days, when he would be drinking champagne and consuming caviar in rooftop bistros, with a lady on each arm. Now, the bistros were all closed for business. I asked him to drive me to the

---

3   Now renamed as the Parsian Azadi Hotel, the Tehran Hyatt opened in 1978 and was one of the tallest hotels at the time.

US embassy where the staff were held hostage[4] for 444 days from November 1979 to January 1981 – just five months earlier. When we drove past, I noticed the perimeter around the compound was still stashed with sandbags and the buildings inside adorned with graffiti. Around the main building was a jumble of broken glass, furniture and other debris from the ordeal.

Returning to the hotel one evening, I was told that there was a wedding party on the top-floor restaurant. Being curious, I took the lift there to see what an Iranian wedding party was like. Strangely, the atmosphere reminded me more of a Chinese wake than what should have been a joyous, matrimonial occasion. I looked in vain to find a face that did not bear a solemn expression. They were simply eating their dinner, accompanied by a mullah reading excerpts from the Koran. There was no music, no song and dance, and of course, no alcohol.

One Saturday afternoon, I went down to the pool for a swim and asked the attendant for a towel. My aquatic plans were torpedoed by a recently ordained Iranian law, for I was informed by the apologetic attendant that it was "women's day". It turned out that the male of the species could use the pool on Monday, Wednesday and Friday while the fairer sex had the pool to themselves on Tuesday, Thursday and Saturday. On Sunday, I assumed, they cleaned the pool.

Business went well and I received an order for several containers of corn oil. As I boarded the Iran Air flight out of Tehran, I felt glad to have survived Iran. However, I came close to meeting my maker after arriving in Dubai. Disembarking, I narrowly avoided being trampled to death by a stampeding crowd – who were my placid fellow passengers just moments ago.

Dodging aside, I watched and wondered as the wild horde tumbled off the plane, sprinted through the terminal, and clambered up a staircase – some even removed their sandals so as to move faster!

---

4 The incident was known as the Iran hostage crisis. Militarised students stormed the US embassy and took more than 60 American diplomats and civilians hostage, in a protest against American intervention in Iranian politics.

When I arrived at the top of the stairs, I saw the reason for the frenzy…it was the airport bar. And the crazed passengers were downing double-shots of whisky – in double-quick time. As I sipped my own shot of whisky, I figured out the reason for the unseemly panic. They were mostly all travelling in transit: from "dry" Iran to a short stopover in "wet" Dubai and then on to…the "dry" kingdom of Kuwait. It was no wonder that they were fuelling up.

I was happy to have achieved my twin objectives on this trip. Some 24 years later, I made another trip[5] to Iran, but under peacetime conditions that made everything so much more enjoyable.

Afghanistan

Afghanistan in 1981 was a country ruled by a puppet, communist regime, riven by civil war and occupied by Soviet armed forces. It was not my first choice for a short vacation, but the business opportunity was very compelling, to be honest.

I was travelling with Steven, a Malaysian who was representing Tejis International, a trading company in Singapore which had a history of doing business in Afghanistan. Tejis was participating in a tender to provide 5,000 tons of vegetable ghee to the Afghan Government Co-op, and my company would be its supplier if our bid was successful.

We had flown to Delhi, India to get our entry visas to Afghanistan. With our visas obtained on 15 June, we were able to purchase tickets from the Afghan national airline, Ariana (nicknamed "Insha'Allah[6] Airlines" by the locals) to Kabul. When we landed in Kabul on 16 June and were ushered through immigration, the immigration officer looked quite pleased to see us. I fully expected him to greet us with "Welcome to our war zone, guys!", but he just mumbled something about exit permits.

We checked into the Kabul Intercontinental, a hotel with more than 200 rooms but only about a dozen of guests, the two of us and some East

---

5 See Ch 11 "The Hardship Group" for my holiday in Iran.
6 *Insha'Allah* is an Arabic expression which means "If God wills".

Germans – the latter vanished after a few days. So we were on our own and enjoyed exemplary service, especially due to the 9 p.m. curfew which meant many staff members were unable to return to their homes.

We were surrounded by both bored and eager service staff as we enjoyed our dinner at the rooftop restaurant. From this vantage point, we could hear sporadic gunfire. Our Afghan companions happily explained that the Russian soldiers were being shot at by Mujahideen snipers. This was a nightly routine, usually followed by soldiers going on house-to-house checks with their fierce and faithful (East?) German shepherd dogs, seeking fruitlessly for long-gone snipers.

Although the Soviet forces were technically in the country at the request of the Afghan president Babrak Karmal, it was difficult to find a single Afghan who didn't despise the Russians' presence. And we were indeed more than lucky to have as our local agent and guide, the President's brother-in-law. This meant we could travel around Kabul after the curfew deadline, passing through the road intersections manned by heavily armed Soviet soldiers, albeit with our own personal guard occupying the front passenger seat...cradling his trusty AK-47. But travel outside of Kabul was not possible.

One day, our agent casually informed us that we were being tailed everywhere we went. To test his point, we abruptly crossed a road and entered a café. Shortly after, two men crossed the road, entered the café and plonked themselves down at the next table, within easy earshot of our conversation. Just what damage did the secret police think that a couple of purveyors of palm oil products from Southeast Asia planned to inflict on the combined Afghan and Soviet military forces?

Our first few days had been spent in meetings and tendering for the contract – the supply of a few thousand tons of vegetable ghee, made from palm oil. Once we had completed our bidding, we had one clear and determined objective – to leave ASAP. Thus we hurried down to the Ariana Airlines office to book our home-bound flights.

The first hurdle came immediately. The airline sales agent said, "I cannot issue a ticket as you don't have an exit permit."

"And where do we get this?"

"From the police H.Q."

At the police H.Q., we hit the second hurdle. The police officer asked us, "Where is your letter?"

"What letter?" we asked, not unreasonably.

"The letter from the Ministry of Home Affairs approving the issue of an exit permit."

At the Ministry of Home Affairs, hurdle number three: "Where is your letter from the Ministry of Commerce?" We asked for guidance. "To confirm that your business here is complete and you are allowed to leave."

It was then I recalled the immigration officer who, upon our arrival, mentioned "exit permit", and I greatly regretted not having paid him more attention. So, we now realised we had been doing everything in reverse. We should have started with our agent confirming to the Ministry of Commerce that we had concluded our business, not committed any crime, had paid all and sundry their dues and thus through the other steps to receive the coveted exit permit. There were also payments to be made for the necessary paperwork. We were told that this full, standard exit process, from start to departure date, generally took two weeks. But entry permits were valid for only 10 days! And, therefore, overstaying fines were a useful, and steady source of income for the country.

Once again, I was reminded of my good fortune with our appointed, well-connected, local agent. He arranged for my exit permit in two days flat – achieved with the assistance of a high court judge who personally visited the various ministries. This and via my agent, the use of a few green-backed notes meant that I was finally awarded an exit permit. I couldn't help flicking to the page in my passport and admiring that little treasure dated 20 June 1981.

With this exit permit, I went back to the Ariana Airlines ticketing office on 21 June and bought myself a ticket to Delhi for the following day. My Malaysian business partner was not so lucky because his company had a commercial dispute with a local agent, so his exit permit application was rejected.

I told Steven that there was not much I could do to help him while I was in Kabul, but I would go to the Malaysian High Commission when I arrived in Delhi to report the case and seek their help. During dinner on the night before I left, he was crying.

However, the Malaysian High Commission in Delhi said there was not much they could do, because this was a commercial dispute. Fortunately, with the help of the same high court judge, Steven obtained an exit permit ten days later.

Looking back, my own escape from Afghanistan wasn't easy either. After check-in, prior to boarding, all passengers were given very thorough body searches – any audio or video recordings were strictly on the no-no list. Even currency was not spared – the guy in front of me was dispossessed of six US$100 bills by the security guards.

Even after boarding, they were not finished with us. Four armed guards entered the plane and dragged one passenger off the aircraft. Everyone else watched in silence, afraid for himself. Then, mercifully, the doors closed and boarding staircase was pulled away – phew…we were off.

But no! The staircase was pushed back, the door re-opened and a technician came on board. Apparently, there was a problem with a cockpit warning light, which indicated that the door was not closed properly. A passenger nearby murmured, "Oh dear, the flight is cancelled." Many hearts sank.

But this glitch was quickly fixed and, finally, we taxied away and took off. When the cabin crew pushed out the drinks cart and offered me a beer, I turned it down. It was only when we had entered Indian airspace that I was truly convinced I had successfully escaped from Afghanistan. I asked for a beer and then another.

And, to rub salt into festering wounds – we didn't get the business.

Three months later, the Mujahideen attacked the Kabul Intercontinental with rockets and bazookas, shattering every window and causing serious damage. So we might have missed out on the contract, but it could have been worse.

Years later, on 28 June 2011, the Taliban mounted an attack on the same hotel. In the ensuing five-hour siege, 21 people were killed, including all 9 attackers. On the night of 20 January 2018, the Taliban mounted yet another attack on the Intercontinental which lasted more than 12 hours, with a death toll of 43 and numerous casualties. I might have been lucky with my timing. When I did an online search in 2020, the Kabul Intercontinental Hotel was still open and thriving with guest reviews on TripAdvisor, and a published room rate of S$178 per night with free breakfast for two, high speed (I wonder how high a speed) internet and free parking.

I would hazard another trip if it weren't for the coronavirus and the chaos resulting from the takeover by the Taliban[7]!

Jordan And Saudi Arabia

In 1982, I left the cooking oil business and joined an aerospace maintenance company the following year, hawking aircraft spares, power plant and overhaul services. We were very keen to offer our services to countries in the Middle East, so I made several trips to that region again over the next three years, including to Jordan and Saudi Arabia.

Whereas I used to call on traders and importers, I would call on the different air force logistics officers and their civilian maintenance contractors. We usually worked through agents who were retired military officers themselves, but backed by some powerful and wealthy businessmen with connections to senior government officials.

One such businessman was Amr Khashoggi. When I went into his office in Riyadh, I noticed a diploma issued by Menlo School and College prominently displayed on the bookshelves behind his desk. Since I was also an alumnus of the Californian private preparatory school and junior college, we connected instantly, exchanging stories about the campus and sports teams.

---

7 In August 2021, the United States pulled its troops out of Afghanistan, leading to widespread panic as Afghans tried to flee from the Taliban's brutal regime.

CLOSE ENCOUNTERS WITH SAUDI ARABIAN
CUSTOMS & IMMIGRATION

My company had an agent in Saudi Arabia who was able to arrange for a visa upon arrival, of the nauseating class that encompasses an entire page of a passport. After diligently filling a whole page with the visa stamp, the immigration officer then filled in the requisite details such as date and port of entry, permitted length of stay, etc. Following this, tax revenue stamps were glued onto the visa-emblazoned page, to record payment.

But a visa on arrival in Saudi, albeit supposedly convenient, was not the norm, as I was to discover on one of my trips. Reaching the end of the process, the immigration officer reached for his revenue stamps, only to find, alas, he had none.

He asked me to wait in the arrival hall while he went off to procure the stamps. He then left…and returned *two* hours later.

Apparently, he had left the airport, driven across the city to the Immigration headquarters to requisition the precious stamps and then driven back to the airport. I watched bleary-eyed as he affixed the revenue stamps to my passport – but vision-impaired or not, I noticed something quite strange. The officer affixed all the stamps he had returned with to my passport – and had none left, not a single one! And so, the next traveller arriving with a visa on arrival would have to wait and twiddle his thumbs for a couple of hours as I did. And of course, this raised certain questions such as what game was the stamp-chasing officer playing? Was he on a time-based remuneration? Taking time off for…what was he up to?

※ ※ ※

On another trip, I noticed a Japanese businessman carrying a large package, nicely wrapped with pretty ribbons. I overheard the customs officer asking the man what the package contained.

"Chocolate," came the reply.

Clearly not convinced, the officer proceeded to cut the ribbons and tear off the gift wrapper. He then opened the box, inspected its contents, selected a piece of chocolate, took a bite – and then spat it into the nearby trash bin.

"Yes, it is chocolate!" he confirmed, handing back the box, with the torn wrapping paper and ribbons to its Japanese owner, waving him away. If the planned recipient of the chocolates received the gift in such a sorry state, he would probably forgive the giver, knowing that such treatment was to be expected for most gifts attempting to pass through the Saudi customs. I made a mental note to leave chocolates at home.

* * *

On another occasion, upon arrival I had taken a copy of the magazine *Cosmopolitan* from the plane, with the intention of bringing it back to Singapore. Rummaging through my briefcase, the customs officer found the magazine and began flipping through its pages, tearing out pages featuring pictures of ladies not wearing headscarves. And of course, there were quite a few. After ripping out more than half the magazine's pages, he handed the depleted *Cosmopolitan* to me, but I begged him to keep it as I clearly no longer had any desire to take it back. He no doubt threw it away – but what he did with the pictures he had torn out is a matter of some conjecture.

* * *

One thing I learned about the excise customs staff in most of these Middle Eastern countries was that they were not really interested in their work. If you walked up to them after you had collected your luggage, they would look at you and ask you what you wanted. However, if you were to just walk by them without acknowledging their presence, they would single you out and ask if you had anything to declare.

During my visits to Saudi, I was driven to housing estates built by the government to house the nomadic Bedouin tribes. So many of these buildings were empty and dilapidated. It was explained to me that the nomadic tribes in the desert still had the habit of sitting around a campfire after dinner, exchanging stories about their ancestors. The problem was, they had difficulty finding firewood in the concrete jungle for the campfire. So, they would tear down the doors and furniture in their apartments and bring them down to the open area near their apartment block and start the fire. When they ran out of doors and furniture to burn, they simply moved out of those concrete apartments and back into their tents in the desert.

Air travellers are probably familiar with the drinks carts on aeroplanes. Most contain the little, 1-oz (30 ml) bottles of liquor that the flight attendant serves with a mixer. On longer flights, the drinks carts are stocked with "fifths" or 700-ml bottles. On a KLM flight from "dry" Riyadh to "wet" Amsterdam, I noticed that when the drinks cart came by, it was stocked with much bigger bottles of liquor. These were half-gallon – almost two litre – bottles, with quite useful handles too! KLM gets my vote.

In 1997, I went to Jordan again with my wife Kwan and some friends, as part of a spiritual trip[8] – we flew into Amman, and then visited Petra, before entering Israel via the Allenby Bridge.

Bahrain

In 1986, I was sent by the aerospace maintenance company on a business trip to Bahrain, which was supposedly a "dry" state. However, I found that we could actually get a drink without much trouble.

As we drove pass the King Fahad Causeway that led from Saudi Arabia to Bahrain, we saw long lines of cars waiting to cross over to Bahrain. These were drivers who were travelling there for a drink after work before they went back to their homes in Saudi Arabia.

The other unusual thing we noticed as we headed to Bahrain was that there were many luxurious cars abandoned on the roadside leading to the causeway. I was told that these were cars involved in minor fender benders and the owners would rather dump their damaged cars than get them fixed.

Oman

Oman is one of the more liberal countries in West Asia. My first trip to its capital Muscat was in March 1986, just five months after Oman

---

8   See Chapter 11 "The Hardship Group" for the spiritual trip that I took to Israel, via Jordan.

hosted the 6th Gulf Cooperation Council (GCC)[9] Summit meeting. The spectacular Al Bustan Palace Hotel was built for that occasion. We had a chance to visit the hotel to appreciate the grandeur of the interior as well as the surrounding landscape.

In those days, there were many expatriates, mostly British, working in Oman. The general manager of our local agent lived in a house over-looking the sea. He had just participated in the local annual Oxford-Cambridge rowing regatta held off the coast of Muscat, and he had the blisters on his hands to show for it. The water off the coast was crystal clear of turquoise blue colour, and the fishing industry had to be flour-ishing. It is no wonder that the Muttrah Fish Market was high on the list of recommended places for all the tourists to visit.

Qatar

Doha, the capital of the small state of Qatar, is home to the national carrier Qatar Airways, which has been regularly voted as the best airline in the world. In 2007, I spent a few hours in transit at the old Doha International Airport on my way to Syria[10] for a holiday. At that time, the airport was not very impressive but rather run-down.

In 2014, the old airport was replaced by the Hamad International Airport, which acts as the hub for the airline's flights from Asia to cities in Europe and beyond. It breaks up the long 12 to 14 hours between major cities in the two continents. We stopped over in this new airport on our way home after our visit to Istanbul and Cappadocia in Turkey. The new airport is modern, clean and generally pleasant.

Turkey

Kwan and I made two separate visits to Turkey[11]. In 1992, before island-hopping in Greece with Christina (Kwan's sister) and her husband

---

9   Established in 1981, the GCC (or the Cooperation Council for the Arab States of the Gulf) is a political and economic alliance of six Middle Eastern countries: Bahrain, Kuwait, Oman, Qatar, Saudi Arabia and the United Arab Emirates.
10 See Chapter 11 "The Hardship Group" for my vacation to Syria, which took place before the terrorist group ISIS destroyed several important cultural heritage sites in the country.
11 In June 2022, the country was officially renamed as Turkiye.

Doug, the four of us flew to Istanbul for some sightseeing. We took in all the tourist sites including the Sultan Ahmed Mosque a.k.a. the Blue Mosque, and the Holy Hagia Sophia Grand Mosque which was built as a cathedral but converted to a mosque during the Ottoman Empire. It was the main mosque in Istanbul until the construction of the Sultan Ahmed Mosque nearby. We had dinner overlooking the Bosphorus Strait, and went on an evening cruise, sailing past key landmarks along both sides of the strait.

In 2014, after attending the Worldchefs Congress in Norway, Kwan and I flew into Istanbul to visit a chef training school, together with Karl Guggenmoss, the dean of Johnson & Wales University, a world-renowned culinary university. As our host was a culinary school, we were brought to taste some of the finest food in Istanbul.

After two days in Istanbul, we flew to Cappadocia, which is a UNESCO World Heritage Site. We hired a car to take us to see all the unique moon-like landscape, underground cities, cave churches and houses carved in the rocks. I found out that the owner of the travel agency was actually an army aviator who had a helicopter maintenance licence. We had a lot to talk about and I even promised to help him find a job as I was in the helicopter business.

Chapter 6
EAST ASIA

Wen we think of East Asia, we naturally think of China, Korea and Japan. Although I have not had the good fortune to visit North Korea yet, I have been to South Korea several times. I find that Japan is a very interesting place to visit and it does not have to be expensive if you know how to go about it. The other places in this region are Mongolia, Taiwan, and of course mainland China which includes the two Special Administrative Regions (SAR) of Hong Kong and Macau.

Japan

My first trip to Japan was an overnight transit in its capital Tokyo because jetliners in 1967 did not have the range to cross the Pacific Ocean in one hop. I had just completed my freshman year at Purdue University, and was due to return to Sandakan for the summer holidays. My dorm pals Wally and David were also summoned home to Hong Kong by their respective families, so the three of us booked a multi-stop flight from San Francisco to Hong Kong (from which I would board a ship to Sandakan).

Along the way, our Pan Am plane landed in Tokyo from Hawaii. We were put up in a hotel and issued with a meal voucher. However, our luggage was left on the plane because we were to continue our journey on the same aeroplane the following morning. To give credit to Pan Am, we were put up in a good-enough hotel that we had to wear suit jackets to dine in the dining room. When we explained to the waiter captain our predicament of not having dinner jackets on hand because they were in our luggage on the plane, he quickly came up with a solution. He found three foul-smelling waiter captain jackets for us to wear, so that we could dine and spend our voucher.

After dinner, we decided to explore Tokyo. Wally, who had just finished reading Ian Fleming's *You Only Live Twice*, suggested that we visit the Mikado nightclub because that was where 007 went to seek some adventure. We jumped into a taxi and told the driver to take us to the Mikado nightclub in Ginza district. The driver knew Ginza well, but he had to ask around to locate the Mikado. After seeking help from many passers-by, he dropped us off in front of the famed nightclub.

Again, on Wally's suggestion, each of us ordered a vodka martini, shaken but not stirred because that was what James Bond would have ordered. Next, the mamasan brought us two young and pretty hostesses. Unfortunately, they did not speak English, so we requested for a change.

This time, she brought us the only English-speaking hostess in the joint. Unfortunately, she was old enough to be my mother. After finishing our martinis, we took a taxi back to the hotel, without further adventure. When we eventually reached Hong Kong, I stayed with David's family for a few days before I went back to Sandakan.

Since that trip, I have been back in Japan numerous times. One of the more memorable experiences was attending the launch of a specialty tanker in Usuki, Oita, which is in the southwestern part of the country. My wife Kwan and I flew there after an overnight stop in Tokyo. We were put up in Kamenoi Besso – one of the best ryokan in Yufuin, Oita. The "rooms" consisted of small cottages with a private hot spring in each cottage.

The night before the launch, we were invited to a traditional Japanese dinner where all of us had to wear a kimono and wooden clogs. We were attended to by a modern-day geisha who did not wear the kimono but a blouse and a skirt. The girl serving us spoke very good English, unlike the one I met in Mikado 40 years ago. When I asked her why she was able to speak so fluently in English, she gave me a wink and said that she had an Italian boyfriend.

The dinner consisted of some very exquisite sashimi, including puffer fish and some very thinly sliced white fish, quite unlike the usual sashimi types of salmon, yellow tail, squid and scallops. The geisha kept topping up my sake cup. Every now and then, she tried to peep under the table to see what I wore underneath the kimono. After dinner, the popular activity was to take a walk along a stream to look for fireflies. When I noticed that our attendant was nowhere to be seen, I asked the mamasan where she was. I was told that she was worshipping the great white throne (toilet bowl).

On the day of the launch, we were driven from the ryokan to the shipyard. As we approached the shipyard, the street was lined with school children, waving coloured pennants to welcome our convoy. Kwan was escorted into an office where she practised chopping off a white string with an ornamental axe bearing the name of the vessel *Chembulk Kobe*. We then assembled at the dock next to the actual vessel. At the predetermined auspicious time, Kwan chopped off the symbolic string that was connected to some heavy chocks which slid away, allowing the vessel to be launched into the water next to the dock.

After the launch, we flew back to Tokyo and stayed in a US$35M house overlooking the Tokyo Bay, which our host bought for US$6M during the property bubble burst. We were also treated to a sumo wrestling tournament where tickets were very hard to come by and expensive. Because we were not regulars, all the points and ranking meant nothing to us, and so we did not stay for the entire duration of the tournament.

Some time later, Kwan and I were invited to attend a tea ceremony held in the city of Nara, except that it was not exactly traditional but meant to be casual. I remember reading up on all the formalities of a Japanese tea ceremony beforehand, but that was not really necessary.

Because it was held on Valentine's Day, wine was served with lunch and the ceremony was actually conducted with the help of a sommelier. The simplified tea ceremony was short and lasted no more than 15 minutes. We were told that there was no dress code, so I went in jeans. It was quite embarrassing when I found out that many of the other men were dressed in Armani suits. Many of the ladies wore kimonos while some had on fashionable and expensive designer suits.

Over the years, we have enjoyed many remarkable meals in the country, including dinner at the three-Michelin-starred Kikunoi Honten in Kyoto. And needless to say, an early morning visit to the Tsukiji Fish Market[1] in Tokyo followed by a sashimi breakfast was always a good way to start the day.

On another trip, we visited the Tsuji Culinary Institute in Osaka, the biggest culinary vocational school in Japan. The institute actually bought a chateau in France so that their students can spend time to immerse themselves in the French culture. We were very impressed with how immaculate their labs were. The students were extremely polite and very neatly dressed. Kwan ended up signing a collaboration agreement with them.

South Korea

I have gone on several trips to the country for business over the years, mainly to its capital Seoul. Seoul was also a convenient stop on the way to San Francisco via Singapore Airlines.

I made some good Korean friends in Seoul during my Bell Helicopter days, so I would drop in to see them whenever I could. Most of the trips just involve good food and heavy drinking. One of my friends, Y.W., was the managing director of a division of a listed company, so he would send his driver to pick me up from the airport when I visited Seoul. All the drivers were dressed in western suits. My friend would address his driver as Mr So-and-So. Very formal indeed.

One of my visits was during the winter season, and Seoul can be very, very cold. I made a special trip there when Y.W.'s son was getting married, so I was able to witness a traditional Korean wedding which was grand and well-attended.

---

1 In 2018, the wholesale section or "inner market" – where tuna auctions took place – was moved to the island of Toyosu. The "outer market" where restaurants and shops continue to operate at Tsukiji.

In the period leading up to the wedding, Y.W. was preoccupied with entertaining his relatives who came from all over Korea, so he sent one of his managers to show me around town. We went up the N Seoul Tower, a communication and observation tower built on a hill in central Seoul. He also brought me to a humongous Lotte department store where the salesgirls stood in the parking lot to welcome and direct the incoming cars. I visited the Gyeongbokgung Palace and watched the changing of the guards ceremony on a glorious sunny day in winter. I was also curious to know what the latest knock-offs Korea was producing, so I spent a few hours walking around the shopping haven of Gangnam.

Having been to the Tsukiji Fish Market in Tokyo, I was keen to compare it with the biggest fish market in Seoul, the Noryangjin Fish Market. Although it was not of the same scale as its Japanese counterpart, Noryangjin impressed me with the different types of live crabs that were on sale, not to mention the dried scallops, oysters and anchovies. There were numerous varieties of sea kelp displayed alongside pans of kimchi too.

In 2017, I went to Sokcho, a seaside city in the northeastern part of South Korea. We were there for the Pan Asia Hash[2] gathering. A few thousand Hash men and women came to the event. One of the runs actually took the runners up to the DMZ[3] which was only 50 km from the city. What I remembered about the place was the abundance of seafood in a fish market there, although it was of a smaller scale compared to the Noryangjin market in Seoul.

Mongolia

I joined a Canadian trade mission to Ulaanbaatar, Mongolia (not to be confused with Inner Mongolia, which is an autonomous region of China). It is a vast country so one could only get to its remote parts by flying in a helicopter or bouncing around country roads in a beat-up

---

2 See Chapter 13 "Hash House Harriers" for what I do on Hash gatherings.
3 Established in 1953 at the end of the Korean War, the DMZ (Korean Demilitarized Zone) is a border barrier separating North Korea from South Korea. While it is heavily fortified on both sides, it is also a popular tourist attraction.

van. Most existing helicopters do not have the required range. In one case, the military installed huge internal auxiliary fuel tanks in a Russian helicopter to increase the range. The helicopter turned into a fire bomb when it crashed in the desert.

While we were there, we were treated to an acrobatic show put on by a troupe of street urchins. These were homeless kids who survived the severe winters by living in the city's sewage tunnels. Some kind soul had rounded them up, trained them in some acrobatic skills and put on these shows to earn some money for their food and clothing. It was heart-warming to see the enthusiasm on their faces while they performed for us. A dinner was arranged for us in a Mongolian yurt (a circular tent house that is portable), where we were served meat that was cooked on heated stones.

Taiwan

Although Taiwan is not considered a country by the United Nations, it is an island with a distinctive Chinese culture that is very different from that in China.

I had my first experience of an earthquake there in 1995. It happened when I was sitting on a sofa, watching TV in a 35th-floor apartment. When I realised what it was, I gripped the armrests of the sofa, expecting to be free-falling from a height along with all the debris from the building. Fortunately, it died down in less than a minute.

In certain parts of the major cities, one can see skimpily-dressed young women wriggling their buttocks and peddling packets of betel nuts and cigarettes, with loud music blasting from their stands. These women are nicknamed *bin lang xi shi*[4]. Cars would drive up, and the drivers would wind down their windows and hand over their cash for a packet of betel nuts.

The habit of chewing betel nuts was still prevalent during my visit in the mid-1990s. It has been claimed to produce a sense of well-being,

---

4　In Mandarin, *bin lang* means betel nut, and Xi Shi was one of the Four Beauties of ancient China. Thus *bin lang xi shi* means "betel nut beauty".

euphoria, heightened alertness, sweating, salivation, a hot sensation in the body and increased capacity to work. However, betel chewing is habit-forming and can lead to addiction and withdrawal symptoms.

As usual, I took any opportunity I had to visit different cities in Taiwan. I rode the train from Taipei north to the port city of Keelung, where one could board a ferry to the Matsu Islands which belong to Taiwan and are just 9 km off the coast of China but 170 km from Taiwan. I also took a flight down to Tainan City and drove down to Kaohsiung City, the third largest city in Taiwan.

On one of my visits, my daughter Oi Leng who spent six months in Taipei co-producing the movie *Au Revoir Taipei* took Kwan and me to a very exclusive restaurant in Yangmingshan[5]. It was near impossible to get a reservation without three months' advance notice. Fortunately, through her friend who was acquainted with the owner, we managed to get a reservation in one day. However, when we hailed a taxi and told the driver the address, he asked whether we had a reservation at that restaurant, because if we hadn't, chances were, we would be riding back in his taxi again. Very impressive.

I remember Taipei as a city of motor scooters. At every traffic junction, there would be close to a hundred scooters waiting for the lights to turn green. Because there were so many of them, no one could really speed, so it was actually quite safe.

Macau (Special Administrative Region)

A former Portuguese colony[6], Macau is a city state inhabited by fewer than 700,000 people on an area of about 30 km^2. It is a major resort city for gambling tourism. Many Hong Kongers make a day trip over to Macau, to cycle around (a lot less traffic on the road compared to Hong Kong) and enjoy the food, which is not much different from that in Hong Kong but priced more cheaply. Macau was also the gateway into

---

5 Yangmingshan is a high-mountain national park known for its hot springs, wildlife and volcanic geological features. It is about an hour's drive from Taipei.
6 In the 16th century, the Ming dynasty government of China leased Macau to Portugal as a trading post in exchange for rent. Sovereignty over Macau was transferred back to China in 1999.

southern China until the Hong Kong–Zhuhai–Macau bridge/tunnel opened in 2018.

In the 1980s, I had a customer in Macau who bought four of our helicopters, hence I had to make very regular visits there. My visits were all day trips crossing over from Hong Kong and returning on the same day. The original crossing into China was a short 100-m walk from the old Portas do Cerco (Barrier Gate) to the Gongbei Border Security Complex on the Chinese side. The historic Macanese structure was built in 1849, and is a crème-yellow, single-arched gate with Neo-classical architectural features, standing on cobblestone pavements. During my crossings, I witnessed many pedestrians ducking behind the gate, stuffing cigarettes and other dutiable goods into their clothing in broad daylight before they proceeded through customs.

One day, I had a Bell's palsy attack when I was in Macau, so I went to see a doctor there. It was comical – although he was of Chinese descent, he spoke Mandarin and Portuguese while I spoke Cantonese and English. In the end, I did not trust his diagnosis and would not take the oral steroid he prescribed for me.

Hong Kong (Special Administrative Region)

Although I was born in Hong Kong, I left the British colony[7] when I was six, so my memory of Hong Kong is kind of patchy. I made short trips there before I became an adult, mostly on transit from America during my summer holidays. My mother also brought my three siblings and me to Hong Kong to visit our relatives when I was 10 and again when I was 14. Generally, I feel very comfortable moving around Hong Kong because I speak Cantonese and am familiar with the food.

Fast forward to 1988. By then, I was married to Kwan and we had two school-age children. My employer, Bell Helicopter Asia, sent me to set up an office in Hong Kong to cover the market in China. Returning to live in Hong Kong was an exciting segment of my life. Although the colony was

---

7   Hong Kong was ceded to Great Britain in 1842 by the Qing dynasty government after the latter lost the First Opium War. In 1898, the British signed an agreement with the Qing government to lease Hong Kong for 99 years. Sovereignty was eventually handed over to China on 1 July 1997.

drastically different from the Hong Kong I once knew, I was able to get around with no difficulty because of my fluency in the Cantonese dialect.

The first task was to find an apartment which we would be calling home for at least the next two years. We were very fortunate to find a 15-year-old, 20-storey, quiet and spacious apartment block that over-looked Deep Water Bay on the south side of the Hong Kong Island. Without traffic, I could drive from our place to Hong Kong Central in 10 minutes.

After we moved in, we found out that the tenants in the 40-unit residential building included mega kungfu actor Jackie Chan and retired kungfu actor Ti Lung. In fact, Pak Seng and Oi Leng had a fair share of celebrity sightings – they met Jackie Chan in the lift a few times. He went to the film studio in the afternoons and only came home in the early mornings because filming was always done at night when there were not so many people in the streets. As for myself, I had seen Jackie Chan's son in the car park on occasion, but I did not meet Ti Lung.

The next task was to find a school for Pak Seng and Oi Leng. Because they did not speak the local Cantonese dialect, we could not enrol them in a local school. So they ended up attending the German Swiss School, where they studied German as a second language. I was informed by my managing director that the company would only pay the difference between the school fees charged by the German Swiss School and their schools in Singapore. When I told him that their school fees in Singapore were $3 a month, he told me not to bother, and that the company would pay the entire sum. During their stay in Hong Kong, my children were also selected by the Hong Kong Swimming Association to join the national swimming squad. As a matter of fact, Oi Leng broke a Singapore national swimming record in one of the local swimming meets.

Weekends were spent exploring Hong Kong Island and the New Territories on the mainland in the north, towards the Chinese border. I also visited my childhood nanny who looked after me from the time I was born till I left Hong Kong when I was nearly six.

The big difference between the Hong Kong that I left behind and the Hong Kong when I went back to live in 1988 was the development of the transport infrastructure, specifically the Mass Transit Railway (MTR) system and the cross-harbour tunnels. Where we used to have to take a ferry or a wooden junk boat to some of the more secluded fishing villages, we could just take the MTR to the nearest station and transfer to a minibus to reach our destination. Even the famous floating restaurant in Aberdeen is now just a 2-minute water shuttle ride from the mainland. When we left Hong Kong in 1956, things were less convenient: we had to take a ferry to cross the Victoria Harbour separating Hong Kong Island from the Kowloon peninsula. If we were in a vehicle, we would have to queue up to take the car ferry.

In 1972, the first of three underwater cross-harbour tunnels was completed. The other two were completed in 1989 and 1997 respectively. Although one could still take the cross-harbour ferry, I suspect that most of the commuters are taking it for nostalgic reasons. With a senior commuter fare card, I could take the ferry for free.

On the mainland side, Lion Rock Hill (495 m) stands between Kowloon and the New Territories. In the old days, motorists had to navigate winding roads to get across this mountain. Finally, in the 1972, the Lion Rock Tunnel (two lanes each way) was opened to traffic, and it cut the travelling time considerably. However, as the population grew, more and more inhabitants were forced to move out to the cheaper suburbs, so several other tunnels were built to ease the traffic. Similarly, the Aberdeen Tunnel was built to connect Hong Kong Central to the southern side of Hong Kong Island.

When we were stationed in Hong Kong in 1988, the Kai Tak International Airport was still in operation. But with a single runway, it was clearly reaching the limits on the number of flights it could handle.

Most airlines only allowed their captain-ranked pilots to command the landing in Kai Tak, due to its notoriously tricky approach. A friend of mine, a Boeing 747 captain, had to shut down (on technical grounds) two engines on the same wing after take-off from Kai Tak. He requested to return to Kai Tak coming for a straight-in approach from the sea. But his request was rejected because the air traffic controller told him that accommodating him would upset the landing sequence of more than 10 other aircraft. As a result, he had to make a dangerous approach from the Lion Rock mountain side of the airfield. He confessed that his whole shirt was drenched when he taxied the aircraft to the terminal after a successful landing.

In 1998, the new Hong Kong Chek Lap Kok International Airport was declared operational, and a third runway was completed in 2021.

Our office in Hong Kong served the company well. We had a very important operator, China Southern Airlines, based in Zhuhai Heliport, China. Whenever they needed an AOG (Aircraft On Ground) spare part, our parts department in Fort Worth, Texas would courier the part to Hong Kong, which usually arrived at 4 a.m. After the package had cleared customs, I would pick it up from the air cargo terminal, hurry down to the pier to catch the 6 a.m. ferry to Macau, cross over to Zhuhai, and turn up at the customer's office with the required spare part, just in time when the engineers come to work at 8 a.m. Such an arrangement earned us a lot of goodwill from this customer. Basing myself in Hong Kong was also very convenient if I needed to make marketing visits in mainland China, as Hong Kong has numerous direct flights to all the major cities in China.

Sadly, after two years, a lot of American companies pulled out of Hong Kong due to the Tiananmen incident, and I was relocated back to Singapore.

China

Between 1982 and now, I must have made several hundred trips to the People's Republic of China. I experienced the transformation of an undeveloped country into what is today the second largest economy in the world. Back in the 1980s, it was not uncommon to find that we were booked on a Russian Tupolev TU-154, or an Ilyushin IL-96 jetliner where the seats could not be adjusted to the upright position and the seat belts could not be buckled. On a typical domestic flight in a reciprocating engine Islander aircraft, both the pilot and co-pilot did not wear their seat belts throughout the 50-minute flight. Steam-powered trains travelled at 50 kph from one end of the country to the other. There would be a two-car lane width on each side of the road reserved for bicycles.

Today, all the Chinese airlines use the latest equipment, flown by local pilots trained in Australia, France or the US. The high-speed trains are cruising at over 300 kph. The rare bicycles you see on the road are from bike-sharing programmes that let users unlock them using mobile phone apps.

My First Trip

For the longest time, China had been closed to the outside world. It intrigued me, but foreign travellers were not welcomed at that time. Then John, a friend whom I made at Purdue University, told me that he discovered a way for me to enter China. John was from Hong Kong but was sent by his family to manage a factory in Nigeria. In fact, he played host to me when I was in the West African nation several months earlier[8].

According to John, I could apply for a Home Return Permit (回鄉 證, *hui xiang zheng*), which facilitated all overseas Chinese to go back to their "motherland". All I had to do was to send him a photograph of myself and furnish him with my Chinese name and my ancestral province, which I promptly did. I was issued with the permit from the Chinese Embassy in Nigeria[9], no questions asked.

Together, we planned to take a trip to southern China, specifically Guangdong province, in February 1982. John and I agreed to meet up

---

8 See Chapter 8 "Africa" for how I survived my escapades in Nigeria.
9 I had to obtain the permit in a roundabout way, because Singapore established formal diplomatic ties with China only in 1990.

THE TROUBLE WITH UPSIZED VISAS

In the 1980s, the Chinese visa was a big rubber stamp imprint that covered the whole page of my passport. The Border Security staff (equivalent to our immigration officers) would then stamp an entry or exit stamp onto this visa imprint.

Once, I requested an officer to stamp it onto the facing page instead because the entry stamp sometimes covered up an important date or letter on the underlying visa imprint. Of course, the officer felt insulted, and he deliberately hammered his entry stamp right on top of my visa imprint.

Undaunted, I showed him how my 6-month multiple entry visa had become a 3-month visa because the entry stamp had covered up the expiry month of the visa. He just shooed me away.

in Hong Kong before entering China. Meanwhile, I contacted another college pal Wing Kee, who operated a factory in Zhongshan, a city right across the border from Macau. He offered to arrange for a car to pick us up on the Chinese side of the border and asked one of his managers to show us around.

When I presented the permit at the Chinese immigration checkpoint, they wanted to know how I had travelled from Nigeria to Macau, and with what travel documents. Nervously, I pulled out my Singapore passport. They studied it for a while and let me into China, where I spent a night. I did not travel very far from the China–Macau border. I was just interested to have set foot on China, and see the other side of the mountain.

When it was time to leave and return to Macau, I went through the same immigration compound. This time, they asked me for my exit permit. Because I was deemed a "citizen of China" (based on the fact that I possessed the Home Return Permit and had "returned to the motherland"), I would need an exit permit to leave the country.

Nervously, I pulled out my Singapore passport and tried to explain to the officer that I was not really a "citizen of China" even though that permit from Nigeria said that I was. Luckily, I recognised one of the lady officers who was on duty when I entered China and she recognised me too. She came over and vouched for me that although I had entered China with that permit, I was actually a Singaporean. After listening to her clarification, her colleague allowed me to leave. That was a close call.

Since that first trip to Guangdong province, I have been to 17 other provinces in China. I have also visited two of its autonomous regions Xinjiang and Tibet with Kwan and our friends[10].

Anhui

Anhui is an eastern province in China and home to Mount Huangshan, a UNESCO World Heritage Site. It is also next to Jiangxi province where the porcelain capital of China, Jingdezhen, is located. I had to visit Jingdezhen regularly for work because one of the two helicopter factories in China is located there.

During the late 1980s and the early 1990s, there were no daily flights into or out of Jingdezhen. Sometimes, I just had to fly to either Wuhan or Nanjing. To get to Nanjing from Jingdezhen, I would have to cross into Anhui province and head northeast along the Yangtze River. To get to Wuhan (before the Poyang Lake No. 2 bridge was built), I had to go around the Poyang Lake to the south, extending the trip by hours. Although Huangshan was a mere 200 km from Jingdezhen, I never did make it there, much to my regret.

Fujian

My wife's ancestors came from the southeastern province of Fujian, although her father moved to Burma later. In 2018, Kwan and I had an opportunity to go back to her father's village for a visit. We also located the overgrown grave of her paternal grandmother.

We spent a day on the island of Gulang (Gulangyu), a UNESCO World Heritage Site. This island in Xiamen city has pedestrianised streets

---

10 See Chapter 11 "The Hardship Group" for my travels to the two autonomous regions.

and 19th-century colonial[11] villas. The Xiamen piano museum here has more than 200 pianos from all over the world, thus earning Gulangyu the nickname of "Piano Island". We located the high school which my mother-in-law attended. We also savoured the local cuisine which Kwan's maternal grandmother would regularly cook at home.

Another attraction we visited in the province was the Tulou or traditional earthern buildings, usually of a circular configuration surrounding a central shrine. They were designated as a UNESCO World Heritage Site in 2008. The provincial capital, Fuzhou, was supposedly visited by Marco Polo during the Yuan dynasty (1271–1368). Just a few kilometres off the coast of Fujian are some islands belonging to Taiwan.

Gansu

Gansu is a province in north-central China. This long province is part of the ancient Silk Road. We came up from Xi'an in the neighbouring province of Shaanxi and travelled the whole length of Gansu (approximately 1,500 km) when we toured the ancient Silk Road in 1993[12].

Guangdong

Guangdong is where my ancestors came from. This southern province played a significant role in the history of China, because her favourite son Sun Yat-sen – widely acknowledged as the founding father of modern China – overthrew the Qing dynasty and established the Republic of China in 1912.

Just south of the capital, Guangzhou, is the Pearl River Delta which is one of the wealthiest regions in the country. Located in this region is Taishan county, where my grandfather came from. For years, I tried to track down his ancestral home, but I had very little success due to the limited information on hand.

---

11 Gulangyu was an international settlement from as early as the 1840s, after Xiamen opened as a commercial port to foreign trade. Many foreigners such as officials, businessmen and missionaries settled on the island, and they shaped the architecture and culture there significantly.
12 See Chapter 11 "The Hardship Group" for my travels on the Silk Road.

After the Manchu regime was overthrown by Dr Sun Yat-sen, my grandfather was appointed as an advisor to the Canton provincial government and later settled down in Hong Kong. None of my father's siblings, him included, could tell me the exact location of our ancestral village. As they were born in Hong Kong, they might not even have been to the village.

In 1988, I made an interesting discovery. I was invited to dinner by my friend Dr Chan Sik at his house in Hong Kong. I met Chan Sik and his wife Wyman on my first trip to Europe with my college pal Wally in 1971, and we became good friends ever since.

Wyman's mother was also present at the dinner, and she found out that I had the same surname – Lui – as her. What a coincidence! She also noticed that my middle name was "Yuen" (元), and so she asked me, "Who was your grandfather?"

When I told her he was Lui Yum Suen, she was taken back and asked what my father's birth order in the family was. When I told her that my father was No. 6, she said she knew Nos. 7, 8, 9 and 10, but she did not know my father.

She related that her father was one of the founders of the Kowloon Motorbus company and he also came from the same village as my grandfather – that was how they were acquainted. She used to go to my grandfather's villa in the New Territories occasionally. She had seen some kids running around there, so I must have been one of them. She said she even brought Wyman there to play with those kids. Small world.

However, she was unable to give me any directions to the village because directions in rural China were not based on maps in those days. After that dinner, I gathered the bits of information and ran them through my mind. I recalled that my Uncle no. 5 once mentioned that the name of our ancestral village was Kam Loong village (锦龙村/錦龍村), but he wrongly told me that it was situated in a locality called Dai Hang (大坑),when it should have been Dai Gong (大江).

I was determined to find the village, so when I was in the area a few years ago, I went to a public security office to ask for directions but was told that there were actually a few Kam Loong villages around. Undeterred, I pushed on, trying to piece together all the bits of patchy directions. Luckily, I recalled having seen a photograph from a distant Lui cousin in Hong Kong, showing a gazebo with the sign "Kam Loong village" at the junction of a small road that led to our village. At last, I found my ancestral village[13]!

Since then, I have been back there two more times, bringing my siblings along. When I paid a visit to the mayor, I found out they were not interested in any donations from me because the Kowloon Motorbus family had already pledged to donate millions of dollars to give the village a makeover.

I had some customers in Guangzhou and Zhuhai, so I visited these cities regularly. Another city in Guangdong province is Shantou (Swatow) where the richest man in Hong Kong, Lee Ka Shing, came from. I made numerous trips to Shantou because our company was planning on building a factory there, but the plan was abandoned due to the bureaucratic hoops we had to go through.

Hainan

Hainan is an island just 20 km south of the mainland. At the turn of the century, trains together with the passengers travelling from the mainland to Hainan would be loaded onto ferries which carry these carriages across the 20-km-wide Qiongzhou Straits. When the ferry reached Hainan, the carriages would be discharged onto the railway tracks and continue their journey down south.

During my early trips to the capital Haikou, planes were still flying in and out of the old Dayingshan Airport which was in the heart of the city. During short final on the landing, the buildings on both sides of the runway looked dangerously close to the aircraft. In 1999, the state-of-the-art Meilan International Airport opened.

On the southern tip of the island is Sanya, a beach resort town and the playground for the rich northerners during wintertime. Halfway between Haikou and Sanya is Bo'ao. This town is famous for the Bo'ao

---

13 Awash with excitement, I went to the local public security office later and obtained the official address of Kam Loong village, just to get the record straight, once and for all.

Forum for Asia, an international platform for political, business and academic leaders to meet annually and discuss the latest issues in Asia, with the aim of promoting economic integration and development.

One year, I was visiting my friend Low, whose ancestral village was near Bo'ao when the forum was being held. Because of the presence of many VVIPs, security in the area was very tight, and all-out-of-state and foreign visitors were told to register with the local police. We went down to the police station, filled out some forms and submitted my passport for inspection. The officer flipped through my passport and went into an office to consult her superior.

After half an hour, I asked another officer what had happened to my passport. The first officer then came out of the office and told me that my passport had expired. What she showed me was an expired Nepal visa on one of the pages. I had to explain to her that the validity period of my passport was on the first page, and what she had been looking at was just a visa issued by the Nepali government. Although she was not completely convinced, she nevertheless accepted my explanation and returned the passport to me and allowed me to go.

Hebei

This province encircles the nation's capital, Beijing. Together with Tianjin, the three divisions form the Jing-jin-ji[14] megalopolis with the combined area six times the size of the New York metropolitan.

I have visited various sections of the Great Wall that stretch across several provinces of China. One such section was Jinshanling, a less crowded but well-restored section of the wall in Hebei. In 2009, I spent the night on the wall[15], initially in open air but was forced to move into one of the watchtowers when it started to rain. The following morning, I was told that those watchtowers were infested with scorpions.

---

14 "Jing" refers to Beijing, "Jin" refers to Tianjin, and "Ji" is an abbreviated name for Hebei, given in reference to the ancient Ji province which encompassed the modern-day Hebei province.
15 See Chapter 13 "Hash House Harriers" to find out why I slept overnight on one of the New Seven Wonders of the World.

I also visited Chengde Mountain Resort, the imperial summer residence of the Qing dynasty emperors.

Heilongjiang

Heilongjiang is China's northernmost province. It is named after the Heilong River (known as the Amur River, in Russian), bordering the two countries.

The capital Harbin is known for its Russian architecture, including the Russian Orthodox Saint Sophia Cathedral, now repurposed as the Harbin Architectural Art Gallery. The city is also famous for its annual International Ice and Snow Sculpture Festival. One of my colleagues told me that during winter, the outside temperature could actually warm up to -15°C in the daytime!

I had to visit Harbin regularly in the 1990s because it was home to one of two Chinese helicopter factories. When the Chinese government decided to move part of the factory in Harbin to Jingdezhen, 2,500 km away, many of the workers had to follow suit and relocate. I was told that two of the technicians were so homesick that they rode their bicycles all the way back to Harbin to visit their relatives in the first summer.

Hubei

Hubei is a landlocked province in Central China. The capital, Wuhan, is the gateway for tourists signing up for a Yangtze River cruise to see

THE NOTORIOUS PUBLIC RESTROOMS OF CHINA

China's public sanitation system has long had a reputation for being inadequate and lacking in many aspects. In 2015, President Xi Jinping proclaimed a "Toilet Revolution" campaign to push for a clean and sound public toilet system. But way back in the late 1980s before China's toilet makeover, I was walking around Tiananmen Square in Beijing with a colleague one evening when I had to find a toilet urgently. After I came out of the toilet, my colleague asked me how many pages of my passport were missing. Wise guy.

the massive Three Gorges dam. Wuhan University is recognised as one of the top universities in the country. It is also well-known for its cherry blossom season every spring. More than 300 m of Cherry Blossom Avenue in the university would be covered in a rain of pink and white cherry blossom petals. Unfortunately, the day that we were visiting the university turned out to be rainy and wet.

Of course, the one thing that is Wuhan's claim to international "fame", like it or not, is the COVID-19 virus that has killed millions of people on earth since 2019. This deadly virus allegedly originated from a wet market in the city.

Hunan

Hunan is another landlocked province in the south-central region of China, and the birthplace of Mao Zedong, who led the country's communist revolution. Born and raised in Hunan, Mao received his primary and secondary school education there before going to Beijing and becoming active with the revolution which eventually led to the founding of the People's Republic of China.

The house in which he grew up and the classroom including his desk are still on permanent display. On the school wall hung a photograph taken of Mao visiting his village and being served lunch by a neighbour. When I visited this village in the late 1990s, this neighbour, riding on her fame from that photograph, had opened a restaurant with supposedly the same menu that she had served to Mao years earlier.

I visited the capital, Changsha, numerous times because I sold two helicopters to an industrialist there. He built a 30-storey hotel in 15 days. In northwestern Hunan, the Wulingyuan District's thousands of quartzite sandstone columns have been the subject of many famous paintings throughout Chinese history. The majestic setting of this UNESCO World Heritage Site also inspired the backdrop for the Hollywood movie *Avatar*[16]. The Heaven's Gate (Tianmen) is a huge hole

---

16 *Avatar* won the 2010 Oscars for Best Art Direction, Cinematography and Visual Effects.

on the side of the mountain. Men and women don wingsuits[17], jump out of a helicopter or from the top of the mountain, glide through the air and aim to fly through this hole in the annual Red Bull Wingsuit Flying World Championship.

Jiangsu & Shanghai

Jiangsu is a coastal province in east-central China. Located in its region is the city of Shanghai, originally an unremarkable little town which developed quickly into a metropolis of trade, banking and cosmopolitanism, and is also known to be at the forefront of fashion trends. Shanghai later became an independent municipality, and is now directly under the administration of the central government.

Because my mother was brought up in Shanghai, we were very familiar with Shanghainese cuisine. When my mother wanted to say something to my father but did not want us to understand what she was saying, she would use the Shanghainese dialect.

Visitors to Shanghai would take time out to visit the canals, bridges and classical gardens of Suzhou, a neighbouring city within the province of Jiangsu just west of Shanghai.

In the western corner of the province lies the city of Nanjing which was the capital of various kingdoms and dynasties in the history of

---

17 A wingsuit resembles a flying squirrel or bat, allowing the wearer to free fall and glide through the air from a height. By adjusting his body position, he can control his flight path and speed.

THE ONLY WAY IS ONE WAY

I was reminded of the time I flew to Nanjing to visit a professor at Nanjing University. This was in the late 1980s. His son informed us that we would not be able to meet his father. The latter had flown to Beijing a month ago and was still there because he couldn't get a return ticket back to Nanjing. In those days, you could not buy a round-trip ticket if you were flying within China. You had to buy a one-way ticket and hope for the best that you could get a return ticket when you were ready to come back.

China. Many monuments and landmarks remain in this city, including the Nanjing Massacre Memorial Hall built to commemorate the thousands of inhabitants who were murdered after the Japanese invaded China in 1937.

Close to the northern border of Jiangsu is the seaport Lianyungang. It is the eastern terminus of the New Eurasian Land Bridge[18] and the proposed Northern East West Freight Corridor[19]. The port is connected to numerous inner cities by rail.

When I visited Lianyungang around 2000, almost all the coal exports from China passed through it. Because of its proximity to South Korea and Japan, many other Chinese products were also being shipped out from this port.

40 km west of the city of Lianyungang is Donghai county, well-named as the "Land of crystals". Home to 70% of the national reserve of the precious material, Donghai produces 80% of China's crystal products. Walking around the port, I was offered sunglasses made with "natural crystals" which were supposed to protect my eyes better than all those Ray-Ban sunglasses that I have always worn. In the heart of the city is Mount Huaguoshan, which is the home of the Monkey King from the Chinese epic novel *Journey to the West* 《西遊記》.

---

18 The New Eurasian Land Bridge is a series of rail corridors to connect Chinese exporters to Europe, and is part of the "One Belt, One Road" initiative.
19 The Northern East West Freight Corridor aims to connect China to the east coast of North America through Europe, using rail and shipping routes.

Jiangxi

Jiangxi is a southeastern province defined by its pastoral landscapes of rice paddies, rivers and mountains. I did not have the opportunity to explore the whole province, but I have been to Jingdezhen, the centre of porcelain-making for over a thousand years. Some of the porcelain bowls on display in the museum were as thin as an eggshell. In the city lies the remains of an imperial kiln from the Ming-dynasty era. Sad to say, I could not find any quality porcelain ware when I was in Jingdezhen because all the good ones were being exported.

Another problem I faced whenever I visited the city was that the host would always present us with a gift from the porcelain producers and I always had to prove to the customs officer at the airport that what I had received was not part of their national treasure trove.

Geographically, Jingdezhen is in a valley surrounded by mountains. The locals boasted to me that the Imperial Japanese Army did not venture into the valley during their invasion in the Second World War because they had heard about the wild animals and poisonous snakes that roamed these mountains.

Liaoning

Liaoning is a northeastern province bordering North Korea and the Yellow Sea. The capital Shenyang was the original home of the Manchu Qing dynasty emperors. The only city in Liaoning that I have been to is Dalian. The weather in Dalian can be brutal in the wintertime as temperatures can drop to as low as -7°C.

We were a subcontractor to a Korean shipyard based in Dalian. However, one morning when my workers went to work, the shipyard was closed and locked up. The Korean managers had left the country overnight because they did not want to face their creditors, the banks.

Shaanxi

Shaanxi is a northwestern province whose ancient capital, Xi'an, was a starting point for the Silk Road. It is also a compulsory stop for tourists visiting China because it is home to the Mausoleum of the First Qin

Emperor (Qin Shi Huang), containing thousands of clay soldiers known as the Terracotta Army (Bing Ma Yong).

Entering the mausoleum, one could see a lot of signs prohibiting flash photography. However, with the advancement of technology these days, cameras or camera phones do not need flashlights to take a good photograph of the terracotta warriors. Seeing the terracotta army begs the question, where else can one find the other contingents of the army. Maybe we have not seen it all yet.

Right in the city centre is the iconic Bell Tower, built in 1384 during the Ming dynasty. On my first trip to Xi'an in 1987, I stayed at the Bell Tower Hotel which was the only international class hotel in the city at that time, and it was right across the road from the actual Bell Tower monument. I revisited Xi'an in 1993, as part of a tour[20] I did along the Silk Road.

Shandong

Shandong, an eastern province on the Yellow Sea, is known for its Taoist and Confucian heritage. One of China's most sacred peaks, Mount Tai (Taishan), is located in the province and features shrines, stone tablets and pilgrimage trails. Mineral water bottled in Taishan are distributed all over the world in small glass bottles.

One of the most famous cities in this province is Qingdao, home to the Tsingtao beer brewery. Set up by the Anglo-German Brewery in 1903, the brewery is the flag bearer for Chinese beer and Tsingtao beer is sold worldwide.

Qingdao was a German enclave, so there is an area near the beach where all the houses were built in the tradition of German architecture. I visited a famous Taoist temple, where a priest offered to read my palm. At the end of the palm-reading session, he took out a book and asked for a donation. Glancing at the records in the book, I noticed that everyone who signed in the book had donated thousands of renminbi. I knew I was had, but taking a chance that he might put a curse on me, I donated RMB100.

---

20 See Chapter 11 "The Hardship Group" for my travels on the Silk Road.

DRINKING IN CHINA – WHAT TO EXPECT

The Chinese like to show their hospitality by plying their guests with ample drinks, alcoholic or non-alcoholic. My colleague used to tell me how much he dreaded having to drink the coffee they offered him. To show their generosity, the Chinese hosts would use up to four teaspoons of instant coffee just to make a cup of coffee. The caffeine rush from that cup of coffee would make my colleague jittery for the rest of the day.

Similarly, the Chinese host would always try to ply us with alcohol during a meal. Everyone at the dining table would take turns to offer a toast to us. I also think that it gives them an excuse to drink as well. The host would use his eyes to convey the message to his subordinates: "OK, you are up next." After a dinner in Tianjin, my colleague had to ask the driver to pull over to the side of the highway three times during that two-hour drive so that he could throw up.

Shanxi

I did not have a chance to explore this province, but the headquarters of one of my customers was located in the capital Taiyuan. I only remember flying into Taiyuan at night while it was snowing. I had my meeting with the customer the following day and flew off in the afternoon.

Sichuan

Sichuan is a southwestern province in China, and its capital is Chengdu. The region is home to the giant pandas, which visitors can observe at several panda breeding reserves. Sichuan is famous for its hot and spicy cuisine[21] which is served all around the world. Among the more famous dishes are Kung Pao chicken, Mapo tofu and those made with mala hot sauce. The province is also famous for the traditional sleight-of-hand art of "face changing (*bian lian*)", where opera performers change their masks rapidly in a short span of time during their dance.

---

21 Chengdu was designated by UNESCO as a "Creative City of Gastronomy" in 2010. It was the first Asian city to be honoured with the status.

My customer in Sichuan conducted basic rotary wing flight training from Xinjin Airport, located 30 km southwest of Chengdu. This is an airfield constructed in 1928 and used extensively by the US Air Force during the Second World War. In the early 1990s when I was making my trips out to the training academy, all that was left of the airfield was just a long concrete runway. What's more, one could usually find bicycles and buffaloes crossing the runway at will, because the perimeter fence was all dilapidated and not serving its purpose.

Another city in Sichuan that I had visited was Panzhihua, an industrial city which used to belong to Yunnan province. I had to take an eight-hour train ride to get there, all because someone notified our agent that he was interested to buy a helicopter.

In an early trip to Chengdu, I had a long, drawn-out meeting with a customer who had already booked a restaurant to treat us to a 52-course dumpling dinner. Because we were late in reaching the restaurant after the meeting, the waiting staff tried to serve us all 52 courses in 45 minutes, so that the company bus sending the workers home could still leave at the designated time. I think we were on the 30th course when the staff decided to just bring out the rest of the dumplings at one go. Needless to say, we could not finish them all, so we told the staff to pack up the unconsumed dumplings for themselves to bring home.

On a later trip to Chengdu, after checking into my hotel, I decided to take a nap. When I woke up, I went down to the main dining room for my dinner. I was told that I still had half an hour before the kitchen closed for the night, so I ordered several of my favourite Sichuan dishes. I was in the midst of enjoying my food when I noticed that as soon as the other diners left their table, the waiter would clear the dishes *and* take the table away.

Pretty soon, I was the only one eating at the only dining table in the dining room. Out of the corner of my eyes, I also noticed a crowd starting to build up on the sides of the room, and a band coming in to set up on the stage. Suddenly, I realised that the dining room was transforming into a ballroom and everyone was waiting for me to finish my dinner so that they could start dancing. Not to embarrass myself further,

I decided to put down my chopsticks, simply finished my drink and asked for the bill.

Yunnan

Yunnan is a province in southwestern China. One of the cities we visited was the Old Town of Lijiang which was designated as a UNESCO World Heritage Site in 1997. Bars lined both sides of a small stream that ran through the town. Groups on each side would challenge each other to compose verses that rhyme. One group saw an American in our group, so they challenged the table next to us to compose something in English. They thought for a while, and then they sang the alphabet song: "A-B-C-D, E-F-G…". That was fun.

On the way to Lijiang, Kwan and I also spent a few days in Kunming, the capital. We visited the scenic Shilin (Stone Forest) which featured limestone karst peaks formed 270 million years ago. Shilin was inscribed as a UNESCO Global Geopark in 2015.

Xishuangbanna is another very popular tourist destination in the province, near the Laotian border. The region is known for its large number of ethnic minorities. We visited a compound where each of the ethnic minorities occupied a building with a restaurant serving their indigenous cuisine and home brew. The famous Pu'er tea is grown on plantations in this region.

AIR TICKET RESERVATIONS – BEHIND THE SCENES

I know someone who was walking to the restroom at an airline reservation centre in China and managed to peek into the room behind the reservation desks with the impressive computers. What he saw shocked him, because he had expected everything to be a seamless computerised operation. There were similar computer screens in the backroom, but there were many clerks filling out 5x3 cards and slotting them into trays, à la the antiquated Kardex system. This must be where "semi-online" booking was invented.

Zhejiang

Zhejiang is an eastern province facing the East China Sea, just south of Shanghai. The picturesque West Lake, which is the subject of many famous Chinese ink paintings and poems, is located in Hangzhou, the capital. The girls from Hangzhou are reputed to be the most beautiful in China. Because Zhejiang is a coastal province, one can find many of its natives in Hong Kong where their trader instinct flourishes in the freeport. Zhejiang cuisine is very similar to Shanghainese cuisine and popular around the world.

In the evening, we attended the famous Impression West Lake Show created by the award-winning film director Zhang Yimou. The light, music and dance spectacle was staged outdoors upon the West Lake itself, and based on Hangzhou legends.

Chapter 7
SOUTH ASIA

Seven countries form the subcontinent known as South Asia: Bangladesh, Pakistan, Sri Lanka, Maldives, Nepal, Bhutan and India. The region is home to major mountain chains, including the Karakoram range and the Himalayas, where Mount Everest stands.

Growing up, I heard a lot of stories about India from my father because he met and married my mother there during the Second World War. He was a very good storyteller and I can still recall some of his anecdotes. In the few years that they lived in India, all my father could remember was how he could count from one to ten in Hindi. *Ick, du, din, jar, bunch...*

He also exaggerated on how spicy Indian curries were. According to him, all you have to do is to smell the curry and your forehead would start sweating. He recalled the time that he bought a refrigerator that came with a three-pin plug, but the sockets in India those days were meant for two-pin plugs. The technician who came to install the refrigerator had never seen one like that before, so he stripped the three wires, mixed the strands together, divided the bunch into two, screwed them into the two-pin plug and inserted it into the socket. That knocked out the power in the whole street.

There were some South Asian students at my university, and the Indian student population was quite substantive, albeit comprising mostly graduate students. I used to meet some of them in the Commonwealth Club, of which I was a member. The Commonwealth Club played in a soccer league on campus but there were hardly any South Asians who played for our team. School work was higher on their priority list. I had an Indian graduate student as a team member in one of my computer courses, but he was quite a few years older than me and had a different social circle, so we did not hang out together.

After joining the helicopter business, I became familiar with all seven countries because I volunteered to cover the South Asian market. I also took a number of vacations there, which gave me plenty of good travel memories.

Bangladesh

My first trip to Bangladesh was in the late 1980s, on a visit to its capital Dhaka. The phenomenon of labour strikes was an everyday affair in those days. Our driver would say, "Oh, another strike. Let's take a different route."

At that time, there were two 5-star hotels, the Sonargon and the Sheraton. The latter was the former Intercontinental Hotel that was taken over by the Sheraton Group in 1983. However, when I stayed there on that first trip, the shower curtain still had the Intercontinental logo. Even the toiletries supplied bore the Intercontinental logo. Maybe someone foresaw that one day, the management of the hotel would revert to Intercontinental again. Because in 2018, after extensive renovations, it re-opened as the Hotel Intercontinental Dhaka.

In 1991, a massive cyclone swept through the country. Apparently, the government had been forewarned about the incoming cyclone because there was a US Navy vessel in the Bay of Bengal that decided to sail away from the delta as the cyclone was building up. The cyclone was accompanied by tidal waves. Bangladesh, being low-lying and surrounded by a delta of rivers that empty into the Bay of Bengal, was very vulnerable to flooding and cyclones. That particular cyclone caused widespread destruction, between 135,000 to 145,000 fatalities and an estimated US$1.5-billion in damage including some new helicopters on the wharf which were still in crates!

I had dealings with the Bangladeshi government. The finance ministry's fiscal year was 1 July to 30 June of the following year. The last few days of June were the busiest time for the government departments. They dragged their feet all year long but then worked around the clock towards the end of June. Every light in the finance ministry building would be lit, all through the night, indicating that the staff were all working extra hard to close the fiscal year. In some countries, this would be the boom time for pizza delivery.

To show me more of the country, my representative took us on a flight down to Chittagong (renamed Chattogram in 2018). This is a major sea port and financial centre in Bangladesh. It is also the second largest city in the country. One of the major money spinners in those days was breaking up tankers to recycle the steel. There were a lot of curios and souvenirs that one could pick up from pseudo-antique shops along the beachfront area, purported to have come off some scrapped steamers.

I was also brought further south to Cox's Bazar, the beach resort playground of Bangladesh's rich and famous. We even had a round of golf on the best golf course there.

Pakistan

I did not have many reasons to visit Pakistan, except maybe to make a transit stop whenever I flew from West Asia to Singapore.

In the 1980s, on one of those transit stops in Karachi, the largest city in Pakistan, my luggage did not appear on the conveyor belt after I had cleared immigration. When I reported this to the lost luggage office, the agent said, "The plane is still there; let's go and see if we can find your luggage."

We walked through security, out onto the tarmac, to the plane. We looked into the cargo hold, and there was my suitcase, lying against a bulkhead. I suspected that my luggage had been targeted to be heisted, because in the empty cargo hold, there was just one suitcase – mine. A baggage handler climbed into the hold, retrieved my bag and handed it to me as if it were no big deal!

In 2004, I revisited Pakistan on a vacation with my wife Kwan and our friends, spending 10 memorable days travelling on the Karakoram Highway[1] from Lahore to the Chinese border.

---

1   See Chapter 11 "The Hardship Group" for my journey on one of the highest paved international roads in the world, that took almost two decades to build.

Sri Lanka

This former Portuguese, then British colony was granted independence in 1948 as Ceylon. In 1972, the country became a republic within the Commonwealth and changed its name to Sri Lanka. Over the years, I have made quite a few trips there, for work and leisure.

Because of my dealings with the Sri Lankan air force, I would visit them once or twice a year, primarily in Colombo, staying away from the war zone in the east. On one visit, after my meetings were over, I hired a car and driver to make an overnight trip down south along the western coast, to the seaside resort town of Hikkaduwa, 110 km south of Colombo. Hikkaduwa is known for its strong surf and beautiful beaches. The beachfront is lined with coconut trees, with ropes strung from tree top to tree top. The driver told me that farmers used these ropes to go from tree to tree to collect the sap of the coconut flowers into big wooden casks mounted on bullock carts. The sap would be transported back to distilleries to be distilled into a popular alcoholic drink called arrack.

In 2017, Kwan and I attended a wedding in Colombo. We arrived a day before the occasion and were invited to spend the night at a seaside bungalow in Galle, located at the southern tip of the main island. It is a fortified old city founded by the Portuguese in the 16th century. Situated right on the beach, the bungalow offered us a most peaceful and relaxing evening.

The following day, we drove back to Colombo where the wedding was held in the iconic Galle Face Hotel. Built in 1864, it is one of the oldest hotels east of the Suez. It was a well-attended wedding, culminated by the groom's grand entrance on a white horse, purportedly to capture his bride and bring her back to his village.

One of the post-wedding receptions was held in the Cinnamon Lakeside Hotel. In 2019, this hotel was one of three luxurious hotels badly damaged in a wave of suicide bombings across Colombo. The attacks targeted Christians during the Easter church services and other guests who were having breakfast in the beachfront hotels.

After the wedding, we took a tour of the Ceylon Tea Trails, 130 km east of Colombo. The owner of the Tea Trails also owned a collection

THE SRI LANKAN DIASPORA IN EUROPE

Although I never had much of a chance to interact on a personal level with Sri Lankans during my work trips there, I learned a lot about the civil war from the minicab drivers in London. A lot of them were Sri Lankans from the northeast of the island, displaced from their homeland by the civil war between the Liberation Tigers of Tamil Eelam (LTTE) and the Sri Lankan army. Those with relatives who had left Sri Lanka in the early part of the war and settled in Europe were lucky, because those relatives could sponsor their migration to Europe. When the war was over, the emigrants were allowed to visit their former homeland, but many of them saw no reason to go back and re-establish their lives, since they had already built a new life in Europe.

of five colonial-era bungalows that used to house British tea planter managers. Restored to impeccable style, these bungalows offer a taste of gracious living with butler service and original furnishings. Although we stayed in one of the bungalows, we were encouraged to travel to the other bungalows to sample their gourmet meals. We also visited a few of the tea-processing factories belonging to the Dilmah Tea Company, one of the largest tea-producing companies in the world.

Maldives

The chain of low-lying coral islands that make up the Maldives offers one of the best diving spots in West Asia. Being a keen diver, I simply could not give the Maldives a miss. On one of my work trips in Bombay, India, I discovered that my return air ticket on Singapore Airlines would be cheaper if I took a detour by transiting through Malé, the capital of Maldives! The choice was a no brainer.

On another business trip, after my meetings were over, I stopped by in Maldives once again for a few days of diving which were simply superb.

Because my visits usually spanned just two or three days, I would stay on one of the nearby islands under an hour's speedboat ride from the Malé airport. However, I did get to stay at a resort further away from Malé once. The resort had previously encountered a fire disaster in which half of the chalets were burnt down shortly after it was constructed. Following an extensive and expensive rebuilding, the resort had a soft opening and extended a special invitation to Kwan and me. We had a great time swimming with and feeding huge manta rays. We also witnessed the feeding of sharks in pretty shallow waters; they were harmless and not more than 2 m long.

Nepal

The 1980s saw me making several trips a year to the Nepalese capital of Kathmandu for business. At that time, Nepal was still a kingdom[2].

I have seen the most unusual luggage on flights into Nepal. Once, I saw a man who wore two scrambler motorcycle tyres around his body like bandoliers. I guessed his luggage was full! I wondered whether he wore his seat belt over or under those tyres. Another time, at the baggage claim, I saw a kitchen sink going around on the conveyor belt. This was a big, stainless steel, double sink with drainer. It made me think that someone had underestimated the expression "Everything but the kitchen sink!".

On a flight out of Kathmandu, I sat next to a young and beautiful Miss Nepal who was flying to Manila for a beauty pageant. She was brushing up on world current affairs in preparation for the Q&A portion of the beauty contest. I glanced over and noticed that she was reading some back issues of *Time* and *Newsweek* magazines that were about five years outdated. I transited in Bangkok for a flight back to Singapore while she continued on to Manila for the pageant, so I did not have a chance to see how she scored on the Q&A portion of the competition.

During a trip to Kathmandu with my director, we were invited to our local representative's house for dinner. We told him that we had to catch an early flight the following morning, so we could not afford to have a late night. He assured us that he would pick us up at 7 p.m. instead of the usual dinner hour of 8.30 p.m. We arrived at his house and

2 The Nepalese monarchy was abolished in 2007, and the country became a secular state in 2008.

he started serving snacks and drinks. By about 10.30 p.m., he asked if anyone was hungry because he would like to start serving dinner. Hallo!!!! We returned to the hotel at half an hour past midnight, which was the norm when a Nepali entertained.

My business dealings went smoothly, and upon signing a US$1-million contract, I felt that it called for some celebrations. I suggested to our representative that we should drive up to a certain resort that faced the Himalayan range and have a beer. He said he could not use his car because the horn was not working. I just could not comprehend how a faulty horn would be such a big problem, so I insisted that we drive out to this resort for our celebration.

By the time we arrived at the resort, I was a complete nervous wreck. Pedestrians, bicycles, auto rickshaws, cars and trucks moved about as if we were not there. All because our horn did not work. I would never recommend anyone else to go through what I did.

During another visit to Kathmandu, I noticed small groups of four or five people in close proximity to each other, standing on the sidewalk. After a while, those groups of people were still there, except that they had shifted further down the road. As I observed this phenomenon, I gradually realised that they were standing in the ray of sunlight that managed to shine through between buildings, probably to keep warm. From their behaviour, they appeared not to know one another. While I am on the subject of keeping warm in the cold and damp winters of Kathmandu – I walked into a bank one day and found all the staff crowding around a fire burning in a wastepaper bin. They were warming their hands over the fire. I just hope that they were not using their customers' deposit slips.

There was once I walked past a bar and saw a sign outside, announcing the availability of draft beer. Of course, I went in to have a taste of the Nepali "Star" draft beer, as it had never been available until then. You could imagine my disappointment when I was told that they had just returned the keg to the brewery for a refill. Apparently, there were only six kegs in the whole kingdom, and being able to find one in your favourite bar was a hit-or-miss affair. Nowadays, from what I see on the Internet, they sell craft beer throughout Nepal.

In the 1980s, the Yak and Yeti Hotel was one of the few premium hotels in downtown Kathmandu. We stayed there once and had dinner at their fine-dining restaurant, The Chimney, where we met an elderly British couple. The gentleman served in Nepal with the Royal Gurkha regiment some time ago. He brought his wife back to Kathmandu to relive his time in Nepal. He told me that he especially missed the borscht served in the restaurant. At the end of his meal, he asked the waiter captain for a copy of the soup recipe. Since the waiter captain gave out the recipe (printed on a 5x3 index card) so readily, I asked for one too. The recipe starts out with peeling 50 kg of potatoes, 20 kg of carrots, and so on. It was then I realised that the recipe was meant for cooking a big pot of borscht, probably in a 200-litre drum!

In the early 1990s, our representative in Nepal told me that his nephew, Deep, owned a safari resort in the Chitwan National Park. Deep invited me to bring my family there for an adventure holiday that included white-water rafting and game viewing, and I accepted it.

Together with two other families, we flew into Kathmandu's Tribhuvan International Airport. After spending a few days in Kathmandu, we took a domestic flight up to Pokhara, the second largest city in Nepal. From Pokhara, Deep arranged a 15-seater minibus to take us down to Mugling where the Daraudi River merges into the Trishuli River, which is popular with white-water rafting activities.

We were loaded into two rubber rafts guided by a local helmsman each, and set off on our exhilarating white-water rafting adventure. Meanwhile, our personal effects were loaded onto the minibus, which drove ahead of our rafts, so that the driver could set up tents for us to camp overnight by the riverside. At the end of each day, we were invited to jump into the cool, fresh mountain waters to bathe ourselves before dinner was being served.

When we arrived at Bharatpur, we were bused over to Deep's safari resort. The chalets were round wooden huts. At night, we could hear the rumbling of rhinoceroses coming into the compound to feast on the bananas hanging from the trees. As there was no electricity in the resort, Deep's 30-year-old GE fridge ran on kerosene.

Deep had an old Land Rover jeep with which he brought us out to the fields, hoping to catch a glimpse of tigers. Our tour guide told us frankly that in his five years working as a guide in Chitwan, he had only seen a tiger twice. We also rode on elephants into the bushes to look for rhinos. Every time the elephant tender saw a rhino urinating, he would jump off the elephant to try to collect the few drops of urine. We were told that the urine had medicinal value. After a week out in Chitwan, we headed back to Kathmandu and flew home.

Some twenty years later, I returned to Kathmandu for a holiday and had quite an adventure on a road trip[3] to Lhasa, Tibet.

Bhutan

In 2017, Kwan and I went trekking in Bhutan. This was not the first time[4] we were in the Himalayan Buddhist kingdom, and many improvements had taken place in the years between.

The road between Paro (where the international airport is located) and the capital Thimphu had been upgraded. Trekking was much more luxurious and elaborate. Horses were deployed as part of our supporting ancillary. Although we slept in tents, warm water showers were provided. The chef even attempted to serve us pizzas during mealtimes.

There was a hotel – the Tashi Namgay Resort – situated on a small hill next to the Paro airport. The flight schedule of all the aircraft landings and take-offs was posted on a board facing the runway. People would come to this hotel, sit on the veranda, sip their tea or beer, and watch aircraft landing or taking off from the airport. That would be their excitement for the day.

Another national pastime was to watch an archery match. All the archers wore the gho[5] as their team jersey, with each team sporting a different colour. There were many rituals before and after each archer

---

3 See Chapter 11 "The Hardship Group" for my Nepal–Tibet journey, in which I battled landslides and altitude sickness.
4 Our first visit to Bhutan took place in the late 1990s, and is also chronicled in Chapter 11.
5 The gho is the traditional and national attire for Bhutanese men. It is a knee-length robe secured with a belt.

took a shot. His teammates would do a little dance routine, especially if his arrow hit the target which was 146 yards (134 m) away. We were told by our guide that the highlight of those matches was the drinking that went on throughout the match. Sometimes, the archers became so intoxicated that it was not uncommon to hear about spectators being shot by stray arrows.

I also noticed that compared to our first trip, there were numerous luxurious hotels built around the country, all operated by international hotel chains. Because of an upcoming national festival – the Thimphu Tshechu celebration[6] – we tried to shorten the trekking portion of our trip by a day so that we could spend that extra day in the capital city for the festivities. We were quoted US$1,000 per night per room for this change in schedule!

All foreigners have to pay a daily tax of US$250 to the government. But not Indian nationals. At that time, they did not have to pay this tax, but they had to pay admission fees to most of the national tourist attractions. In general, I found that the locals are very nationalistic; they are proud of their heritage and they have great respect for their king.

Our 12-day itinerary included 6 days of trekking and many pints of red rice beer. On the second day, we had an acclimatisation trek that took us up to a pass at 4,100 m altitude before coming down to a nunnery (3,500 m) where our transport was waiting for us.

On the third day, we started our trek up to Phajoding Monastery (3,650 m) which was established more as a refuge for orphaned and underprivileged boys. Situated at such a high altitude, it was not a monastery that received many visitors. The principal of the monastery, Lama Namgay Tenzin, told us that when he was assigned to Phajoding, his peers expressed their sympathy as they felt that he would have a hard life there. On the day that we were there, the monks were busy cleaning up the building and sweeping the floors because they were expecting a visit from the Chief Lama of the monastery.

---

6 The Thimphu Tshechu is a three-day religious event and the biggest festival in Bhutan. Through prayers and rituals, participants hope to usher in blessings and rid themselves of bad karma.

We were supposed to set up camp at an open field next to the monastery, but the field was flooded from rain. We had to climb up another 200 m almost in the dark before we could set up camp. Our tour guide was the president of the Bhutanese Tour Guide Association, so that evening, sitting around a campfire, he had many folklore stories to tell about his country.

The following day, we ascended to 4,300 m altitude before climbing down from the other side of the mountain to get to the famous Tiger's Nest Monastery (Paro Taktsang). On the way down to our minibus, we met the Chief Lama of the Phajoding Monastery and his entourage coming up for his visit to Phajoding. We almost missed him because he was a reincarnated pre-teen. We would not have recognised him if not for the special coloured robe that he was wearing.

As we returned from our trekking, we were joined by the rest of the group in our party. Because they did not want to go on the long trek, they timed their arrival to coincide with the end of our trek. After they had their half-day trek to Tiger's Nest a day later, everyone came together for a birthday party lunch set up next to a river, to celebrate the 70th birthday of Kwan's older brother, Dennis. On our way back to the hotel, our driver showed us a patch of marijuana crop growing in the wild by the roadside.

Over the next few days, we attended part of the Thimphu Tshechu festival, which was unfortunately marred by rain. We also visited the Great Buddha Dordenma, a 54-m tall Buddha statue. While we were there, the highest-ranking monk in the country spoke for three days straight on the teachings of Buddha. People from all over the country came to listen to him.

At the end of 12 days, we flew out of Bhutan with fond memories.

India

India is the biggest country in South Asia. Over the course of 20 years covering the Indian market for Bell Helicopter, I must have made close to 100 trips there, both for work and for leisure, not discounting the fact that my parents met and were married in India.

Since gaining independence in 1947, India has seen an explosion of its population, from 361 million (the first census in 1951) to 1.39 billion in 2021. Correspondingly, the number of states grew to 28 as new states were carved out of larger states for the ease of governing. I have been to 17 of the 28 states. Those that I missed out were mostly the new states, many of them in the eastern part of the country.

Andhra Pradesh

Andhra Pradesh is a state in southeastern India, and Hyderabad used to be its capital[7]. However, in 2014, the state of Telangana was carved out and Hyderabad went with the new state.

The curries of Andhra Pradesh are famous for their spiciness because the state is known for producing Guntur chillies – one of the spiciest chillies in the world. The local cuisine is tasty and easy to gulp down, but the sting comes on 15 minutes later. Another specialty is their coffee. It is so strong that they serve it with a pot of hot water. If you attempt to drink it straight up, it tastes sour.

Visakhapatnam, also commonly referred to as Vizag, is one of the oldest port cities in the state. Situated in the heart of Andhra Pradesh, Visakhapatnam is known for its picturesque beaches and serene landscape. Due to some unexpected developments on a work trip[8] that turned out to be rather fortuitous, I spent a night in the Sheraton on the beach. In the afternoon, the fishermen would come ashore and sell their fresh catch to the hotel, so I had a chance to savour the best chilli prawns I have ever tasted in India.

Assam

This northeastern state is famous for its tea[9] plantations. In the late 1990s, we had the fortune of driving through Assam when we went by

---

7   There have been plans to create three different capitals in Andhra Pradesh, but for the moment, Amaravati is its capital.
8   See the box story "Travelling with a copter, from state to state" in the later part of this chapter.
9   The popular and widely consumed breakfast teas are usually a blend of Assam and other tea leaves.

road from Bhutan to Sikkim[10]. Miles and miles to the left and right of the road were just lined with tea plantations.

On the Indian Airlines[11] flight out of Bagdogra after the trip, I read in the inflight magazine about a man who went around Assam performing in circus freak shows, rubbing raw crushed chillies into his eyes. He had been doing this act for over 30 years and he had a certificate from an eye surgeon attesting that his eyesight was as good as the day when he was born.

Delhi

The union territory of Delhi is in north-central India and it contains the capital New Delhi and other districts. As a major industrial, commercial and financial hub, Delhi is well-connected domestically and internationally with road, rail and air links.

Back in the 1980s, most imported goods were liable for taxation, and it was especially high for electronic goods. I was on a flight to Delhi and happened to be sitting next to a local lady who clearly did not believe in paying taxes. She began secreting all sorts of items on her person – calculators and gold bangles tucked into her bra, pens hidden in her shoes and a Sony Walkman nestled inside the front of her saree. She brazenly carried out her plan despite knowing that I was witnessing her every move. When she was finished with the concealment, she turned to me and gave me one of those looks that said: "If you say or mention anything about this, I shall have to kill you".

What's more, she really bullied an old man sitting next to her. The bossy lady put all her carry-on bags underneath the seat in front of this old man, leaving him with very little legroom. For some reason, he dared not protest. I really felt like blowing the whistle on her to the customs officer.

On one occasion, I arrived at Delhi Airport, and the immigration officer, as per usual, removed my disembarkation card which I had con-

---

10 See Chapter 11 "The Hardship Group" for my Bhutan–Sikkim road trip.
11 Indian Airlines was formed in 1953 to fly the domestic and regional air routes. It was merged into Air India in 2011.

veniently placed to help him locate my Indian visa, and proceeded to take his sweet time flicking through my passport looking for my visa. This seems to be a standard procedure for most immigration officers worldwide. Next, he asked me the usual questions: "…Your first time in India?...how long are you staying?...what is the purpose of your visit?... what business are you in?..."

Having been advised of the sector that I worked in, presumably impressed, he then caught me completely by surprise with a most unusual question: "Can I have a job?" I was lost for words – except those silently spoken to myself, which went something like "With the speed at which you work? You expect me to give you a job? Hallo…?"

Luggage arriving at the Delhi Airport were X-rayed in the secure area before being delivered to the conveyor belt. According to a friend, when the X-ray indicated anything suspicious inside, the operator would mark an "x" on that suitcase…with chalk. The savvy locals knew this and simply rubbed off the chalk mark with their shoes before presenting their luggage for the standard customs inspection.

In the 1980s and 1990s, the most common way to get from any major airport in India to your hotel was by pre-paid taxi. These were usually beat-up, ageing cabs but the drivers were willing to wait in line for hours to pick up a fare. Payment was made within the terminal. When the taxi approached the parking lot exit barrier, the attendant would ask the hirer for his name, and record it in a notebook along with the taxi licence plate number. This was to facilitate tracing during a search should one become waylaid, disappear or be killed. He also wrote down the taxi number on a little piece of paper which would be handed to the hirer, in case something was left behind in the taxi. One night at the Indira Gandhi International Airport, a friend came to receive me and we hired a pre-paid taxi to get to my hotel. When we reached the exit gate and he was asked his name, he replied, "Mao Tse Tung". The attendant diligently recorded that name in his record book.

After a work trip in Delhi, I was at the airport, getting ready for my flight home. There were a few lines for the passport check, and I was waiting in one of the lines. Unbeknownst to me, there was an Indian

GETTING TO KNOW INDIA'S OLD TAXIS

An interesting feature of these old taxis was that they generally had just one working windscreen wiper, on the driver's side. The other wiper would be blade-less and wrapped in cloth so that when activated, the metal holder would not scratch the glass.

Also, I noticed that most taxi drivers in India had a habit of shutting off the ignition in a traffic jam in order to save fuel. When the traffic inched forward by a foot, he would start his engine and move the taxi by a foot, then shut down the engine again. Perhaps that is why some modern cars are also designed to shut off the ignition whenever the cars come to a complete stop, even in traffic. The manufacturers must have borrowed the idea from Indian taxi drivers.

woman travelling with her son and daughter, and she had placed her children in different lines – her son happened to be in front of me.

My line advanced until her son was about to be called up. Sure enough, the woman pulled her daughter over and stepped in front of me. Now I have a system for selecting a certain line. If I had known the boy represented a family like hers, I would not have selected that line. Because the woman and her daughter joined the boy in my line, I was now behind a whole family!

So, I did what any seasoned traveller would do – I ratted her out. "Lady, you were in the other line," I said.

"But my son is in this line," she retorted.

I told her, "You might as well put a child in each line."

To which she again retorted, "I don't have that many children."

Just then, the immigration officer called out, "Next". She quickly gathered her whole family and stepped up to the officer's counter.

"She cut into our line!" I walked up to the officer and told him.

"Yeah, she was in that other line!" The rest of the people behind me called out. The immigration officer had no choice but to send the woman and her kids back to the line where she had moved over from. Out of the corner of my eye, I noticed that she was holding a Canadian passport as she was walking away, so I asked, "Would you do this in Canada?"

On another trip from Delhi back to Singapore, after I had cleared immigration, next up was Customs & Excise where the inspection to ensure that passengers were not attempting to flee the country with excess Indian rupees was conducted. On previous occasions, I was usually waved through, but this time round, I was stopped by the duty officer who asked me to follow him to his office – via a 4-passenger capacity shoe-box lift.

Once we were in the privacy of his office, he handed me two US$10 notes and told me to buy two bottles of White Horse Scotch whisky from the duty-free shop. He also requested me to leave my briefcase in his office – presumably to ensure that I didn't abscond with his money.

At the shop, I discovered that the White Horse whisky was out-of-stock. As I was contemplating my next move, there, in the next aisle was

---

THE INVISIBLE BAG

At Delhi Airport, every piece of hand-carried luggage had to be tied with a tag. After the hand luggage had passed through the X-ray machine, there would be a security personnel whose lifelong job was to stamp on that tag to show that it had been scanned. Before boarding, there would be another security personnel checking to ensure that no unstamped items were carried into the cabin.

Simple, yes, but...A friend of mine was about to board a plane and, travelling light, she had no hand-carry bags. Not willing or able to think out-of-the-box, the security officer at the X-ray machine put a "hand carry" tag around her wrist – and stamped it.

When my friend reached the final security check just prior to boarding, she almost missed her flight. All because she had to spend much time trying to convincingly convey her story to a super-sceptical security officer who kept on asking, "Whatever happened to the piece of hand luggage that came with this tag?" One wonders how the performance of the X-ray machine security officer was rated. Was the stamp chopped squarely on the tag? Or was the clarity of the stamping consistent?

that same officer, watching me like a hawk. I told him that the shopkeeper had recommended Johnny Walker Red Label as an alternative, and he readily agreed.

After paying for the whisky, we returned to his office. He explained that with Christmas coming up, it was customary for him to present his superior officer with a suitable gift. If not, he would face the prospect of being transferred to some remote outpost in the back of beyond – he even mentioned, as an example, Port Blair in the Andaman and Nicobar Islands. By tapping on a traveller's privilege to buy duty-free liquor, he managed to save himself some money. With no more requests, my briefcase was returned intact. Finding it hard to convince myself that I had just performed a truly noble deed – I continued on my way.

During the winter months, not long after sunset, Delhi Airport becomes shrouded in fog. The fog affects all flights, in and out of Delhi. Realising this, Singapore Airlines usually adjusts its winter flight schedule so as to arrive and take off earlier, thus avoiding the fog. During the years in which I flew in and out of India for work purposes, Indian Airlines and Air India never seemed to have figured this out – or perhaps they didn't care – even though they were at their home base. Invariably, their flights which were scheduled to depart around midnight would be delayed until the morning sun had burned off the fog. This had a knock-on effect and delayed the departure of all the other flights in the following day. It didn't make good business sense at all.

Goa

This west Indian state is a former Portuguese colony, similar to Melaka in Malaysia. It boasts of some fabulous beaches which, sad to say, have not been very well preserved. Many jetsetters from India, especially those living in the west coast, would fly there over the weekend for some fun in the sun. The landmark of the beach was a tanker which had run aground in 2000 and had been lying there for 12 years. It has since been removed after my visit.

Goa also produces a wide variety of frangipani flowers in different colours and shapes. Some of these are made into fragrant massage oils and a local liquor.

Gujarat

One of the big cities in the west Indian state of Gujarat[12] is Ahmedabad, which is accessible from Singapore via a direct flight on Singapore Airlines. Legend has it that the rulers in Ahmedabad were so decadent that they did not even want to chew their food, so the kebabs were made so fine and tender that the rulers could just swallow the meat.

In one year, I went on a trip to Ahmedabad with Kwan, because she wanted to visit the textile museum there and also sample the legendary tender kebabs.

Haryana

Haryana is one of the north Indian states bordering New Delhi. On the way from the Indira Gandhi International Airport into the city of Delhi, we could see the familiar road sign pointing to Gurgaon in Haryana. To get to Gurgaon (renamed Gurugram in 2016), we would drive onto a viaduct that leads us to this new financial and technology hub just outside of Delhi. The city is very modern and vibrant, and we were there to visit a new culinary school, the Indian School of Hospitality.

Karnataka

The capital of the southwestern state of Karnataka is Bengaluru (formerly Bangalore). At about 1,000 m, it is the highest among the major cities in India and enjoys a pleasant, cool climate throughout the year. Bengaluru is also known as the beer capital of India as one can find pubs all over the city, serving craft beer.

Often called the "Silicon Valley of India", Bengaluru is a fast-growing technology and innovation hub, attracting major companies as well as startups. It is also an aerospace hub – top aerospace companies have a presence there, including Boeing, Rolls-Royce and Airbus. Hindustan Aeronautics, India's oldest and largest aerospace and defence company, is headquartered there.

---

12 Gujarat was the birthplace of Mahatma Gandhi, who successfully led India's non-violent independence movement against British colonial rule.

BUZZ OFF, WINGED PASSENGERS!

I boarded an Indian Airlines aircraft that was transiting at the Bengaluru airport. After all the passengers had disembarked, the crew left the passenger doors open. The aircraft sat on the dispersal area for half an hour before the passengers were told to re-board the plane.

As we took our seats, we discovered that we were now sharing the cabin with hordes of jumbo-sized, Indian mosquitoes. We were literally breathing in mozzies. After the doors were closed and the aircraft was accelerating down the runway for take-off, the mosquitoes were drawn to the rear bulkhead and then sucked into the environmental control system a.k.a. air-conditioning. How often, I asked myself, was the airline forced to replace the airworthy, certified filters? Why not install temporary screen doors that would be far cheaper than replacing the filters? No prizes for the correct answer...

Every other year, Aero India would be held at the Yelahanka Air Force Station, 22 km outside of Bengaluru. The air show is organised by the Defence Exhibition Organisation under the Ministry of Defence of India, and is the event of the year in that region. Entire villages would come to the air show. One year when I was there, the Regimental Police had to use Alsatian dogs to keep the crowd from literally gatecrashing the exhibition.

In the 2000s, the Indian government decided to upgrade the Bengaluru airport to an international "point of entry" status. I was on the inaugural flight into the capital, arriving at around 10 p.m.

Clearly, the upgrade had caught the airport staff somewhat by surprise. Four rostrums had been placed there to serve as makeshift immigration counters. I was first in line at one of them. The officer took my passport, pulled out the disembarkation card – which for convenience I had inserted next to the page stamped with my India visa – and proceeded to flick through the passport, from back to front and vice versa...looking for my visa! Having finally satisfied himself that everything was in order, he then flourished his all-important arrival rubber stamp. Next, he strolled across to rostrum no. 1, where he wetted his stamp on that officer's ink pad, and returned to his station to stamp my passport.

This action was then repeated by the other two officers – all four rostrums at an international airport sharing just one single ink pad. It was amusing to watch the officers wandering back and forth – as if performing a kind of civil-service circus act. What, I mused, happens when the precious pad runs dry? Do they send a colleague into town for fresh ink supplies? Or go next door and use the departure hall's ink pad? This time-consuming stamping coupled with the over-zealous examination of passports clearly pointed to a wage system based on hours spent and not duty performed. Or, to be kind, perhaps it was simply the result of these officers being exposed to passports for the very first time.

Kerala

Although Thiruvananthapuram is the capital of the southwestern state of Kerala, the more famous city in that state is Kochi, formerly known as Cochin. It is a city carved out of the lowland surrounded by the flooding backwaters. During the monsoon season, the water level can rise by 10 m and all the inhabitants of the villages around the backwaters have to move out of their houses to higher ground. When the flood subsides, they move back in, but they first had to clean out all the mud and debris left in their houses by the flood.

A popular tourist activity is to hire a houseboat to cruise around the backwaters. These massive houseboats with air-conditioned living and dining rooms plus two or three bedrooms are propelled by small 5-horsepower outboard engines, hence they are very quiet and peaceful when cruising. Paul and Stella McCartney spent their honeymoon on one of these, and I am sure there are dozens of houseboats (including the one we chartered) with a thank-you note purportedly signed by Paul and Stella hanging on the wall, praising the wonderful service from the crew on board.

Madhya Pradesh

Most tourists go to the central Indian state of Madhya Pradesh to visit the Hindu and Jain temples at Khajuraho, better known as the Kama

Sutra carvings. I made a visit[13] to this UNESCO World Heritage Site in the early 1990s, as part of a trip on the Maharashtra/Rajasthan Trail.

I also visited Bhopal, the capital of the state. Bhopal is famous in its own right, albeit for a completely different reason. In early December 1984, a Union Carbide pesticide plant leaked at least 30 tons of toxic gases into the city, leading to the worst industrial catastrophe in the world. The disaster reportedly killed 20,000 inhabitants of the city.

I had to make several trips to Bhopal to pursue a helicopter sale to the chief minister. The city is not much different from other Indian cities, but travelling around it makes one wonder what it was like when the industrial disaster struck.

Maharashtra

Maharashtra is the third largest state by area in India. Located in the west-central region, it is home to two UNESCO World Heritage Sites, the Ajanta and Ellora caves[14]. It is also the most industrialised state in India, while the state capital Mumbai (formerly Bombay) is the country's most important financial and commercial capital.

As a tourist in Mumbai, going to the Gateway of India monument is a must. From the jetties there, you could take a ferry boat out to the Elephanta Island, then come back for an ice-cream soda at the Taj Mahal Palace Hotel. A short walk from the hotel takes you to the main train station, the Chhatrapati Shivaji Maharaj Terminus. Formerly known as Victoria Terminus, it was built in 1887 and designed in Italian Gothic style. I can still remember having dinner at the nearby Khyber Restaurant where I ordered a tandoori lobster for US$5.

If your host has a car, he might take you for a drive around the Bandra area where all the rich and famous Bollywood actors and actresses live. In the old days, before the Rajiv Gandhi Sea Link (also known as the Bandra-Worli Sea Link) was built, driving along Marine Drive to the international airport could turn into a gut-wrenching experience.

---

13 See Chapter 11 "The Hardship Group".
14 Ibid.

This was because at the wrong time of the day, the 6-km drive along the coast – from the southern end of the bay to the northern end – could take 3 hours, causing thousands of travellers to miss their flights.

One of my trips to Mumbai coincided with an outbreak of a strain of pneumonic plague. Most would-be visitors gave the city a miss, but plague or no plague, I was there on important business. Pneumonic plague is highly contagious and can spread via airborne particles. Whilst there, I had to take precautions – especially when in close contact with other people. Whenever I stepped into a lift, I would hold my breath for as long as it took me to reach my desired floor. That was quite crucial because most lifts then had a limited capacity of just five or six passengers – who were often crammed together, breathing all over each other. As luck would have it, I was not required to visit any tall buildings, and so my lift rides were sufficiently short to enable me to maintain breathless mode. This no doubt helped me to successfully avoid the deadly Mumbai plague.

On a subsequent business trip, I arrived in Mumbai at 2 a.m. On the way to the hotel, my taxi driver decided to use the fast lane, even though the road was basically deserted. A faster car came up behind us and clearly wanted to pass, but my driver refused to budge and did not change lanes. The car behind then overtook us from the inside, re-entered the fast lane in front of my taxi, and slowed down. My stubborn driver then copied this action, regaining his position in front of the fast car, and slowing down.

Soon, we came to a halt at the traffic lights. Three guys sprang out of the other car, came over, grabbed my driver by his collar and gave him a good slapping before driving off. I told my driver how stupid he was and that he had been let off lightly this time. There was no way I would have physically defended him – although my very presence might well have saved him from a more severe beating.

On one trip, I stayed at the Holiday Inn in Juhu, near the Santa Cruz Airport. For the first time in my life, I was stuck in a lift with seven or eight other people, who were mostly guests at the hotel. Nobody panicked, so it must have been a regular affair. We were in between two floors of the hotel, but fortunately the hotel maintenance crew managed

---

HOW NOT TO NAME AN AIRPORT TERMINAL

There was one year when I flew into a new airport terminal in Mumbai. Instead of naming it "Terminal 2" and the original one "Terminal 1", the authorities called it the "Boeing terminal". The old one must have been the Airbus terminal. What about the McDonnell Douglas terminal, or the Tupolev terminal, I wondered?

---

to pry open the doors so that we would not suffocate. They told us that they had informed the lift maintenance company and help was on the way, from Mumbai. They said that they would be there in 1½ hours. Meanwhile, on the urging of some of the lift passengers, the hotel maintenance crew (four or five of them) tried to raise the lift with their bare hands. Of course, they failed. We were finally freed after the maintenance contractor crew arrived.

In 2008, some terrorists came ashore Mumbai and attacked several sites, including the Taj Mahal Palace Hotel and the Oberoi Trident Hotel. One of our friends was staying at the Oberoi when this happened. He had gone down to the cake shop in the lobby earlier to buy a cake to bring to a dinner party that he was to attend that evening. He charged the cake to his American Express card. When he went back to his room to clean up before dinner, the terrorists stuck. Not long after that, he received a call from the Amex office in Singapore (who knew he was in the hotel because of the cake that he had charged to the card), telling him to remain in his room as there was an ongoing terrorist attack in the hotel. This goes to show, never leave home without your Amex card.

Odisha

Formerly known as Orissa, Odisha is an eastern state on the Bay of Bengal known for its tribal cultures and many ancient Hindu temples.

I had a manager based in the India office, who is a descendant of the Odisha royal family. In 2013, he invited Kwan and me to attend the wedding of his son, and arranged a trip for us to do some sightseeing as well. We were brought to the famous Konark Sun Temple, which is a 13th-century temple located on the coastline of the state, about 50 km south of Bhubaneswar, the state capital. There are twenty-four stone chariot wheels – each with a 3-m diameter – engraved on the walls of the temple. These wheels are similar to the one featured on India's national flag.

From Konark Sun Temple, we drove for an hour to visit the Shri Jagannath Temple which is strictly out of bounds for non-Hindus. Not even for someone who looks Indian. Our friend, a Singaporean Indian, tried to enter the temple but was rejected when they sensed that she could not be a Hindu from the way she was dressed (too westernised).

To look into the temple, we were brought to the rooftop terrace of a 6-storey library building next to the temple. In the library hung photographs of famous international personalities who had also been refused entry into the temple, so they had to resort to coming to this roof top to get a glimpse of the inside of the temple. Even his Holiness, the Pope was denied entry. He had to meet the High Priest of the temple on the rooftop terrace of the library building.

We rented a car to go around the city. Whenever we passed a temple, the driver would press his hands together and take a bow. The only problem was, the front-wheel alignment of his car was so far out that the car would pull to the left whenever he took his hands off the steering wheel. He would have to quickly grab the steering wheel again to straighten the car. That was quite comical.

Rajasthan

Located in northern India, Rajasthan is the largest state of the country in terms of land area. It is known as the "Land of Kings", and was formerly ruled by Indian royalty.

Famous for its historic palaces, majestic forts and holy temples, this state has a long and colourful history. Travellers from all over the world are especially drawn to four Rajasthan cities of colour: white (Udaipur), blue (Jodhpur), gold (Jaisalmer) and pink (Jaipur).

In the early 1990s, Kwan and our friends visited all the four cities during a trip[15]; I could only join in the fun halfway through the journey due to a prior business mission in another part of India. Among the highlights were staying overnight in a palace by the lake, and joining the annual Pushkar Fair, where camels and livestock are traded. It is a huge carnival, with bazaars, dancing, rituals and even beauty contests for camels.

Sikkim

We had heard so much about the northeastern state of Sikkim being a heavenly state with fantastic views of the Himalayan mountain range. However, we were utterly disappointed when we reached there[16] in the late 1990s, mainly because we had just visited Bhutan. Although the populations of Sikkim and Bhutan were comparable in size, the streets of Sikkim just seemed so much more crowded and dirtier. After just two days there, we were ready to head home.

Tamil Nadu

The majority of Indians in Singapore are Tamils who have descended from settlers originating from the southern Indian state of Tamil Nadu, hence we are familiar with their food, dress and customs. As a matter of fact, one of the four national languages in Singapore is Tamil.

In the 1980s, the Tamil Nadu government supported the Tamil Tigers (LTTE) who tried to overthrow the Sri Lankan government. In 1991, because the then-Prime Minister Rajiv Gandhi was assassinated by an LTTE suicide bomber in Tamil Nadu, security was tightened and Indian support for them diminished.

I have made more than 20 trips to the capital Chennai (formerly Madras). Chennai was also the point of exit for me whenever I was heading home from other parts of India. The Singapore Airlines flight left

---

15 See Chapter 11 "The Hardship Group" for my holiday in the land of the Maharajas and its colourful cities.
16 This visit to Sikkim is covered in more detail in Chapter 11.

Chennai at around 1 a.m., so I would fly in from other parts of India just to catch this flight back to Singapore. On numerous occasions, I would call the Sheraton Hotel in Chennai in advance to order a couple of tandoori leg of lamb (raan) for takeaway, then hire a taxi to go from the airport to the Sheraton to pick them up and return to the airport to continue my journey.

On another occasion, I was required – with just a 24-hour notice – to travel to Kolkata in West Bengal to sign an important contract. The only way to reach there in time was first to fly to Dhaka, Bangladesh, stay there overnight and then catch a 7-a.m. flight to Kolkata. I arrived on time for the signing ceremony and reception in the afternoon.

Immediately after this, I boarded an evening flight from Kolkata to Chennai. My aim was to catch a midnight flight from Chennai back to Singapore. So in actual fact, I had been in India for a little more than half a day only.

Unusual? Well, perhaps. It certainly seemed so to the immigration officer at the departure counter. I had a really hard time convincing him that, no, I did not have an address in India on this trip because, no, I did not spend a night in a hotel. Despite seeing the totally legitimate immigration entry stamp on my passport, it was beyond his comprehension as to why anyone would spend such a short time in India. As the clock ticked, I was beginning to worry that I might miss my flight home and then have to spend a night in India after all... but, still shaking his head, Doubting Thomas stamped my passport and allowed me to depart.

I also remember travelling on one of the roads near the beach where the Chennai municipal government wanted to expand from a two-lane road to four. However, they also decided that the mature trees along this road should not be chopped. So the road would run in four lanes for 50 m, then narrow to two lanes to avoid the need to chop down a mature tree, and quickly widen to a four-lane road again.

On one of my later trips to Chennai, I actually had a chance to experience the new and very unusual road structure, and a thought came to my mind: they should organise a road race on this road to test the skill of the local drivers.

The Red Sea, with Aqaba/Eilat in the background. I was one of the members of the Malaysian Palm Oil Trade Mission in 1981. (Photo courtesy of Lim Liew King)

In the mid-1980s, I visited a farm in the desert in Saudi Arabia, with Ong Keng Yong (the Chargé d'Affaires of the Singapore Embassy in Saudi), the owner of the farm (in white robe) and his friend.

Memorable visa stamps in my passport.

Top row: 5 May 1981 Iran visa issued in Jakarta; 1985 Saudi Arabia visa-on-arrival with four revenue stamps.

Bottom row: 15 June 1981 Afghanistan entry visa issued in Delhi; 20 June 1981 Afghanistan exit permit issued in Kabul.

More uncommon passport visa stamps for some of the Hardship Group trips.

Clockwise from top left: 23 August 2004 Pakistan visa; 18 October 2005 Iran visa; Iran entry and exit stamps; 7 February 2007 Syria visa; 28 March 2007 Syria entry stamp and 7 April 2007 Syria exit stamp.

Standing in front of the Singapore Flying Club's Aerospatiale Tampico TB-9 light aircraft during one of the fly-ins organised by the Malaysian Department of Civil Aviation. The photo was taken by one of our friends.

With Don Pantle, the managing director of Bell Asia, in front of the Potala Palace, in Lhasa, Tibet, in the early 1990s. Don and I were stuck in an elevator in the Lhasa Holiday Inn on that trip. Coincidentally, we were also together when we were stuck in an elevator in the Juhu Holiday Inn in India.

On a dive trip to the Komodo Island in Indonesia. (Photo courtesy of Keng Beng)

Some of the voodoo charms that Kwan and I bought in Benin – cowrie shells sewn onto a leather pouch (left), and a seed.

I bought this 80-cm long voodoo stick in Nigeria and presented it to the Seletar Hash as the "Whip Stick".

Swami Dhirendra Brahmachari (above) was a well-known yogi with political clout in India. He was also my prospective client and gave me this autographed photo.

In the early 1990s, we went white-water rafting on the Trishuli River, followed by a safari tour of the Chitwan National Park in Nepal.

We went on a safari in Tanzania in 2014. Under the tree, from left: Suzy, Kwan, Pak Seng, me and our guide Elisa. On the tree, from left: Zack, Sam and Max. (Photo courtesy of Pak Seng)

Spotting wildlife on a game drive. From left: Me, Max and Kwan. (Photo courtesy of Pak Seng)

Family reunion on a trip to Bhutan, 2017, with members coming from Thailand, Malaysia, US and Singapore. (Photo courtesy of Amankora Hotel)

One of our relatives owns a house by the sea in the British Virgin Islands and invited us to spend Christmas there in 2004.

The Hardship Group explored Bhutan in 1998. From left: Kim Lean, Chong Wah, me, Kwan, Dora, Beet, Leen and Linda. (Photo courtesy of Leen and Beng)

In 1992, the Hardship Group went to India. One of the highlights was a morning cruise along the Ganges River in Varanasi. From left: Kwan, Linda and Edward. (Photo courtesy of Leen and Beng)

Kwan dancing with Uighur performers during the Hardship Trip to the Silk Road in 1993. (Photo courtesy of Leen and Beng)

On a visit to Sikkim in 1998, I wanted to buy that humongous kukri but then, there was no way I could have brought it back to Singapore. (Photo courtesy of Leen and Beng)

Kwan with the Kyaiktiyo Pagoda (Golden Rock) behind her. We visited her birthplace Myanmar in 1991, on the first Hardship Group trip. (Photo courtesy of Beng)

The Hardship Group visited Jordan and Israel in 1997. Behind us was the Al Khazneh (Pharaoh's Treasury) in the ancient city of Petra, Jordan. (Photo courtesy of Leen and Beng)

The Hardship Group went from Kathmandu, Nepal to Lhasa, Tibet by road in 2003. We were at the Gyatso La Pass (at more than 5,000 m), the highest point in the road from Kathmandu to Lhasa. From left: Beng, Leen, Beet, Dora, me, Kwan, Oi Leng and Jerome. (Photo courtesy of Jerome)

In 2004, the Hardship Group set off on a road trip on the Karakoram Highway, which connected Pakistan and China. At the border of the two countries, there was a slab that said "China (中國)" on one side and "Pakistan" in Perso-Arabic and English on the other side. From left: Jerome, Beng, Kwan, Leen, Beet and me.
(Photo courtesy of Leen and Beng)

The Hardship Group visited Syria in 2007. While driving to Palmyra, we came across this road sign and debated jokingly whether to head to Baghdad instead. (Photo courtesy of Jerome)

At the Temple of Bel. From left: Beet, Kwan, Kat, Leen, Dora and me. (Photo courtesy of Leen)

My grandfather was born in Kam Loong Village, Taishan, Guangdong province. This was the entrance to a newly renovated heritage hall there.

The gazebo was the landmark that led me to the village, after many years of searching.

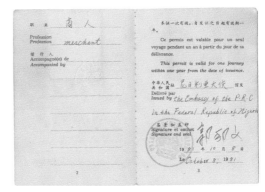

I made my very first visit to China in February 1982 with the help of a permit issued by the embassy of the People's Republic of China in Nigeria. From left: Front cover of permit booklet, inside pages.

Family vacation at Land's End, United Kingdom, 2021. From left: Pak Seng, Suzy, Max with pet dog Archie, me, Mika, Lena and Kai (both seated), Zack, Kwan, Sam, Oi Leng and Thorsten. (Photo courtesy of Suzy)

Telangana

This south-central state has been carved out of the old state of Andhra Pradesh, but Hyderabad, the old capital, also followed the realignment and became the capital of the new state instead.

The historic city of Golconda was renowned for being a centre for trading diamonds and an important source of diamond mining in the world. However, the Kollur diamond mines where most of these diamonds came from are located on the Andhra Pradesh side of the Krishna River.

Uttar Pradesh

Anyone who has been to India would probably have been to the northern state of Uttar Pradesh (U.P.), because this is where one of the New Seven Wonders of the World – the famous white marble mausoleum known as the Taj Mahal – is located. U.P. is also home to Varanasi, supposedly the most ancient city in India. I have been to the Taj Mahal on numerous occasions and Varanasi during a trip[17] with Kwan and our friends.

Uttarakhand

Uttarakhand, a state in northern India crossed by the Himalayas, is known for its Hindu pilgrimage sites. Rishikesh, a major centre for yoga study, was made famous by the Beatles' visit in 1968. In the late 2000s, Kwan and I visited our friend Raj, who meditated in Rishikesh for three to four months annually. Oi Leng and Thorsten came over from London to join us. We attended the evening Ganga Aarti[18], a spiritual gathering on the bank of the sacred Ganges River.

The orphans of many Indians who had died in the 2004 tsunami which hit the coast of Tamil Nadu and Andhra Pradesh sought shelter in the Rishikesh ashrams. During the Aarti, these orphans put on a perfor-

---

17 See Chapter 11 "The Hardship Group".
18 The Ganga Aarti is a spiritual ritual that uses fire as an offering to the goddess Ganga. Small oil lamps with flowers are floated down the river as part of the ritual.

mance, chanting mantras, singing bhajans (spiritual devotional songs), reciting prayers and performing sacred rituals that all took place around a fire.

The ashram that we stayed at was strictly vegetarian and alcohol-free. After a couple of days, we sneaked out and dropped by a 5-star hotel on the hills, where there was a bar.

Uttarakhand is also home to the Doon International School which the former prime minister Rajiv Gandhi attended. Over the years, I have met some alumni of that school and all of them claimed to have access to the Gandhi family in one way or another.

While on the subject of access to the Gandhi family, I almost sold a helicopter to Swami Dhirendra Brahmachari, the highly influential yoga mentor of Indira Gandhi[19]. Because of the difficulty for him to get an import license for the helicopter, I advised him to buy it and register it to an Non-Resident Indian (NRI). He said to me, "Leon, you are brilliant. You are my god!"

Unfortunately, the sale did not go through, because when he was flying his own single reciprocating engine light aircraft in 1994, it crashed and he died in the accident.

West Bengal

West Bengal is a state in the eastern region of India along the Bay of Bengal. With over 91 million inhabitants, it is the fourth most populous state in India. The state capital Calcutta (now Kolkata) was where my father met my mother and married her during the Second World War.

When I started visiting West Bengal for work in the 1980s, it was known as the "Communist State" because the then-chief minister was from the communist party. There was daily labour unrest, including strikes and demonstrations in the streets.

The Kolkata Metro was the first planned and operational rapid transit system in India. It was initially proposed in the 1920s, but construc-

---

19 Mrs Indira Gandhi was the only woman to have served as India's prime minister to date. She was elected to office from 1966 to 1977, and 1980 to 1984 (the year she was assassinated).

tion only started in the 1970s, and the metro finally opened in 1984. It was just a straight 2.5-km north-south line with three stops, taking six minutes for the whole journey. Looking at the crowds in front of the stations, I did not dare to try out the Kolkata underground.

On another note, there is a thin strip of land in West Bengal, approximately 20 km wide, that separates Bangladesh from Nepal. This would be an ideal route for smugglers to dash across in the air from Bangladesh to Nepal, bypassing India. Naturally, India built an air force station, Bagdogra, right next to this strip of land, with fighter planes ready to shoot down any such attempts.

The Union Territories

I have also visited the union territories of Jammu and Kashmir (J&K), as well as the Andaman and Nicobar Islands. In J&K, Kwan and I stayed on a houseboat for a couple of nights. The whole lake was overcrowded with other houseboats, so it was neither romantic nor serene.

Because we were guests of one of the ministers, we were escorted by armed guards wherever we went. Part of our itinerary included a visit to the local golf course, and we were puzzled to see huge steel cages on the side of the fairways. The caddie told me that those cages were used for trapping brown bears that came down from the mountain occasionally.

Our trip to the Andaman and Nicobar Islands was a liveaboard dive trip. Getting to the capital Port Blair would require us to transit at the Tamil Nadu airport for six hours. In order to avoid the long wait, we decided to charter a plane to fly directly from Singapore.

On that very day, our dive boat which originated from Phuket, Thailand, also arrived at Port Blair, the capital. Unfortunately, the immigration office was incapable of handling two arrivals on the same day, and this led to much delay in our schedule. It did not help matters when our host brought along more than 40 bottles of wine for the one-week trip.

When we finally cleared immigration and customs, we sailed around the islands over the next seven days, making many beautiful dives in the spellbinding seascapes.

TRAVELLING WITH A HELICOPTER, FROM STATE TO STATE

Once, I took a helicopter to India for sales and demonstration purposes, and travelled across several Indian states in the process. Because of all the spare parts and oil, etc., that had to accompany the helicopter, we weren't too excited about going through the customs check. Technically, we needed a permit for *everything* that entered the country. Every bolt, every nut and every can of oil.

Our state-to-state itinerary went like this: West Bengal–Odisha–Andhra Pradesh–Tamil Nadu–Telangana–Maharashtra–Delhi–Uttar Pradesh–Bihar. We also devised a plan to minimise the hassle of the bureaucratic customs checks at our point of entry, Kolkata (West Bengal).

From Singapore, the helicopter pilot flew the aircraft and the engineer there via several stops in Asia (due to the limited range of helicopters). As for myself, I arrived via a commercial plane. The three of us were received by our India office manager and a staff member from our India representative, and we began to put our plan into action.

We told the customs office at Kolkata that we were heading to Chennai (Tamil Nadu) to demonstrate the helicopter to the chief minister, and would clear customs there. The Kolkata customs sealed the helicopter for a night, so we couldn't remove any items. To unseal the aircraft and leave the airport, we asked the pilot to get our customs form stamped so as to clear us for take-off. Our strategy worked. And when we arrived in Chennai eventually, we would tell the customs agents that we had already cleared customs in Kolkata and show them our stamps as proof.

While waiting for the helicopter to be refuelled at Kolkata, we told the fuel operator that we needed to uplift fuel in our second stop, Bhubaneswar (Odisha). We asked them to contact his counterpart in Bhubaneswar and tell them that we were coming and would be paying for fuel in US dollars in the form of cash.

"Okay, no problem," they said. We proceeded to split into two groups: the pilot and the engineer flew off in the helicopter, whereas the rest of us took a commercial flight. This was to be our travel arrangement throughout the whole itinerary.

But when we landed in Bhubaneswar, we were told: "You cannot pay in US dollars because we can only receive payment in rupees." The fuel operator sent a man on a bike into town to find what the exchange rate was. He came back with the required information, and we paid for the fuel in US dollars based on the rupees-US$ exchange rate he had from the bank in town.

Next, we flew to our third stop, Visakhapatnam/Vizag (Andhra Pradesh). We had asked the fuel operator in Bhubaneswar to call ahead and let them know that we were coming and would be buying fuel in US dollars. Once again, when we arrived in Vizag, the fuel operator said he would only accept rupees.

So every one of us emptied our pockets to see if we had enough rupees to pay for the fuel. We did, but the fuel operator said he would also need to see the foreign exchange receipts. Of course, we did not have all the receipts, as some of our rupees came from our representative and office manager who lived in India. The operator said we could take our US dollars to a hotel in town and change them to rupees, and we had to get an exchange receipt. By then, it was almost dark and we were beginning to be concerned that they would be closing the airport by official sunset[20].

I found a motorised three-wheel vehicle called an auto-rickshaw. I asked the driver to take me to town. "I have to get to the Sheraton, and fast," I said.

"Okay, no problem," he said, as he shook his head in the typical manner. "Hold on!" The driver revved the engine, merged into the traffic, and took off at top speed. Then he intentionally drove onto the wrong side of the divided highway and stuck half his body out of the vehicle, weaving in and out of the traffic as he waved at the oncoming vehicles to give way to him.

There we were, going down the highway on the wrong side, full-throttle. "I'm in a hurry, but not that big of a hurry!" I exclaimed. "Slow down!"

We arrived at the Sheraton and I asked to change US$2,000.

"I'm sorry, we only exchange money for guests," the representative said.

"Well, how much is a room?" I asked. The representative checked and said a room would cost US$40. I paid for a room and then asked if I could change my money then.

"Oh, yes sir!"

With the required rupees and receipt in hand, I took a hotel car back to the airfield. Before I left, I told the hotel reception, "If I do come back later, I will need an additional four rooms." Sure enough, we could not take off because it was after official sunset and the airport was closed by then. We ended up staying overnight and enjoyed the best shrimp dinner I had ever eaten.

---

20 In aviation, any flight that takes place after official sunset is considered a night flight. Some airports, such as the one at Vizag, are not opened for night flights.

The following day, we continued our flight to Chennai (Tamil Nadu), Hyderabad (Telangana), and then on to Mumbai (Maharashtra). Getting to Mumbai was not a lot of fun as a very huge storm had developed. Those of us who took a commercial flight arrived safely in Mumbai, but the helicopter, its pilot and engineer had to set down on a ridge high above Mumbai and wait for the storm to pass. We were all worried about them until we spoke with the control tower and learned that they were safe.

In the morning, our pilot took off and landed in Juhu airport, where the rest of us were waiting. He and the engineer recounted that some villagers had surrounded them within minutes of the helicopter setting down. The villagers asked them for biscuits and sodas! He was very surprised, because he had thought that no one would notice their presence in the pouring rain, especially in a seemingly remote area.

The fuel base in Juhu would not accept rupees nor US$ as payment. They would only accept a cashier's order for fuel! We took things in our stride, and proceeded with the rest of our itinerary. At the conclusion of our demo tour, our local representative begged us not to send an aircraft to India for a demonstration again, ever.

Ironically, it was a fruitful demonstration as we sold a multi-million helicopter to the chief minister of Tamil Nadu and some helicopters in Mumbai.

Chapter 8

AFRICA

Africa is the second largest continent in the world, in terms of land area. It is also home to the largest, tallest and fastest land animals[1]. To be frank, I never thought I would have many opportunities to visit Africa. As it turned out, I have visited eight countries in that continent to date, covering parts of North, East and West Africa. My first trip was to Egypt (which straddles both Africa and the Middle East) as part of a palm oil trade mission in 1981. The following year, I went to the West African nation of Nigeria to find out how to sell my cooking oil. Thereafter, my trips to Africa were for leisure, such as going with Kwan to visit our daughter who was stationed in Benin, and doing some animal-spotting on a safari organised by our son.

Nigeria

My ticket said "Lagos, Nigeria", but to be honest, I was wary of what to expect after hearing many horror stories about the country. In the end, I still went ahead because this gave me a chance to visit another country that I had not been to before.

Nigeria was a former British colony that declared independence in 1960. It has the highest population among the African countries, and is one of Africa's largest economies. My flight from Amsterdam into Lagos touched down at the Murtala Muhammed International Airport at 3.30 a.m. – not my favourite time of day and certainly not when arriving at an African airport for the first time.

---

1 These are the African elephant, the giraffe and the cheetah, respectively.

Following my travel agent's guidance, I had obtained the mandatory Nigeria entry visa in Singapore, but as soon as I proffered my passport at the immigration counter, I was pulled aside and into a room where I was told by the officer that I had no entry visa. Then, after his attention was directed to the relevant page in my passport, he grudgingly led me back into the entry process.

Next, I was asked to present my vaccination papers. Alas, it suddenly dawned on me that Yellow Fever inoculation was compulsory for entry into most African nations and I didn't have one. I was escorted to another room, where a health officer announced, "No shot, no entry."

After making a mental note to take up the issue with my travel agent when I returned home, I asked the officer, "How much for a shot, here and now?" I guessed he was after some pocket money. Why would he be any different from his immigration counter pals? And I was right.

"If I give you a shot, you must be quarantined for one week," he said with a smug grin. The quarantine factor was his trump card and we both knew it. So, with my back firmly against the wall, I fed him my tried and tested. "What else can you do for me?"

He pointed to another passenger whom he said was offering US$300 for his shot but that I only had to pay US$200. "I don't have that kind of money, but I can offer you $100," I replied with a tone of finality.

"Okay!" he shouted, stamped my passport with the entry visa and disappeared from view, leaving me to clear my entry into Nigeria.

I collected my luggage and walked, a little poorer but triumphantly, out of the customs area en route to my connecting flight to Port Harcourt, and into a country rife with Yellow Fever…without Yellow Fever immunity at all.

As I exited the customs area, I was immediately surrounded by a pack of thuggish touts offering me a wide choice of "services", from accommodation to women and…transportation. On hearing of my connecting flight to Port Harcourt, the taxi thugs took over and told me that I was at the wrong Lagos "airport" – I needed the domestic version which was "very far" and, of course, I'd need a taxi to get there.

Not inclined to trust a single one of them, I told a cabby to follow me to the information counter. Here the Info Lady, in the presence of the cabby, announced that the fare to the domestic "airport" was 10 nairas[2].

Off I went with the cabby to his taxi. I loaded up my gear and leaned back into my seat. As we pulled away, my driver, without so much as a glance via his rear-view mirror, announced, "Domestic Airport, 20 nairas". I protested, reminding him that he was there when the Info Lady said 10 nairas. His reply: "Who's driving, she or me?"

The *very far* domestic "airport" was in fact situated on the other side of the aerodrome, a mere kilometre away from the main building. I was annoyed with my driver, but I handed him 20 nairas because my luggage was still in his car boot. He wasn't through yet. Refusing the nairas, he told me that the particular naira note was no longer legal tender and I had to pay in US dollars. The exchange rate meant that 20 nairas was worth about US$12.50. He took my US$20 note, saying he didn't have change and without so much as a thank you and goodbye, pocketed the money and went on his way.

I was comforted that I had arrived at the domestic terminal well in time for the 7 a.m. flight. With my confirmed ticket in hand, I felt I was in good shape. I was told that the check-in counter would only open at 6 a.m. when, in exchange for tickets, free-seating boarding passes would be distributed. So I sat down to relax for a while.

Fifteen minutes before the check-in window was due to open, I joined an orderly queue. Then, seconds before 6 a.m., they struck – the queue was swept aside as the mob rushed in from all directions, pushing, shoving, arms flailing – assaulting the check-in counter window. Reaching close enough, some waved their tickets with over-the-counter (in lieu of under-the-table) money attached, while others shouted, "No luggage, brother, no luggage!"

---

2 At that time, the exchange rate was approximately 10 nairas to US$6.25.

Rewarded with boarding passes, they dispersed sufficiently for me to reach the window where I presented my ticket. Without looking at me or said ticket, the counter staff said, "Sorry, flight is full." My vehement protest that my confirmed ticket meant I should be on the flight was met with "Next flight 8 a.m." and a slamming in my face of the counter window.

Great, except that the so-called next flight scheduled for 8 a.m. was cancelled, and the next-next flight was at 10.30 a.m. Since I was right outside the check-in window and was first in line, I was so sure that I would be on that flight. However, the same jerk who slammed the window on me earlier now prised it open at 9.30 a.m., and after a quick look at my ticket, told me I was booked for the 7 a.m. flight and "It has left and you have missed your flight!" I expressed my views of him in my most eloquent Cantonese, but I was unable to reach through the window to show him how I really felt.

I was not alone. After me, a Scotsman went through a similar routine, muttering "This is no bloody good", and invited me to follow him to the first-class window. We bought tickets, checked in my suitcase with a priority first-class tag, and proceeded to the lounge for coffee. He clearly had been here before; when it was near to boarding time and he suggested we move to the gate, I was happy to follow. He further suggested that to avoid drawing attention to our motives and causing a mad rush, we should separate and slowly approach the gate in a pincer movement down opposite sides of the room. It worked, for none of the growing horde so much as stirred. We were right next to the gate where we could see our aircraft out on the apron: a gleaming Boeing 727 just 100 m away, its staircase invitingly slotted into position and the cabin door wide open…

Here we met two orthodox Jews in traditional dress of long black cassocks and hair in long ringlets over their ears. They were diamond dealers, and instead of a planned hour-or-so flight, these poor guys had been marooned in this lounge for four days, as was obvious from close quarters, since shower facilities were not available (the lounge did have toilets, although one could not bear to spend sufficient time in these to even think about showering).

They told us that when boarding the Friday flight and half-way up the stairs, everyone not actually inside the cabin was informed that the flight was full and had to return to the lounge. They quickly learned that the possession of a boarding pass meant nothing when it came to guaranteeing a seat on the plane. The next day being Saturday and the Sabbath, as orthodox Jews they were forbidden to travel. And it became worse. There were no flights scheduled for Sunday, so here they were on Monday, four days later – and in front of us at the boarding gate. They were clearly more than a little determined to get out of Lagos and get to Port Harcourt – or anywhere – for a shower and change of clothes.

Then the gate supervisor walked by, and we heard his walkie-talkie crackle: "Tower to Boarding Station!" This was the signal that our Jewish friends were watching out for. Not waiting for the gate supervisor to make an announcement and open the gate, they burst through the access door and sprinted towards the Boeing, ringlets and cassocks swirling in their wake. Following suit, I also took off with my Scottish companion. As we dashed towards the airstairs, I turned back for a split second to see a hundred or so stampeding brothers behind us.

PLAYING MUSICAL CHAIRS IN LAGOS

A few years later, in the basement bar of the Kathmandu Sheraton, I talked to an English pilot working for Singapore Airlines over some drinks. After listening to my Lagos domestic "airport" tale, he topped it off with one of his own.

He was then flying for Air Nigeria, and before starting up the engines at the same Lagos domestic "airport", he peeked into the cabin. He saw that all the seats were occupied but five or six passengers were standing in the aisle, just as if they were on a local bus.

Drawing from childhood memories of the game of musical chairs, he ordered all passengers to disembark onto the apron and had them walk in an orderly procession, encircling the aircraft. At his command "Now!", the lucky requisite number of passengers closest to and moving in the direction of the staircase, climbed up and into the cabin – with the unlucky tailenders sent back to the departure lounge to try again for "the next flight".

On board, we buckled ourselves into our seats, waited for the ensuing boarding chaos to run its course – and unbuckled only after the aircraft was in the air.

My college friend John picked me up at the Port Harcourt International Airport. As we drove away, I told him about my morning's fun and games. He chuckled and said, "Knowing that it's your first time in Nigeria taking a domestic flight, I was sure that you wouldn't be able to get on that 7 a.m. flight, so I didn't even bother to come to pick you up until now!"

I also recounted my Yellow Fever-US$100-phantom-shot experience. He said I could have offered as little as US$5 to pay off the health officer and he would have accepted it! But he did solve my Yellow Fever problem by arranging, in exchange for a few nairas, an inoculation certificate, courtesy of a local doctor, stating that I had received a Yellow Fever shot, which, of course, was not strictly true. Now all I had to do was to avoid any over-zealous health officials…and mosquitoes.

Soon, I had first-hand experience of the highway code, Port Harcourt style. We were driving through town on our way to lunch, with John at the wheel. After crossing an intersection, we were waved down by a traffic cop. He told John that he had committed an offence by not signalling his intentions in crossing the intersection. Seeking clarification, John was informed that: "When turning right, a driver must use the right signal blinker; when turning left, the left signal. But when going straight on, across the intersection, the emergency blinkers – the right and left signals – should be flashing". Two minibuses then appeared and boxed us in, presumably to ensure we did not flee from this serious crime scene.

The cop then climbed into our car and ordered John to drive to a police station where he would be charged. When given the address, John told the cop he was familiar with it as the commanding officer, Inspector So-and-so, was a personal friend. On hearing this, the cop then gave

John the address of another police station and told him to turn the car around and head there instead.

"Sure," said John, appearing quite unconcerned with his new instruction. Sensing this, the cop asked if John knew anyone at this second police station, to which John answered in the affirmative, giving the name of a senior officer who happened to be a personal friend too.

By then, we had travelled about 2 km from the site of the "arrest". The cop said, "Okay, I let you go this time. Just take me back to the intersection." Being in a less-than-charitable mood, and with the upper hand, John said he was too busy, pulled the car to a halt and told the cop to alight – and find his own way back. Grudgingly, the cop complied.

Soon, we arrived at the restaurant for lunch and John asked, "Have fish?" The waiter replied, "Never have."

John asked again, "Have chicken?" The waiter answered, "Yes, have chicken."

And so we ordered two plates of chicken. We were in the middle of our meal when the waiter came over and asked, "Don't finish?" John confirmed, "Never finish."

After we had finished our meal, the waiter returned. "Don't finish?" John said, "Yes, don't finish." The waiter immediately removed our plates – and I learnt a lesson in local lingo:

"Don't finish" means "Done/finished".

"Never finish" means "Not (yet) finished".

"Never have" means "We don't have" i.e., "We are temporarily out of stock".

Remember this if you ever eat out in Nigeria. It could save you from starvation.

Then it was time to get down to business. I did not expect it to be difficult to sell cooking oil in Nigeria because I knew that Nigerian buyers would come to Singapore and pay less than US$2 for a 2-kg tin of palm oil, and yet I saw the same tin of palm oil on the supermarket shelves in Nigeria being sold for US$8. But the buyers from Nigeria (usually Indians from Hong Kong or London) would still press our prices down to the last penny. They would tell me, "If I want quality, I will buy from Europe or the US. I come to Singapore for the price."

I found out later that the whole trade was just a money-laundering scheme to siphon money out of Nigeria. For example, when I was leaving the country, John said, "I shall buy you another plane ticket from here. Whatever refund you can get on the unused portion of your original ticket, please deposit it into my bank account in Hong Kong. The scheme is, I shall spend some naira for you here, and you deposit some foreign exchange for me in Hong Kong or London." It did not matter what exchange rate I was going to use. When they could buy something for S$1.40 (approx. US$1.12) and sell it at US$8, there would be enough margin to pay off all the middlemen in the scheme.

I heard of a case where someone in Singapore had shipped them a container of discarded Yellow Pages[3]. Another person shipped them plain water in bulk instead of free fatty acids. Why not? The corrupt representative from the buyer's office had been paid off and had no intention of showing up again in Nigeria.

After wrapping up my business dealings, I had some free time on hand. Having just passed his private pilot licence test, John flew me out to the coast in a Cessna for an aerial tour of Port Harcourt.

For my return trip, I transited in London instead of Amsterdam. The departure from Port Harcourt directly to London was uneventful, because by then, I had a local Nigerian Airways ticket and a brand-new Yellow Fever inoculation certificate. Things were also more orderly because it was an international flight. Except that one of the security guards reached out his hand and said, "10 dollars!". I did not bother to ask him for what, because I had been in Nigeria for a full 10 days to fully understand and not to ask "Why?".

---

3 Before the advent of the Internet, the Yellow Pages were an essential part of every office and home. They were thick telephone directories updated annually and printed on yellow paper, listing businesses and their contact details by categories and in alphabetical order. In Singapore, the print directory ceased publication in 2018.

Comfortably seated on the plane and waiting for the inflight service to begin, I looked through the menu and saw a chicken dish among the options. I recalled how tough the chicken was from that lunch experience on my first day in Port Harcourt. Just then, a passenger called for the cabin attendant and complained loudly, "How do you expect me to eat this piece of chicken? I can bounce it on the floor and it will jump right back onto my plate!"

Benin, Togo & Ghana

After graduating from university in mid-2000 and securing a job that allowed her to defer the joining date, my daughter Oi Leng decided to take several months off to work for an NGO in Benin, a former French colony in West Africa, so that she could do some good while immersing in a French-speaking environment.

She stayed in a village that did not have a landline or network coverage for mobile phones. To contact her on a weekday, we had to call her in the village where she worked. That village had two telephones: one in the mayor's office and the other in the local bar. Mindful of the time difference, we would call the bar in the early afternoon, local time. We would tell the proprietor of the bar that we wanted to speak to our daughter Oi Leng. He would tell us to call back in 15 minutes. Meanwhile, he would send this little kid who hung out at the bar to run over to Oi Leng's workplace and tell her that she had a call from her parents. The two of them would then run back to the bar and wait for our call.

On weekends, things would be less complicated because she spent most of her weekends in Cotonou, the commercial centre of the country. There was actually a service provider for her mobile phone, so I was able to call her directly on the mobile phone I gave her.

Later in the year, Kwan and I decided to visit her and find out more about how she was doing. To get to Benin, we transited in Paris and flew down to Cotonou, after another transit stop in Lagos, Nigeria. Not forgetting the favour that the local bar owner did by allowing us to call Oi Leng on his phone, I bought a bottle of duty-free Chivas Regal whisky for his bar.

Getting into Cotonou was not a hassle, and Oi Leng was there to meet us at the airport. She booked us into the grand old hotel in town, where the rooms were housed in individual cottages. The inside was dark and damp. The shower curtain was disgustingly mouldy and dirty, and the shower drain was of course clogged up.

The trip to Benin was not complete without a visit to the voodoo[4] village. Unfortunately (or fortunately), the voodoo chief was on leave that day and his son was standing in for the chief. He blessed us with something that looked like a feather duster. He also showed us how he talked to the gods. He would throw two clam shells[5] into the air. If they both landed on their back or their front, the gods had shown his pleasure in whatever we were asking for. If one shell landed on its back and the other on the front, that meant the god was not happy and we had better retract whatever we were asking for.

Next, he put together three packages of black magic ritual items, which we were supposed to keep with us when we travelled. These items would protect us from heavenly and earthly harm. They included a big seed from some African plant, an animal tooth, a small rock that glistened in the sun and several other odd items. None of the common chicken blood because these witch doctors were educated enough to know that it would be confiscated by the health authorities in many countries at the point of entry.

After he had laid them down nicely, he said "US$180 for the lot or US$60 per set". Now, I was born at night but not last night, so we knew that he was trying to take us for a ride. Kwan offered him US$30 for all three sets. He acted like he was insulted, so Kwan told him to ask his god whether he should accept our bid. This young man's advisor standing behind him tried to tell him not to accept our counter proposal, but on Kwan's urging, he agreed. He threw two shells up in the air and lo and behold, they both landed on their back. His face turned black or red (it was hard to tell) but his god had spoken. Reluctantly, he accepted our

---

4 Voodoo is a traditional religion widely practised in Benin. In 1996, it was officially declared a religion. Voodoo Day is a public holiday and observed on 10 January.

5 This is slightly similar to the wooden divination blocks used in Chinese traditional religions.

US$30. We picked up our winnings (opposite of loot) and left his tent. I am sure he started to put a curse on us after that.

After one night in Cotonou, we left in a hired van for our drive up north, where Oi Leng lived and worked. Firstly, she brought us to the house she had been staying in for the last four months. What we saw really shocked us. The kitchen was just a tap sticking out from the wall. There was no sink beneath the tap. The kerosene stove sat on the concrete floor. With this, one could boil water or cook rice! There was no electricity in the house, so lighting at night came from a pressure kerosene lamp which I had not seen for 50 years. Needless to say, there was no refrigerator, so her diet was mostly cooked rice and vegetables. When bottled water became unaffordable, she alternated between constipation and diarrhoea.

She made a lot of friends in her four months there. When the villagers heard that her parents were visiting, all of them came out to welcome us. All the topless women went home to put on their cleanest dirty shirts. Each of them presented us with a bunch of bananas. We must have collected a ton of bananas. If we were to finish all of what they had given us, we would be producing a whole ton of soft fertilisers for their next banana crop. They formed a circle around us and performed a tribal dance which resembled a fighting cock which had just won a fight. The father of the bar owner actually came down to the bar to thank me personally when I presented the bottle of whisky to the bar.

We visited the beach at Ouidah, where the government had erected a monument – The Door of No Return memorial arch – commemorating the slaves who were captured and shipped out to work on plantations in the West Indies. To ensure that their souls would return to their homeland after they passed on, the slaves would walk backwards in an anti-clockwise direction around a particular big tree near the beach three times before they were headed out onto the slave ships anchored near the shore.

We visited the Ouidah Museum, which used to be the palace of one of the local warlords. He would trade slaves for firearms so that he could capture more slaves. Villagers equipped with spears, bows and arrows were just no match for these warlords. We could not bear to imagine the scenes in those villages when the wives and children came to send off the men whom they knew they would not have a chance to see again.

Oi Leng wanted to show us the neighbouring countries of Togo and Ghana, which were her stomping grounds on weekends. So we headed further north in the hired van all the way close to the northern border with Burkina Faso, and then we crossed over west to Togo. This tiny West African country had a colourful history; it was colonised by Germany, then Great British and France before becoming independent in 1960.

Along the way, we spent the night in a hotel. At the tennis court, we met an American helicopter pilot flying an Evergreen Helicopters BO-105 helicopter fitted with spraying equipment. I found out that he was a one-man operation funded by the World Health Organization to spray chemicals into the stagnant waters around the country to combat the West Nile virus. Hats off to him.

The landscapes we saw during the following day's drive was very similar until we reached the southern shores. Whereas the southern shores of Benin were quite barren with some beach motels sprinkled here and there, the southern shores of Togo were quite well developed and inhabited.

In Lomé, the capital of Togo, we went to a local restaurant and had a schweinshaxe (German roasted pork knuckle). At the next table were some Chinese engineers having the same dish. It must surely remind them of home as the schweinshaxe is identical to our Chinese roast pork.

Lomé is right next to Ghana. As a matter of fact, there was no border wall or fence between them, so we were able to just drive up the road and cross into Ghana which was a bigger and wealthier country, judging from the condition of the buildings.

After a short drive around, we headed back to Cotonou in Benin. That night, we decided we would pay a bit more, and so we stayed in the Hotel Novotel Cotonou Orisha, a modern hotel under international management standards.

Oi Leng was supposed to stay in Benin for a total of six months. However, when we were about to leave Benin, she told us that she would like to cut short her stay and follow us to Paris and meet up with Pak Seng and Suzy who were flying over from America to spend the Thanksgiving weekend with us in Paris. We were a little surprised, but very happy to have the whole family together again, so we did not probe further.

Later, we would find out the real reason for her decision. Every weekend, she would catch a shared taxi to go from her village to either Cotonou or Lomé in Togo. The taxis that plied between these cities were known as "pirate taxis" and were unlicensed. There were "agents" who tried to pull in passengers for a commission, and the taxi would depart when it was filled up.

One weekend, Oi Leng boarded one of these taxis with three other American college kids. There was a dispute between the driver and an "agent" over compensation and the two of them started a knife fight. The crowd pulled them apart and told the taxi driver to drive off. Just as he drove off, he said something to the agent who then chased after the taxi, hung onto the door post and started to rain punches onto the driver through the wind-down window. Just like a scene out of an Indiana Jones movie, the driver tried to shake him off by jerking the steering wheel back and forth. After a short distance, the taxi smashed into a lamp post!

The passenger in the front seat slammed his face into the windshield. Oi Leng, who was sitting in the middle of the back bench, broke a rib when she was thrown forward. The driver was also seriously injured. Who had ever heard of seat belts in West Africa!! To add insult to injury, as the driver was being carried away on a stretcher, he offered to refund the passengers their fare.

Because of the injury she sustained in that accident, Oi Leng felt that she should cut short her stay in Africa and go home so that she could have a thorough medical check-up. So much for her planned escapades in Africa.

Although she was afraid to tell us about the accident when it happened, she called her brother and confided in him. We only found out in Paris when we decided to climb the Eiffel Tower because the queue for the elevator was too long, and she said she would give it a miss. At that time, Pak Seng asked if that was because of the injury she had sustained in the accident. "What accident?" both Kwan and I exclaimed, and only then did she tell us all about it.

Morocco

In March 2014, Kwan and I made a trip to the kingdom of Morocco, flying into the capital Marrakesh and driving up to Casablanca after a few days. The visit to Morocco was not really that memorable. The cities were dusty and hot. We stayed at the Naoura Barriere Hotel, supposedly the best hotel in Marrakech.

We rented a car to drive up to Casablanca. Along the way, we saw the famous goats which climbed the Argan trees. On close examination, we saw that the villagers had built little footings with twigs for the goats to stand on while they chew on the fruits of the Argan trees. For that, the villagers would hassle you for tips if you took pictures of those goats.

Since Casablanca is a seaside city, we drove along the coast to admire the beaches. Lunch was at a village by the sea. Finding sea urchin on the menu, we naturally ordered some for sampling. We were utterly disappointed because the sea urchin there had no *uni* at all.

Drivers in Morocco were very aggressive. However, since I was driving a rental and it was fully insured, they must have wondered about this foreigner who was just as aggressive as they were and would not be bullied on the road.

An African Safari

In December of the same year, we were invited by Pak Seng to join his family on a safari trip to the East African state of Tanzania. The plan was to meet up with them in Nairobi, Kenya, then take another flight together to Tanzania the following day.

We had heard terrible things about safety and security in Nairobi, so we had no plans to sightsee there. On the day that we had wanted to fly over, we could only take Kenyan Airways from London. It was somewhat puzzling as British Airways supposedly flew the same route. Later we would know why.

We were met at the Nairobi airport by a representative from the Muthaiga Country Club, an old colonial club where we had planned to stay for the night. Part of the movie *Out of Africa*[6] was filmed in the club. It was here at the club that I saw a waiter with literally a cone head.

After we had settled in, we received a message from Pak Seng that their British Airways flight was cancelled several months ago, but no one from the airline had notified him. That explained why they could not check in online! They only found out when they showed up at the airport to take the flight. With no other choices, they also booked themselves on a Kenyan Airways flight, showing up 12 hours later.

Being guests of an old traditional colonial club, we had to be properly dressed in coat and tie to dine in the main dining room. My three grandsons had on their prep school coat-and-tie uniforms, but alas, did not have covered leather shoes to go with the uniforms. We managed to convince the manager that we came all the way from Singapore, and he decided to let us sit at a table in one far corner so that we were out of sight from the other members of the club.

After a good night's rest, all of us proceeded by van to the airport to take the flight to Tanzania. At the airport, we found out that we had left a duffle bag in the van. There was a panic as it was 6 a.m. and there was no one to call to get the van to come back.

Fortunately, the driver discovered our bag as he was cleaning up the van. He was on his way to bring it back to us on his own initiative after informing the club. We found out about this when we called the club,

---

6 The romantic drama was a box-office hit, and won seven Oscars in 1986, including Best Picture, Best Director, Best Original Score and Best Cinematography.

as it had arranged for the transfer. Soon, the boarding call was sounded, but there was still no sign of the bag. So, one by one, we told the staff at the gate that we had to go to the restroom. We managed to stall the boarding till the bag showed up at the airport. On that first night in Kilimanjaro, we celebrated Suzy's birthday at the Onsea House with a beautiful cake baked by the chefs there.

In the span of a week, we travelled through the Tarangire National Park, the Lake Manyara National Park, the Ngorongoro Crater and the Serengeti National Park. At the entrance to one of those parks, our 4-wheel drive stopped at the gate so that we could use the washroom. The car doors were left opened and suddenly, a fierce-looking baboon popped up from the front seat, baring his fangs and giving me the shock of my life. Apparently, he had come into our car looking for food.

We did the usual safari activities, such as going on trails both on foot and in a 4-wheel drive where lions, elephants, leopards, cheetahs, rhinoceroses and giraffes were sighted. We slept in luxurious tents or chalets with carpeted floors and even had hot water for our showers.

Our tour guide/driver was a burly man with an unusual (and feminine) name, Elisa. He had a lot of pride in his work. After I criticised him for always following where the other 4-wheel-drive safari vehicles went, he made great effort to finally peel off from the convoy and brought us to a big tree where a leopard had just dragged a wildebeest carcass high up on the tree.

Then I challenged him to show us a pangolin. He took up the challenge, but there was none to be found. However, he brought us to see some rhinoceroses and the rare African wild dog. When we strolled through the parks on foot, we were usually escorted by a Maasai warrior. These Maasai warriors carry their sticks and are rumoured to be so strong and skilful that even lions are afraid of them.

During our first outing on foot, there was a lioness who lurked in the vicinity, but kept her distance probably because of our Maasai warrior escort. In one of our camp sites, we heard lion roars throughout the night, and discovered lion footprints in the morning. We also saw the king of the jungle mating with a lioness, oblivious to the twenty-odd 4-wheel drives surrounding the couple. As the king reached his climax, he let out a roar, to which many of the onlookers responded with thunderous clapping.

At one camp, we were told that a party of two 4-wheel-drive vehicles were bogged down by heavy rain, and the camp had to send out some additional utility vehicles to rescue the party and lead them back to the camp.

All too soon, our safari came to an end and we flew back from Kilimanjaro to Nairobi. The aircraft, a DH-6 Twin Otter was piloted by two female pilots. The captain was a local Kenyan and the co-pilot, also wearing four bars, was an American. After a two-hour layover in Nairobi, we flew back to London uneventfully. Pak Seng took a lot of photos on the trip and these are framed and hung on the walls of his apartment in London.

Chapter 9
AUSTRALASIA

Australia is so near and yet so far away from Singapore, familiar but alien at the same time. It is the largest land mass in Australasia, a region that also includes New Zealand and islands in the surrounding seas. This part of the world has a wide range of ecosystems, such as coral reefs, rainforests, deserts and glaciers. Many of its animal species are unique, such as the kangaroo and the kiwi.

In the 18th century, Australia and New Zealand became colonies of Great Britain. Today, they are constitutional monarchies with parliamentary democracies and elections are held periodically. Their head of state is the sovereign of the United Kingdom.

Australia

My very first exposure to Australia and its culture came from the principal of my primary and secondary schools in British North Borneo. Mr Brummel was from Sydney with an accent to match and we all felt that he didn't really speak English. Maybe they have improved the language over the years. According to him, tomorrow is a "holi-*die*". Since we all loved holidays, we did not really care what he called it. His daily attire was a white shirt, a pair of white shorts, white stockings and black shoes. He could be strict at times but he definitely earned our respect. Indeed, quite recently, he came back to visit the school after 40 years to attend a reunion.

A couple of my classmates left the country to attend boarding school in Australia. We heard great tales of them attending classes in blazers and trousers, and it reminded us of the *Famous Five* and *Secret Seven* novels by Enid Blyton. My classmates prospered and came back to Southeast Asia with highly regarded professional qualifications.

My first visit to Australia took place in 1977. I was the engineering officer for a Republic of Singapore Air Force (RSAF) flight of eight aircraft, going on a five-week detachment to Australia. All the support staff and support equipment were individually weighed, and then loaded onto two transport aircraft.

We had to make a refuelling stop in Bali, Indonesia on the way to Darwin, our point of entry into Australia. The airport services in Bali were ill-equipped to handle the refuelling of our planes that required gravity refuelling nozzles. So with the help of some rupiah (it always helps), the fuel supplier managed to locate the only gravity refuelling nozzle on the island, and after a slight delay, we were en route to Royal Australian Air Force (RAAF) Base Darwin.

Even with the refuelling delay, we still had enough daylight to visit downtown Darwin. My memory of this city in the northern part of Australia was that it had a relaxed atmosphere, with many people in the streets walking barefooted and casually dressed.

However, we were staying in the officers' mess, and so we had to dress formally for dinner. After the meal, we spent some time sampling various unfamiliar Australian beers and then participating in a speed drinking contest with the RAAF officers. When there was money on the table to be won, we Singaporeans could always put up a good fight and come away respected.

The following morning, we took off for RAAF Base Amberley, southwest of Brisbane, Queensland, with a quick refuelling stop in Townsville. Amberley was home to RAAF's No. 1 Squadron. All the facilities were very new. One thing we learned was that it was a chargeable offence to walk out to the tarmac without ear defenders and the RAAF personnel were very disciplined about this.

While we were there, we had the opportunity to tour Canberra, the capital of Australia. It was here that we saw our first furry friend, the koala. We also saw kangaroos as we rode the bus into the city. Over the weekend, we went down to the seaside resort of Surfers Paradise and the Gold Coast.

After 10 days in Amberley, we re-deployed to another air base, the RAAF Base Williamtown in Newcastle, just north of Sydney, in the eastern state of New South Wales. By this time, the temperature had turned cold by Singaporean standards and we had to don a jacket whenever we were outside. Sydney was a four-hour train ride away, so we were there every free weekend, taking in the Sydney Harbour Bridge, the Opera House, Bondi Beach and of course Kings Cross, which is known for its night entertainment venues and red-light district.

The mess warrant officer owned an oyster farm in Nelson Bay, so we waited in the mess bar every Tuesday for a new supply of freshly shucked oysters. Each of us would eat at least two dozens of oysters that night.

While we were in Australia, the following year's national budget was announced over the radio. What amazed me was that just about everyone took a great interest in the budget. All the streets were cleared. The whole city kind of shut down because everyone was glued to the television or the radio to learn about the new budget. I also found out that Australians were big gamblers. I met a punter who flew around the country, going to all the big horse races and making a living out of betting on the races.

All too soon, our five-week detachment came to an end, and we had to pack up and prepare for the flight home. The flight plan called for a one-stop flight from Williamtown to Townsville for fuel, and then onto Darwin. The refuelling stop was uneventful. But during the second leg from Townsville to Darwin, one of the aircraft had a technical fault which forced the pilot to make an emergency landing in RAAF Base Tindal.

Tindal Air Base was just a long, long runway built out of nowhere. There was not even a terminal building. The technicians had to sleep underneath the wing of the aircraft after the problem had been rectified. It was cold, and they were not even fed.

Early next morning, the aircraft continued her flight to Darwin, accompanied by another aircraft acting as her escort. After the two aircraft landed, all the aircraft were prepared for the final leg home to Singapore albeit one day behind schedule because of the diversion. That night, I went to the officers' mess and tried to sample all the different Australian beers available. I remember trying as many as 13 types of beer.

When we landed in Singapore, there were congratulations and celebrations all around, and I rolled out the not-so-fresh oysters brought back from Nelson Bay.

In 1999, our family went down to the northeastern state of Queensland to scuba dive in the Great Barrier Reef. We had heard so much about the big potato cods and the abundance of sharks. We made the trip on a liveaboard yacht. Since it was a private charter, we went straight for the outer reefs. Those potato cods were huge, yet tame. I was told that cods are territorial fish that will attack intruders, but not the ones we met. They just leisurely stayed where they were, and we could pat and swim next to them.

We also wanted to swim with the sharks, so whenever we saw one shark, we would make Pak Seng jump into the water with his mask and find out if that area was infested with sharks. If he spotted a whole school, he would give us a signal so that we could all suit up and jump in as well to swim with the sharks. The weather was just fabulous, and being at the outer reefs meant that there were not so many other divers around. We had a very enjoyable fortnight.

Also in 1999, I participated in a Pan Asian Hash[1] held in Perth, Western Australia. That was my first trip to the city even though it is less than five hours away by flight from Singapore. Part of the Hash run entailed swimming across a river. The river was not that wide, but the water was icy cold. Jumping in for the swim after an hour of running was torturous, and I came down with a runny nose for the rest of the trip.

---

1 See Chapter 13 "Hash House Harriers" to know more about this hobby of mine which has taken me to various lands and enabled me to make friends from all over the world.

Some four years later, our friends invited us to cruise[2] around Collins Pool on a houseboat. This is a lake located south of Perth, and has good fishing spots and abundant wildlife.

In 2005, I revisited Sydney with Kwan and our children, years after my air force detachment in 1977. The occasion was the wedding of the daughter of our ex-neighbours, Pierre and Sandra Moccand. Having grown up with Jaqueline, our daughter Oi Leng was asked to be one of the bridesmaids. At the wedding, we also met another family who lived in the same condominium in Singapore around the same time. This family repatriated back to New Zealand after a few years in Singapore and came up to Sydney for Jaqueline's wedding.

The largest demographic group in Australia consists of people of European descent; indigenous peoples[3] are a minority. Australia also has a substantial Asian migrant population. In Perth, there is a huge Singaporean community. Some Singaporeans send their children to Perth for secondary school because they could not do well in their second language, which is a mandatory subject in Singapore. Many Singaporeans own property in Perth because real estate there is comparatively cheaper than in Singapore. They would use it as a base to play golf, go deep sea fishing or simply stay when they visit their children who were studying in Perth.

Even Kwan and I had thought about buying property in Australia. We spent a week in Melbourne in the southeastern state of Victoria, looking at the property market there. But we decided against it because of the distance from Singapore and the restrictions a foreigner faces when owning a property in Australia.

---

2 See Chapter 11 "The Hardship Group" for my houseboat holiday in Collins Pool.
3 Aboriginal and Torres Strait Island peoples were the first inhabitants of Australia, prior to colonisation.

New Zealand

The majority of New Zealand's population is of European descent, with the indigenous Māori people forming the largest minority group. The coat of arms was revised in 1956 to feature a Māori chief and a European woman facing each other across a British crown and shield. Since 1987, Māori has been an official language in the country.

In 1999, I had an opportunity to see New Zealand for the first time when Kwan and I transited there on our way to a reunion with her extended family members in the South Pacific island of Bora Bora (see box story). To get there, we embarked on a multi-flight journey. From Singapore, we flew to New Zealand, Fiji and Tahiti. Then we took a smaller plane to reach the resort at Bora Bora.

Our transit point in New Zealand was the city of Auckland, on the North Island. We did the usual touristy things, starting with an exploration of the city. While I was there, I contacted my maternal cousin Zuo Hui, the youngest son of my mother's third brother, whom I had never met before. Zuo Hui migrated from Shanghai to New Zealand and gained his permanent residence status through his daughter, who had studied in New Zealand for her MBA and stayed on after graduation.

Zuo Hui played tour guide and drove us around the city, even though he did not speak much English. He brought us to the New Zealand Maritime Museum on Hobson Wharf, where the yacht, NZL 32 (or Black Magic), which won the 1995 America's Cup[4] by beating Team Young America, was on display.

After a short stay in Auckland, we went on to Bora Bora. On the way back after the reunion, we transited in New Zealand again – this time on the South Island. In Queenstown, we did bungee jumping. Then we rented an aircraft and I flew around the glaciers with an instructor plus Kwan and Oi Leng in the back. We also drove out to Milford Sound and rode the ferry to take in the scenery of the fjord.

When we disembarked from the ferry, we tried to beat the crowd by jumping into the car right away, and was one of the first to hit the

---

4 America's Cup is a prestigious international sailing yacht competition with a long history, and New Zealand won it for the first time in 1995.

A RESORT-STYLE FAMILY REUNION

Bora Bora is just an expensive resort which is part of a commune of French Polynesia in the Pacific Ocean. Close to 20 of us – Kwan and her siblings, their spouses and the next generation of nephews and nieces – gathered at Bora Bora in 1999 for a special reunion. Most of them had flown in from the United States. Pak Seng, his then-fiancée, now-wife Suzy and Oi Leng also joined us.

We celebrated two occasions there: the 60th birthday of Kwan's sister, Elaine, and Christmas. All activities were confined to the resort and its vicinity. Although the water was very clear, we did not go diving as there was not much sea life.

At the end of the gathering, we all went our separate ways. Kwan, Oi Leng and I flew into Queenstown, New Zealand, to celebrate the New Year.

road going back to Queenstown. After 15 minutes, judging from the way my fuel gauge needle was behaving, it was obvious that I would not make it back to Queenstown on that slightly less-than-half tank. Recalling that I did not see any petrol (gasoline) station on the road out to Milford Sound, wisdom took over from there. I accepted defeat, and turned around to head back to Milford Sound to refuel. Along the way, I met all the incoming cars whose drivers were probably laughing at my predicament.

We celebrated New Year's Eve in Queenstown. There were signs all over the city that there would be a 100% breathalyser test for all drivers on the road that night. Roadblocks were being set up everywhere. The message was: "Don't say we didn't warn you". On New Year's Day, bright and early, we went jetboating. The driver of the boat looked like the partying type and I prayed that he did not have a heavy night before that. Anyway, we survived. The following day, we flew to Auckland to catch our onward flight back to Singapore.

More than 20 years later, I went back to New Zealand to visit an ex-colleague, Joe Keegan. He was an exchange engineering officer from the Royal New Zealand Air Force, and we first met when he was sent to Singapore from 1977 to 1978.

Joe was happily retired in the North Island, living in a beautiful house in Porirua, a suburb north of Wellington. Although Auckland is the commercial centre of New Zealand, Wellington is the capital of the country. We drove around the Parliament buildings, the various ministries, the High Court and the Cathedral, all of which were a stone's throw from the major sporting venue, Westpac Stadium (Wellington Regional Stadium).

One day, Joe drove us down to Cape Palliser, two hours away from Wellington. We visited the Cape Palliser Lighthouse, which provides the guiding light for all ships navigating through Cook Strait as this was the southernmost point of the North Island. Joe told me about the abundance of lobsters just off the beach there and showed me a photograph of more than 50 lobsters that he caught within two hours in the area.

Chapter 10

THE WEST INDIES

O ften referred to as the Caribbean, the West Indies is a region with numerous islands, islets and reefs set in the Caribbean Sea and the North Atlantic Ocean. With a tropical climate and great biodiversity, it is especially popular with divers.

For centuries, different European powers have colonised the region, bringing over enslaved people from Africa to work on plantations. Many of the islands have since gained independence, while others remain as dependent territories.

The culture of the West Indies has evolved with time, and has been influenced by traditions and practices from Africa, America and Europe, resulting in a unique blend. Over the years, I have enjoyed exploring various parts of the region, which is grouped into three archipelagos: the Greater Antilles, the Lesser Antilles and the Lucayan Archipelago.

The Bahamas

During my second year at Purdue University in 1967, I was very fortunate to have a roommate, Dave, whose father was posted to the Bahamas – part of the Lucayan Archipelago – for work. Dave's parents, Mr and Mrs Rogers, invited me to join their son on a short trip down to Grand Bahama to spend Christmas with them, and even bought me a plane ticket to fly back to Indianapolis at the end of the Christmas school break.

It was the first time I set foot in the West Indies, and I had a grand time. We went snorkelling and waterskiing during the day and hung out at the discos at night. It was here that I first learned how to water ski.

Gliding over the clear blue waters, I could see from beneath my skis the coral scenery whizzing by, and it was a sight to behold.

Mr Rogers managed a cement factory in Grand Bahama. On a visit to the factory, I saw signs with the slogan "Keep the green side up" all over the facilities. When I asked Mr Rogers about the significance of the slogan, he said with a twinkle in his eyes that it was a reminder for his workers to use their brains when working, just like one should always keep the green side of the turf facing upwards when it was being planted.

Jamaica

The island of Jamaica is part of the Greater Antilles, and used to be a colony of Spain until it was seized by England in 1655. In 1962, it gained independence successfully.

Kwan (who was my girlfriend at that time) and I joined a church group for a working trip to the country in 1970. A school bus ferried the group of us (Purdue students) from Indiana to Miami, where we would board a plane to fly over to the Jamaican capital of Kingston.

Unfortunately, the bus blew an engine along the way, leaving us stranded in Mississippi, far away from any town and such things as hotels. But a kind local church group organised shelter for us and we were billeted in various homes while the bus had an engine change.

When we reached Jamaica eventually, we stayed at a school outside of Kingston. We would work for eight hours in the day and then swim in the pristine clear waters afterwards. Our project was to build a workshop where the locals could learn some skills in machining so that they could gain employment later.

One unforgettable experience was going to the national stadium in Kingston and watching a football match between the Jamaican national team and the Santos from Brazil, featuring the legendary Pelé. Every time Pelé touched the ball, everyone in the stadium stood up. After he passed the ball off, everyone sat down again. Earlier, when we were lining up to buy tickets for the game, some of the more curious Jamaican girls came up to us and stroked Kwan's hair which was long and straight, and quite unlike theirs which was short and curly.

The roads outside of Kingston town were very narrow, and yet the vehicles were driven very fast. When the cars, buses or trucks barrelled down the road, the drivers would sound their horn and the poor pedestrians would jump into the ditch on the side of the road to avoid being killed or maimed.

During our week in Jamaica, I drank a lot of Red Stripe pilsner and dark beer. However, travelling in a group with limited budget, we did not get to sample the local cuisine such as jerk chicken and curry goat.

The Cayman Islands

Being an avid diver, I absolutely could not turn down an invitation from my maternal cousin William, a dive instructor at one of the local YMCAs in Dallas, to join him on a dive trip to the Cayman Islands in 1987. Located in the Greater Antilles, the Cayman Islands are a British Overseas Territory. The three islands that make up the Caymans are renowned for their underwater scenery and attract countless of scuba divers and nature lovers from all over the world.

Unfortunately, the weather was not very cooperative during our stay there and our diving was limited to the more sheltered areas. Although the visibility was fantastic, the sea life could have been better. Several years later, I went back to the Caymans for another dive with Kwan and Pak Seng, but the weather was not much better than the previous trip.

British Virgin Islands

The Virgin Islands are a group of islands in the Lesser Antilles. The eastern island chain is known as the United States Virgin Islands, while the western chain is known as the British Virgin Islands (BVI). There are four main islands and many smaller ones in BVI.

One of our relatives has a house on the beach in Virgin Gorda, the third largest main island of BVI. In 2004, we were spending our Christmas holidays there when a tsunami – caused by an undersea earthquake in Aceh (on the Indonesian island of Sumatra) – struck the various beaches in the neighbouring countries.

We watched the destruction on the TV news halfway around the world, and could not imagine the damage it was causing. According to Oxfam, five million people were affected, of which 1.7 million were made homeless, half a million were injured and more than 230,000 were killed. Having been to Phuket, Thailand, numerous times, I am quite sure the number of fatalities would not have been so high if all those makeshift stalls that lined the side of the beachfront road were not there. A lot of people lost their lives when they were crushed by the debris made up of beach chairs, umbrellas, huts and other objects.

Puerto Rico

On the trip to BVI, we transited in San Juan, the capital of Puerto Rico, in order to change to a smaller aircraft. Located in the Greater Antilles, Puerto Rico was formerly a Spanish colony until 1898, when it came under American rule. Later, it became an unincorporated organised territory of the United States, a status which it maintains today.

We did not venture into the capital, but I happened to notice that there was a Hooters Air Boeing 727 on the tarmac. So the airline did exist. Many people only know Hooters as an American restaurant chain that puts its female waiting staff in revealing outfits; the airline was less well-known and eventually ceased operations in 2006.

Chapter 11
THE HARDSHIP GROUP

In 1991, my wife Kwan met a gentleman from Myanmar (formerly Burma), U Hla Khaw, who offered to organise a trip for us to revisit her birthplace. Joining us were a few close friends. We had to abide by the curfew imposed by the government. As for our accommodation, we stayed in a dilapidated hotel in Yangon which had withstood the test of time, as they were exactly as she had remembered them when she left the country in 1963. The grand old Strand Hotel was under heavy renovation at that time. After the trip, we all felt that we had lived through a lot of hardship, hence the name "The Hardship Group" was coined.

The core of the group consisted of Kwan and me, and four other friends. Raj was an elderly Indian lady who spent time meditating in Rishikesh, India, in between our Hardship Trips. Bee Tin (or "Beet", as we like to call her) is a financial controller by profession, and was tasked with keeping an account of our expenses on the trips to make sure that we had enough funds left over to splurge on a sumptuous meal at the end of each trip. Leen is a philanthropist who enjoys travelling all over the world, and her husband Beng is a photography enthusiast, having spent many years taking beautiful photographs of the places they had travelled to and the people they had met on these trips.

Occasionally, we were joined by Linda, an administrator who lives in Hong Kong; Kim Lean and Chong Wah who owned a regional market research firm; plus Jerome, an IT consultant, and his wife Dora. We took turns to organise the Hardship Trips and once the itinerary had been set, the group was small enough such that we never had arguments over the activities in which we partook on these trips. On some trips, one of the core members would invite a close family member or friend to join us.

THE HARDSHIP TRIPS

1991	Myanmar
1992	India: The Maharashtra/Rajasthan Trail
1993	China: The Silk Road
1996	Cambodia: Angkor Wat
1997	Jordan & Israel
1998	Bhutan & Sikkim
2003	Nepal & Tibet
2003	Australia: Perth
2004	Pakistan: The Karakoram Highway
2005	Laos: Luang Prabang
2005	Iran
2007	Syria
2009	Indonesia: The Banda Islands

Myanmar

This was the inaugural trip for the group. It was also the first time that Kwan returned to Myanmar since leaving her birth country in 1963. Just applying for the visa took longer than usual. The embassy wanted to know the flight number and itinerary of her departure in 1963. Of course, she could not remember those details, especially since she was only 12 years old at the time.

When we arrived in Yangon (formerly Rangoon), there was another round of interrogation for Kwan that lasted almost an hour. After the officials were satisfied that she did not return to start a revolution, she was cleared to enter. All visitors were required to exchange US$200 at the airport at the official exchange rate of 6 kyats to US$1. However, the prevailing black-market rate was 120 kyats to US$1.

Kwan had a chance to revisit her former residence and places she had frequented while growing up. She noticed that nothing had changed in the 30-odd years. The whole nation had stood still all this while.

Obviously, the buildings could use a new coat of paint. In fact, the building where her grandmother used to live in had not been re-painted at all.

Because the country was still under martial law, curfew was imposed from dusk to dawn. The moment when curfew was lifted early in the morning, hundreds of runners began training in earnest for the annual marathon, where the first prize was a colour TV. Some of them could not afford proper jogging shoes, so they ran barefooted. For breakfast, we were brought to the restaurant that served the "best Mohingha (local staple fish soup) in Yangon". The owner proudly displayed the certificate to that effect, issued by the mayor of Yangon.

On the second day, we flew north to Mandalay and worked our way south in a minibus. We spent a day in Bagan, a UNESCO World Heritage Site famous for its 5,000 pagodas. Then we travelled east to Meiktila, a city in central Myanmar. Going further east, we came to Taunggyi, the capital of Shan State and the hometown of Kwan's uncle.

Turning south, we travelled to the Kyaiktiyo Pagoda, a popular tourist attraction and pilgrimage site for Buddhists. The pagoda was built on a massive boulder (15 m in girth and 7.6 m in height) perched on the edge of a cliff.

According to local folklore, the rock floats on air, defying gravity. The legends also said that the rock is actually supported by a strand of hair from the Buddha, and that is why hundreds of thousands of Burmese come every year to venerate it. One used to be able to pull a thread through the underside of the boulder, but that is no longer possible because devotees had been throwing coins at the rock for years, which ended up clogging the gap.

Getting to the pagoda required a 1,100-m hike. A palanquin service was available, so we hired one for Raj who was over 70 years old. Because of pride, she declined to ride on it, so the bearers carried an empty palanquin up and down the mountain. After spending a night up on the hill, we treated the bearers to lunch at the restaurant where we were eating. They had so many second helpings of rice that the restaurant owner had to put a stop to that.

We continued our journey back to Yangon, passing by Bago, home of the largest reclining Buddha (55 m long and 16 m tall) in the country.

This Buddha was lost in 1757, but was rediscovered beneath jungle vegetation in 1880. From there, it was just 90 km back to Yangon, where the ladies endowed themselves with rubies and jade gemstones that Myanmar is famous for. After an enjoyable dinner arranged by Kwan's maternal aunt, Rosalind (her mother's youngest sister), we flew home.

India: The Maharashtra/Rajasthan Trail

In 1992, Raj agreed to organise our next Hardship Trip, and that was to travel along the Maharashtra and Rajasthan Trail from Bombay (now Mumbai) to Delhi. I had been to many Indian states for work, including Maharashtra, but it would be my first time exploring the sights on the itinerary planned by Raj, so I looked forward to an interesting trip. Unfortunately, I had a prior work mission in another part of India and could only join them halfway.

Because of the extensive scope of the itinerary, we decided to invite more people to join us on the trip, and the group size grew to 15. They flew into Bombay and spent the first two days enjoying a city tour, including a boat ride over to the Elephanta Caves. Bombay had a wealth of Victorian Gothic architecture, which is still present to this day. Many of the buildings were built from stone, with façades of arcaded verandahs and porticoes.

As the road conditions in India were poor, Raj arranged for the group to fly between some of the cities, starting from Bombay to Aurangabad (both in the state of Maharashtra), where the group made a side trip to the Ellora and Ajanta Caves, which are UNESCO World Heritage Sites. The former is the site of ancient Hindu, Jain and Buddhist monasteries and temples dug into high basalt cliffs. The latter features ancient Buddhist monasteries and religious art carved into a massive rock wall.

Next, they flew up to Udaipur, the former capital of the Mewar Kingdom. This city in the state of Rajasthan is often called the "White City" because of its marble architecture. Set around a series of artificial lakes, it is known for its lavish royal residences. The City Palace overlooks Lake Pichola, and is a monumental complex of 11 palaces, courtyards and gardens, famed for its intricate peacock mosaics.

My fellow Hardship Group members had the fortune of spending a night in the famous Taj Lake Palace Hotel. It is built on a man-made island in the middle of Lake Pichola, giving the impression of a white palace floating on the lake. Formerly used as a royal summer retreat, the Taj Lake Palace was converted into a hotel in the 1960s.

During their stay in the Lake Palace Hotel, they celebrated the birthday of Edward (who had joined the Hardship Group on this trip) with a big dinner. After the palatial stay, the group was bused over to Aodhi Hotel, which was in close proximity (and thus served as a gateway) to the mighty Kumbhalgarh Fort. That night, another birthday bash was organised – this time for Raj. The following day, the group visited Ranakpur, where the Adinatha Temple, the best-known Jain temple in India, was built.

After the visit to the temple, the group flew over to Jodhpur. This is another city in Rajasthan, and home to Mehrangarh Fort, a former palace that is now a museum which displays weapons, paintings and elaborate royal palanquins. Set on a rocky outcrop, the fort overlooks the walled city, where many buildings are painted in the city's iconic shade of blue, thereby earning Jodhpur the nickname of the "Blue City". The blue buildings signify the Brahmin Quarter.

This city is where jodhpur pants originated. Also called breeches (English riding pants), these are tight-fitting trousers that reach to the ankles, where they end in a snug cuff and are worn primarily for horse-riding. In one of the receptions at Delhi during the later part of the trip, we actually met someone wearing a pair of jodhpur pants although he did not come on a horse.

After spending some time sightseeing, the group took a bus ride to Jaisalmer, the western-most city of significance in India. Dominating the skyline was the Jaisalmer Fort, a sprawling hilltop citadel buttressed by 99 bastions. Jaisalmer is known as the "Gold City", as the fort is made of sandstone and shimmers in a golden hue at sunset. Behind the massive walls of the fort stands the ornate Maharaja's Palace (Raj Mahal) and intricately carved Jain temples. The group spent the night in the Jaisal Castle Hotel.

From Jaisalmer, they returned to Jodhpur and spent the night in Rohetgarh, a palatial lakefront hotel 40 km south of Jodhpur. This was where I finally met up with everyone. The following day, we rode our bus to the Pushkar Camel Fair. The Pushkar Camel Fair is an important event in which all the camel and horse traders gather once a year to trade their livestock. We stayed in "luxurious tents" with hot-water showers and toilets lined with carpets in the sand.

After that, we moved on to Jaipur and toured the Amber Fort. Jaipur is the capital of Rajasthan. The Old City, also known as the "Pink City", earned its name from its trademark building colour. At the centre of its stately street grid (notable in India) stands the opulent, colonnaded City Palace complex. Jaipur is home to many jewellery craftsmen, and the ladies in the Hardship Group had a good time bargaining for a deal.

The next site we visited was one of the wonders of the world, the Taj Mahal in Agra. From Agra, it was just a four-hour bus ride to Delhi. One of my favourite tourist attractions in this city is the Indira Gandhi Memorial Museum where the former prime minister of India lived until she was assassinated by her own bodyguards. Her bedroom and office were on display. So were photos and letters from the various stages of her life, including a postcard from Uncle Ho[1].

From Delhi, we flew to Varanasi, in the state of Uttar Pradesh. Because of work commitments, some members of the group returned to Singapore from Delhi, without joining us on this part of the trip. Varanasi is supposedly the most ancient city in India. Situated along the Ganges River, Varanasi is where the Ganges turns north for 5 km before turning south again to flow out to the Bay of Bengal. Hindus believe that because the river is flowing north, it will carry the holy water towards heaven which is somewhere up in the Himalayas. In the olden days, all the maharajas in the country would build a palace on the banks of the Ganges River at this spot so that after their passing and the subsequent cremation, their ashes – when sprinkled into the river – could be sent to heaven.

Everyone we met there held a little silver vase filled with this holy water to be brought home. Our guide told us that the water there was

---

1 Ho Chi Minh, the Vietnamese revolutionary leader who later became the president of North Vietnam, was also known as "Uncle Ho". He fostered close bilateral ties between Vietnam and India when he was in political office.

so holy that even bacteria would not grow in it. I think that no bacteria would survive in the river because of all the human waste and ashes that were being dumped into it.

A rowboat ride up and down the Ganges River just before dawn is a unique activity that everyone should experience. As the sun rose in the east, the mist over the river slowly dissipated as we witnessed all the sun worshippers meditating on the west bank of the river after a bath in the river. Mixed in the action were flocks of buzzards flying overhead, looking for parts of human carcasses that were not completely burnt during cremation.

After a two-day stay in Varanasi, we took an aeroplane to Khajuraho in the state of Madhya Pradesh, where the famous Kama Sutra sculptures in the temples are located. We saw figurine after figurine of gods in compromising positions.

Later on, we flew back to Delhi for a sumptuous dinner at the Bukhara Restaurant in the Delhi Maurya Sheraton Hotel, as per the practice of giving ourselves a treat at the end of every Hardship Trip. It was a satisfying way to cap things off before heading back home.

China: The Silk Road

Kwan met Xiao Pan in Singapore, and he used to be a tour guide in China during his college days. In 1993, Xiao Pan agreed to arrange a tour of the Silk Road for our group. Raj's daughter Vidula joined us on this trip.

The Silk Road was an ancient network of routes used by traders from the time of the Han dynasty. Stretching across deserts, steppes and mountains, the network comprised mountain passes, trading posts and markets that facilitated the flow of spices, gemstones, silk and other goods between the east and the west.

We started out flying to Xi'an, the capital of Shaanxi province, with a transit stop in Beijing. Our flight from Beijing to Xi'an was delayed because the incoming aircraft suffered an inflight lightning strike which cracked the windshield.

On the second day, we paid a customary visit to see the Terracotta Army warriors and the Mausoleum of the First Qin Emperor (Qin Shi

Huang). On the third day, we visited more museums and the old city wall. That night, we took an overnight train to Lanzhou, famous for its beef noodles (*la mian*).

From Lanzhou, it was another overnight train, this time to Jiayuguan (Jiayu Pass). Hygiene on the train was horrendous. The men in our group had to flush the floor of the restroom for the ladies in our group before every visit. I happened to celebrate my birthday on the train, and Xiao Pan went to the kitchen to order some longevity noodles[2] for us. We all took our share, but Xiao Pan would not touch the noodles. We thought he was just being polite, until he explained that after seeing the hygiene conditions in the kitchen, there was no way he could eat the noodles.

Jiayuguan is the western end of the Great Wall, and beyond that fort is the vast Taklamakan[3] Desert. It was rumoured that in the old days, caravans and convoys that plied the Silk Road would stop at Jiayuguan for prayers before they headed out west into the desert. Traders and travellers would throw a pebble at the fort. If the pebble bounced back at the thrower, it was believed that he would return safely one day. If the pebble dropped down at the foot of the fort, chances were the thrower would not come back alive.

We were supposed to reach Jiayuguan sometime in the morning, but there was no announcement on the train that we had arrived. Suddenly, I saw the signboard at the station, and yelled at the rest of the group, "We are here! Better get off." One of the members of our group was actually brushing his teeth in the bathroom when he heard my call. We just threw our luggage out the window and jumped off the train before it started moving again. That was close.

After visiting the fortress, we were taken by coach to Dunhuang where we visited the Mogao Grottoes, located at a strategic point along the Silk Road. This UNESCO World Heritage Site features shrines con-

---

2 Longevity noodles are often eaten during Chinese birthday celebrations and other special occasions, as the long noodle strands symbolise a long and good life.
3 Common and ominous interpretations of "Taklamakan" include "The Place of No Return" and "The Desert of Death".

structed by Buddhist monks accompanied by very ancient Buddhist paintings and architecture serving as aids to meditation.

Leaving Dunhuang, we took another overnight train to Turpan. Turpan is the wine-producing region in Xinjiang province. Although the landscape looks like a desert, our noses could catch the scent of raisins being dried all over the land as we travelled around in a van. To irrigate the land and grow grapes, the people of Turpan constructed a grid of underground tunnels made up of a horizontal series of vertically dug wells that are then linked by underground water canals to collect water from the base of the Tian Shan Mountains and the nearby Flaming Mountains (Huoyan Shan). They make some very fine wine, something that we could all attest to.

After Turpan, we reboarded the van and reached Ürümqi, the capital of Xinjiang. We were all glad to be back in civilisation again. Here, we visited some farms and were invited to tea by some of the farmers.

After a day exploring Ürümqi, we flew to Hotan to visit the famous jade factories. A few members of our group decided to give Hotan a miss, and they prepared to board the next flight out. While Chong Wah was queueing up for security check, I walked up behind him, grabbed his elbow and said in a low voice in Standard Mandarin, "Comrade, follow me". He almost fainted.

We backtracked to Ürümqi to catch a flight to Beijing and then another flight home to Singapore. At the Ürümqi airport, we were kept waiting at the boarding lounge, way past the scheduled boarding time. We were then informed that all of our luggage had been loaded onto the wrong aircraft. Some clever dispatcher then made a quick decision to swap aircraft since both were of the same Ilyushin IL-86 model.

After we were ushered onto this other IL-86 parked on the tarmac, we thought things would proceed smoothly, but we were made to return to the lounge again for another half an hour – because someone realised that the substitute aircraft had too much fuel for the sector. They had to offload part of the fuel so that the aircraft would not be landing with more than the maximum allowable landing weight. After two weeks in China, we finally reached home.

Cambodia: Angkor Wat

In 1996, Leen organised a short trip for our group to visit the UNESCO World Heritage Site of Angkor Wat. Located in Siem Reap, Angkor Wat is a huge temple complex that was originally built as a Hindu temple, but later became a Buddhist temple.

Part of the itinerary included a pre-dawn visit to the Wat to wait for the sunrise from the east, so as to catch the silhouette of that ancient temple with the rising sun in the background. All of us were sitting on the steps of the temple waiting patiently and quietly for the sunrise, when a group of tourists from China announced their arrival with loud chattering and the sounds of throat clearing. That was something we certainly did not bargain for.

We also observed a lot of locals on crutches as a result of stepping on land mines left over from the Vietnam War. We even ventured out to a secluded hill overlooking some fields that our tour guide told us might be mined.

Jordan & Israel

In February 1997, Kwan organised a trip to Jordan and the Holy Land. I have been to Jordan (but never been to Israel) several times in the 1980s for work, so I was excited about exploring more facets of the two countries on this sightseeing trip with the Hardship Group.

The trip started off with a Royal Jordanian flight to the capital Amman, arriving there in the early morning at a freezing -2°C. Stepping out of Queen Alia International Airport, I could not help but notice that all the taxis on the road were the same locally assembled model and were all painted in yellow. No exceptions. They reminded me of the Hindustan Motors Ambassador car models in India.

After a warm breakfast, we started our bus ride towards the south, heading for the town of Wadi Musa where Petra, the historical and archaeological city is located. Petra is one of the New Seven Wonders of the World. On the way there, we passed through the ancient town of Madaba. A 10-km car ride took us to Mount Nebo where we had a spectacular view of the Jordan Valley, Dead Sea and the hills of Jerusalem.

We drove on and came to Shobak and its Crusader castle – Montreal (Mon Reals), constructed in the 12th century A.D.

The following morning, the weather was just perfect when we set off for Petra. This UNESCO World Heritage Site is also known as the "Rose City" for the pink sandstone that Petra was carved out of. Our Jordanian guide led us on horses to the entrance of the Siq, the narrow 1.2-km gorge that opens up into the monuments of Petra. Finally, we had our first glimpse of Petra's grandest monument, the Treasury (Al-Khazneh)! The architecture is a unique mixture of Hellenistic, Middle Eastern and Egyptian influences. We spent the rest of the day exploring various temples on the site, then retired to the Petra Forum Hotel for the night.

We set off early the following day, crossing the Allenby Bridge[4] over the tiny Jordan River into Israel. Our first stop was Jericho. From there, we headed north to Nazareth, where we spent the night. In the morning, we went to Tiberias where we boarded our boat for the Sea of Galilee cruise. When we returned to Tiberias, the tour guide took us to a diamond jewellery shop. The ladies went into a buying frenzy. The diamond salesman introduced himself as Isaac Jacob, and was enterprising enough to ask us for the rest of our itinerary. Little did we know, he had not finished selling his wares yet.

After shopping, we went by road to Tabgha and Capernaum, two towns on the northern shore of the Sea of Galilee. Tabgha was where Jesus fed five thousand people with five loaves and two fishes. In Capernaum stood the House of St Peter.

We continued north and went as far as Banias which is close to the Lebanese border passing through the Golan Heights, seeing Syria in the background. That evening, we had dinner at the Kibbutz Ayelet Hashahar, where a plane was shot down during the Six-Day War and the wreck was on display in a children's playground.

After a good night's rest, we went to the Mediterranean Sea and visited the sea walls of Akko. Travelling south, we came to Jaffa Port and

---

4 The Jordanians also call it the King Hussein Bridge, while the Palestinian Arabs call it the Al-Karameh Bridge.

spent the night in Tel Aviv. The following day, we visited Jerusalem, the Holy City for the world's three greatest religions – Judaism, Christianity and Islam. At the Wailing Wall, we witnessed a Bar Mitzvah (coming-of-age) ceremony of a young Jewish boy.

After that, our guide took us to the Temple Mount, the Dome of the Rock, and the Basilica of the Holy Sepulchre. Although we did not visit all the stations of the Cross, our guide showed us the location and significance of each station on a map.

Mixed in with all these walking tours was an essential visit to the main souk. Among the group of us, there was always interest in the type of breads, sweets, desserts, herbs and spices sold. For me, I also wanted to try out the local brew.

After two days of sightseeing in Jerusalem, we drove over to the Dead Sea for a swim. Why were we not surprised when Isaac Jacob, the diamond salesman we met several days ago, showed up at our hotel that evening with more diamonds for sale? With his opening line of: "Today is your lucky day…." he managed to sell more diamonds to the ladies in our group.

We stayed for another night, and then returned to Jordan for our night flight back to Singapore, but not before we had our sumptuous dinner at a restored castle, as per our Hardship Group tradition.

Bhutan & Sikkim

Back in 1998, there were no direct flights between Singapore and Bhutan, so we had to spend a night in Delhi, India before we could fly to Bhutan. However, that gave us a chance to have dinner at the Bukhara Restaurant in the Delhi Maurya Sheraton Hotel again[5]. They made the largest naan in the world. For those who love lamb, they also made the best tandoori leg of lamb.

The following morning, we flew into the Paro airport, which is the main airport serving the capital Thimphu. The runway is located in a

---

5 The Hardship Group dined there in 1992 to celebrate the great times we had on the Maharashtra/ Rajasthan Trail.

valley. It must be a tricky airport to fly into because the planes have to snake their way between hills and ridges down the valley during descent. There was simply no straight-in approach.

Thimphu is a two-hour drive from the airport. Back then, Bhutan was just a sleepy country. The best accommodation in town was no better than a 3-star hotel in most other countries. Tourists visited monasteries and trekked through the hills and meadows. I don't remember going to any cultural shows then. And there was nothing to do in the evenings. Every day – for five days straight – we went to museums and monasteries. One day, we were driven to a lookout point overlooking the Thimphu Valley. When we climbed back into our mini-bus, Linda screamed suddenly, and we saw blood all over one of her shoes. Looking closely, we found a leech stuck to her ankle, and that was the cause of all that blood.

After that, we were ready to head to our next destination, Sikkim, a small state in India. Instead of flying out from Paro, our tour operator arranged for a minibus to take us down to the Indian border so that we get to see the Indian state of Assam along the way. From there, he made arrangements to take us by road to Gangtok, the capital of Sikkim.

This road coming down from Bhutan must have been featured in many National Geographic TV shows as one of the most dangerous roads in the world. It hugs the side of the mountains, and the drop off was mighty steep. The whole road was unpaved, and became slippery when it rained, not to mention that most vehicles plying this road had bald tires. Parts of the road became a single lane because of landslides. Some of the sharp curves around the side of the mountains made it seem like the nose of our bus was hanging out over the edge of the cliff!

After the long, tiring and hair-raising bus ride, we arrived at the immigration checkpoint at the border town of Phuentsholing. Here, we cleared customs and immigration for both Bhutan and India. Once that was done, we were allowed to head to the Bhutan Gate, where the actual border crossing was located some 5 km away. The Bhutan Gate is just a structure in the middle of a road in the heart of Phuentsholing. On one side is India, and the other is Bhutan. However, in those days, there were no fences or walls on either side of the gateway to control access. You either walk through the gate or simply walk around it.

On the Indian side of the road, the shops would be very busy and the sidewalk would be bustling with people. In contrast, the other side of the road would be very quiet, with fewer people walking about. That side was Bhutan. On the way down, we saw a sign that said: "Urinating is strictly prohibited in this area. By order." I think prohibiting pooping in this area is more appropriate because of the hair-raising hairpin turns on the roads coming down from Bhutan.

Gangtok is the capital of Sikkim and a 5½-hour drive from Phuentsholing. As we actually drove through Assam to get to the foothills, we passed by acres and acres of tea plantations.

However, Gangtok itself was a let-down for us, especially having just come from Bhutan. The city was overcrowded, over-built, and very dirty and noisy. The outdoor scenery was not very different from what I had seen in Bhutan or on previous trips to Nepal.

After just two days in Sikkim, we took a 4-hour minibus ride down to Bagdogra Airport, which was also an air force base. From there, we flew out to Delhi to catch a flight home.

Nepal & Tibet

We had heard about the possibility of travelling by road from Kathmandu, Nepal all the way to Lhasa, Tibet. This was an adventure right up the alley of the Hardship Group. As my work took me to Kathmandu very often, I had a friend there who owned a travel agency, and he put together an itinerary for us. My daughter Oi Leng joined us on this trip.

So in 2003, eight of us met up in Kathmandu. Although the linear distance between the two cities was only 609 km, the actual distance travelled by road came up to 1,300 km. The weather was not particularly promising; it was raining continuously when we left the Kathmandu valley. Before we could even make it halfway to the Chinese border, we came upon a landslide and the road was completely blocked by boulders and mud. Our tour operator managed to hire a group of porters to carry our luggage in the rain, and we all climbed over the slush and boulders to get past the landslide.

On the other side, there were some Toyota Corollas waiting to fetch us to yet another landslide just one kilometre away. Once again, we had to get out into the rain and climb over this second landslide. The Corollas were doing a roaring business just ferrying passengers and goods between the two landslides, and they would continue doing it until the landslides were cleared.

There was a minibus waiting to ferry us to the Chinese border. After clearing immigration and customs, we checked into a hotel in the border town of Zhangmu[6], all tired out.

The following morning after breakfast, we loaded up into three Toyota Land Cruisers. Although we were promised new Land Cruisers, those three were definitely more than 10 years old. We looked doubtfully at the vehicles, but it was too late to turn back, and the three seasoned drivers assured us that their 4-wheel drive vehicles were fully capable of bringing us to Lhasa in one piece.

Our first journey was a five-hour drive to Xegar (2,500 m) where we spent the night. The following day was a hard climb to Shigatse (4,350 m). It was on this last leg that we had to go over the highest point on the whole route, the Gyatso La mountain pass at more than 5,000 m. When we were at the pass, we stopped and went down from the cars to take pictures at the marker. As luck would have it, one of the cars would not restart when it was time to go. The drivers gathered together and pooled all the used spark plugs that they had and chose the cleanest one to be fitted into the engine that would not start, cylinder by cylinder.

Miraculously, they restarted the car, but all of us had to spend more than two hours at that high altitude without acclimatisation. We paid the price for that in the evening – all of us had altitude sickness, accompanied by splitting headaches.

In the morning, we visited the Tashi Lhunpo Monastery and continued on to Gyantse, a town which was only another 260 km from Lhasa. However, the altitude sickness affected all of us badly and no one was in the mood to explore the town which was the third largest town in Tibet at that time. So we went back early to rest for the night.

---

6 I found out that the Chinese had commissioned and built a dam in Zhangmu in 2014, about 11 years after our trip. So the border crossing was relocated further south.

On the final day of our road trip before we reached Lhasa, we travelled on the road running alongside of Yamdrok Lake, also known as the Heavenly Lake. According to local folklore, a fairy maiden left her home in heaven and transformed herself into Yamdrok Lake. The turquoise colour of the water enabled the local villagers to claim that it is the most beautiful lake in the world.

By the afternoon, we arrived in Lhasa. Fortunately, the headaches that had afflicted us went away gradually. Over the next three days, we did all the touristy activities, visiting monastery after monastery. We also insisted that our tour guide, Norbu, bring us to his home village. His mother was very surprised to see him because he had not been home for half a year. His whole family was harvesting in the field, and we had a chance to sample the food and home brew typically served during the celebration of a good harvest. Leen has stayed in contact with Norbu after all these years. On the fourth day in Lhasa, we flew home via Hong Kong uneventfully.

Australia: Perth

In the later part of 2003, Leen and Beng hired a houseboat and invited the Hardship Group to cruise around Collins Pool, a 30-km long lake located 70 km south of Perth. We were joined by Jerome, Dora, Leen's daughter Imin, and Beet.

Jerome used to be a naval officer in the Singapore Navy, so he was nominated to captain the houseboat. The plan was to cruise up and down this lake and visit the various lakeside settlements.

Unfortunately, it rained non-stop for the few days we were there. So we came back on land and drove down to Cape Leeuwin Lighthouse, overlooking the southwestern tip of Australia where the Indian and Southern Oceans meet.

I was simply amazed by the abundance of fresh seafood in Western Australia. There were lobsters, scallops, oysters, sea urchins and all kinds of fish. However, we also learned very quickly that the flies in that area liked the seafood, just as much as we did, and were more than happy to join in when we were having our feast.

Pakistan: The Karakoram Highway

In 2004, we went on a 10-day road trip on the Karakoram Highway, driving northwards from Lahore to the Chinese border in Khunjerab Pass. Also known as the National Highway 35 or the China–Pakistan Friendship Highway, this roadway took almost 20 years to build and is a joint project between the two countries.

We picked up a bottle of port wine at the airport duty-free shop in Singapore before our departure, planning to enjoy it while sitting outside a tent on a cool, starry night. Unexpectedly, we were told by the customs officer at the Lahore airport that we were not allowed to bring in any alcohol because Pakistan is a Muslim country. We were instructed to leave the bottle with the customs office, but we could retrieve it when we leave the country. Of course, I had serious doubts whether that same customs officer would be on duty when it was time for us to leave Pakistan, so I looked upon the situation as donating the bottle to the customs office for their research on the effects of the evil alcohol.

After clearing customs, we met up with our tour guide Fazal. He said that he had been forewarned that I loved my beer, so he had a crate of Heineken and a crate of locally brewed Rawalpindi beer, all chilled and waiting for me in the bus. I actually developed a liking for the Rawalpindi beer over the next two weeks because it was a superb beer brewed in a prohibition country[7].

Before we set off for the northern tip of the country, Fazal brought us to witness the Wagah–Attari Border flag-lowering ceremony[8], during which soldiers from Pakistan and India lower their respective national flags. The atmosphere of the whole place was most emotional and the ceremony was a once-in-a-lifetime experience. Having been arch-enemies ever since the British granted them independence in 1947, the two countries nurse a rivalry that have never gone away.

The spectators on the Pakistani side of the border (where we sat) were outnumbered by those on the Indian side. Even the grandstands

---

7 Until 1997, it was legal for Pakistanis to buy alcohol.
8 This ceremony takes place every day before sunset, and attracts civilians from both countries, as well as tourists.

were smaller. However, the spirit was no less enthusiastic. Spectators on both sides were chanting and waving their national flags with fervour. The Pakistanis were chanting "Zindabad" and the Indians were chanting "Jai Hind". It felt like the fanaticism could spark off another war at any moment.

The following day, we set off for the Karakoram Highway. Our minibus drove right by the city of Abbottabad. We could not in our wildest imagination have known that Osama[9] was actually hiding there as we drove past. We continued our drive, passing the city of Mansehra before reaching Besham for our night stop.

In the morning, we continued northwards, passing by the Rakaposhi Mountain (7,772 m) and the town of Gilgit. In Gilgit's city centre, we saw an Indian Army Chetak helicopter which had been on displayed since October 1997. There were many stories circulating around on all the heroic deeds carried out by the Pakistani Army to capture this helicopter. Then there were just as many stories about the heroic and daring attempts by the Indian Army pilots to escape.

However, from talking to an Indian Air Force pilot friend of mine, I learnt that the pilots were lost in the fog (GPS was not available to the Indian Army at that time). Since the Pakistanis also flew the Chetak, the local regiment assumed that the helicopter that had landed was one of theirs. Only when they saw the insignia on the pilots' flying suits did they realise that the Chetak belonged to the Indian Army. As the story went, the Indian pilots were invited back to the Pakistani officers' mess for tea, while the Army headquarters from both countries sorted out the protocol so that the pilots could return to India. However, the helicopter had to be left behind.

That evening, we settled down in Karimabad (2,500 m) which is the capital of the Hunza District. Fazal told us that until the Karakoram Highway which cuts through Hunza Valley was completed in the 1980s, the Mir (monarch) of Hunza forbade his citizens to venture out of the

9 In 2011, Osama bin Laden – founder of the terrorist group Al-Qaeda that was responsible for the September 11 attacks in America – was killed in Abbottabad by United States CIA operatives.

valley. However, during the construction of the highway, there was an influx of civil engineers and construction crews, so the opening up of the valley was inevitable. Fazal, who came from the area, had sandy hair and green eyes, so he could have been a descendant of soldiers lost from Alexander the Great's army when he invaded India in 4th century B.C. Fazal told us that on his first trip to the United States, the immigration officer just would not believe that he was Pakistani.

We spent a couple of days exploring Hunza Valley and the nearby meadows where the inhabitants were known to have an average life span of close to 100. We were told that the secret to their longevity was in the water. Looking closely at the water that was channelled from the surrounding mountains to the valley for irrigation, we found tiny metallic flakes glistening under the sunlight. As we walked around the town, Fazal would just jump over a low fence to pluck fruits that looked so yummy, and we had a chance to taste some plums. Those fruit trees belonged to someone else, but then everyone knew everyone else in the valley, and so all the fruit trees became communal property.

We visited the Baltit Fort which was once the epicentre of the Hunza Kingdom. This fort fell into disrepair before being preserved. Leen has stayed in touch with Ejaz, the curator of the Baltit Fort Museum, after all these years. We also visited the Hasegawa Memorial Public School which was established in March 1995 based on the wishes of the late Tsuneo Hasegawa, a famous Japanese climber who died in the mountains in October 1991. His fall was witnessed by his widow who was watching from the school grounds in Hunza Valley because it was a brilliantly clear day. After her husband's death, Mrs Hasegawa solicited donations to sustain the operations of the school and the Japanese government also contributed in the way of educational equipment, building material and furniture. The students were taught simple Japanese as a second language. We also met climbers coming back from the Everest base camps, with many amazing stories which they shared with us.

From Karimabad, it was another six-hour drive to reach the Chinese border at the Khunjerab Pass (4,800 m). We took some pictures in front of a 2-m tall slab that said "Pakistan" on one side and "China" on the other side. Satisfied, we backtracked on the Karakoram Highway, taking two days to reach Rawalpindi, and then Lahore. Much of the scenery along the way was snow-capped mountains and ice glaciers. As expected, the customs officer who confiscated our bottle of port was not on duty the day we left Lahore to fly back to Singapore.

Laos: Luang Prabang

Luang Prabang is designated as a UNESCO World Heritage Site, hence the attraction for the Hardship Group to make a trip there. Because of work commitments, I was not able to join the group on this trip in 2005. They visited all the architectural, religious and cultural sites. They also tried the pastries and breads baked by the locals who had learned the techniques from the French during the colonial era.

Iran

In 2005, I made my second trip to Iran after about a quarter of a century – this time with the Hardship Group. I found the country to be much more civilised and settled; not being at war[10] is a definite advantage. As it has been compulsory for women to wear headscarves in the public since the 1979 Iranian Revolution, the ladies in our group adhered to the dress code and covered their hair with either a headscarf or shawl. One of them forgot to wear her headscarf once, and was shouted at by someone who drove by in a car.

Since Iran was no longer engaged in warfare, we were quite free to travel all over the country. On a trip north to the Caspian Sea, we were walking along the waterfront during the day when a man, reeking of alcohol in his breath, approached us and said, "Hey, you want caviar? 100 grams for US$100". He was one of the workers from the state-owned caviar factory, who stole some caviar out to sell on the black market just to earn a few rials or to barter for some black-market vodka.

Not knowing whether we could trust him, we gave him a US$100 note and were told to wait for him in a nearby alley. He returned with a small plastic tub and said, "There are 140 grams here but you can have

---

10 Although the Iran-Iraq war ended in 1988, a peace agreement was signed only in 1990.

it." That had to be the tastiest caviar we had ever eaten. It was so fresh, and had to have been processed right there in the factory down the street. We really regretted not buying more.

Later, back at our hotel, we bought some caviar again, but it was produced in Azerbaijan. Compared to the black-market Iranian caviar, this version costed twice as much, and yet did not come close to the taste of what we had earlier. The moral of the story? If you really like caviar, a trip to the Caspian Sea is well worth the trouble. The following day, sturgeon steak was on the menu of a restaurant that we dined at, and it tasted delicious too.

We continued on our journey and went south to Shiraz, where the popular wine varietal originated. Although Muslim armies conquered Iran in the 7th century A.D., the territory only became a stronghold of the Shi'a Muslim faith around the 15th century. Zoroastrianism, the ancient pre-Islamic religion of Iran, survives in isolated pockets of the country. The descendants of Zoroastrian Iranian (Persian) immigrants are known as Parsis. We visited a Zoroastrian temple as part of our tour and saw a Zoroastrian high priest feeding the perpetual fire in the temple with some logs. Our tour guide told us that we were very lucky because in all her years leading tours, she had never seen a Zoroastrian priest.

From Shiraz, we headed north to Isfahan. Known for its Persian architecture, we visited all the famous mosques and the Vank Cathedral, which was covered with mosaic tiles and calligraphy. Despite Iran's conversion to Islam, many of the paintings, murals and carpets depict wealthy Iranian families enjoying their wine (probably Shiraz but could also be grape juice) accompanied by music and dancing ladies.

Travelling through Iran in 2005, we met some Americans who were working in Saudi Arabia. Come holiday time, they hired a car and drove around Iran, taking in the sights. These people – Americans – were actually vacationing in Iran! It was indeed strange to meet Americans in Iran, even more so that they had chosen to vacation there. Another example of how Iran has improved? No doubt.

Our tour guide for the trip was actually a glider pilot. We spoke much about glider flying. Some time after our tour, she came to Singapore for a visit and I took her on a flight in a Cessna to Melaka, Malaysia.

Syria

Getting a Syrian visa was not much of a hassle. There was an embassy of the Syrian Arab Republic in Kuala Lumpur, Malaysia, so Leen – who organised the trip – collected all our passports and arranged for them to be sent there for the visa to be affixed onto our passports.

Back in 2007, the most convenient way to fly to Damascus from Singapore was to take Qatar Airways with six-hour layover in Doha. Unfortunately, the flight left Singapore at 3.20 a.m. and arrived in Doha at 6 a.m. local time. The Doha airport terminal at that time was quite run down (unlike the current Hamad International Airport), and there was not much to see or do while we were in transit. The connecting flight from Doha to Syria put us into Damascus at 3.25 p.m. local time.

We were met at the airport and transferred to our hotel in the heart of the old city, minutes away from the Bab Touma (St Thomas Gate), the Umayyad Mosque and the Old Souk (Al-Hamidiyah Souk). After a good night's rest, we visited the National Museum, the Umayyad Mosque, the Al-Azem Palace, and a Roman bath. We also strolled around the old city. In the evening, we were brought up to Mount Qasioun for a night view overlooking the city.

The following day, we left for Palmyra after breakfast. As we drove along the main desert highway heading northeast, we came across a road sign indicating that the junction ahead branched into Palmyra, Homs and Baghdad. We jokingly debated whether we would want to make a diversion to Baghdad but that was more than 700 km away. How were we to know that eight years later, there would be all this turmoil in the two countries? Convoys of ISIS fighters might have driven across the desert on this same road on their way to Palmyra, where they left behind a trail of destruction.

Over the next two days, our tour guide took us to all the famous ruins in Palmyra which were designated as UNESCO World Heritage Sites. We took a group photograph with the Temple of Bel[11] in the background. We also climbed up to the ruins overlooking Palmyra.

---

11   In 2015, ISIS tried to flatten the whole temple with dynamite.

After that, we headed out to the Krak des Chevaliers, which was a Crusader castle built in the 11th century A.D. Perched on top of a 650-m-high hill, this medieval castle was said to be the best-preserved castle in the world, according to T.E. Lawrence. We took a look around the castle, came down the hill and spent the night in Homs.

In the morning, we continued north to the city of Hama, famous for its waterwheels used for irrigation. Then we moved on to Apamea, to see the 2-km-long Great Colonnade, which ranks as one of the longest colonnades in the world. We stopped in on the archaeological discovery of the lost city of Elba, which dated back to the 3rd and 2nd century B.C. Before settling down in Aleppo that night, we visited the Church of Saint Simeon Stylites that could be traced back to the 5th century A.D.

We spent the following day exploring Aleppo, visiting mosques, the citadel, the National Museum of Aleppo and souks. One place that I found interesting was a traditional olive oil soap factory. A mixture of olive oil, water and lye was boiled for three days in what looked like a big Chinese wok to me. The next step involved adding laurel oil and pouring the thick green mixture over large sheets of waxed paper set on the floor. Before the soapy mass could harden fully, workers would walk over it with planks of wood strapped to their feet, so as to spread it out evenly. The smoothened mass would be left for a day to cool and solidify.

After that, the workers would cut the soap into cubes using a process which reminded me of the way farmers plough the land. The cubes would be stacked in towers using a staggered formation, to allow maximum air circulation where they would be aged for six months to a year.

Soon, it was time for us to head back to Damascus. On the way south, we passed by a village where our tour guide took us to a small shop that sold home-pressed olive oil. He bought two 18-kg tins of the olive oil. All of us also bought some, and it had to be one of the freshest and most aromatic olive oils that I had ever come across.

Another interesting local product was their mutton. The local sheep – known as the Awassi breed – have fat tails that looked like flaps. The breed has existed for at least 5,000 years. The meat of the Awassi sheep largely lacks the characteristic flavour associated with mutton in Europe, hence it has a less gamey taste.

As we drove through the desert, we saw groups of Bedouins digging in the sand at the foot of some rocky mounts. We were told that they were digging for desert truffles (known in Arabic as *kamah*). These are a species of the mushroom family and are distantly related to their more pungent, and far more costly European cousins. We bought some in a market and brought them to a restaurant to be cooked as part of our dinner that night. To our disappointment, they turned out to be quite tasteless.

The following day, we arrived in Damascus in the mid-afternoon, just in time for lunch. Our tour guide took us to a boutique restaurant set in the courtyard of a typical Syrian house. The waiters were clearing up after a lunch party, and we were told that the guests included Nancy Pelosi[12], hosted by the Syrian government. Her entourage had just left for the airport when we arrived. If the restaurant was good enough for the Syrian government to host a VIP like Nancy Pelosi, it had to be good enough for us. And it was.

We spent two more days exploring Damascus, shopping for spices in the souk, and sightseeing at the Roman amphitheatre of Bosra. We did consider making an impromptu day trip over to Beirut, the capital of Lebanon, which was only two hours away by road from Damascus. However, as we were at the tail end of our trip, our adventurous spirit had dampened, and we were just anxious to get on a flight home.

The following day, we boarded a Qatar Airways aircraft to Doha, where we had another long layover, after which we were flown home.

Indonesia: The Banda Islands

Kwan's friend, Patti Seery, who was an American naval architect, built an Indonesian phinisi sailing boat, hand-crafted from tropical hardwoods in Indonesia and named it *Silonona*. The boat was originally designed to look like the traditional Indonesian trading boats that sailed along the historical Spice Routes. Patti married old-world style with

---

12   Pelosi is a prominent American politician who was the first woman to become the Speaker of the House. At the time of our trip, she had just started her speakership.

contemporary indulgences, including a spacious deck, day beds and five air-conditioned suites.

In September 2009, we chartered the *Silonona* for a week to tour the original Spice Islands of Banda. In addition to the core group, we were joined by Kwan's sister Christina and her husband Doug. As the world's sole source of the valuable spices of nutmeg and mace, these nine tiny islands attracted traders from China, Southeast Asia and the Middle East, as early as 2,000 years ago. However, by 1667, the Dutch had established a virtual monopoly on nutmeg and the English relinquished their claim by trading the tiny island of Run (pronounced as "r-o-o-n") in the Banda Sea for Manhattan in the New World. Pulau Run, although small, was strategically located where all the spice ships heading to Europe had to sail by. The Dutch wanted this island so that they could control the passageway of the spice ships, thereby preserving their monopoly on the Asian spice trade.

We boarded the *Silonona* in Ambon, the capital of the Maluku archipelago, and sailed overnight to the Banda Islands. Over the next six days, we explored the cluster of islands, big and small, known as the Spice Islands. The Banda Sea had an abundance of sea life, and we enjoyed diving in the pristine clear waters.

We went ashore on Banda Neira, the only island with an airstrip. Right next to Banda Neira is the active volcano on Pulau Gunung Api, which last erupted in 1988 after lying dormant for centuries. The lava flowed north from near the summit into the sea, cooling in gentle undulating waves, destroying both nutmeg gardens and corals. The coral growth is phenomenal largely due to the nutrient-laden currents and clear waters that encircle Banda. The lava itself seems to be conducive to speeding up coral growth, and this spectacular growth has amazed scientists and coral specialists the world over. We called on Des Alwi, the owner of the Maulana Hotel on Banda Neira. He was also known as the King of Banda. Leen was acquainted with him when she visited these islands in 1988. He personally drove us around the waters surrounding the Gunung Api in his outboard.

We also visited Pulau Run. We were brought to see the old church and wondered at the quirk of fate that moved Run from the centre of world trade to become a very isolated dot that is home to only one remaining family.

There was another island, Pulau Ai, which is larger and remains amongst the most traditional of all the islands in the region. It has one large village boasting of the perpetually winning team of 40 men who paddled their sacred ceremonial war canoes called *kora-kora* to the rhythm of the drum and chanting. Patti made prior arrangements so that we could witness such an event. She was also known to sponsor real village weddings when the happy occasions coincided with the arrival of her tour groups, so that the latter could immerse themselves in an authentic experience.

At the end of the week, we bade farewell to the crew of the *Silonona* and took a flight to Makassar and onwards to Bali to head home. This trip was a fitting end to the Hardship Trips that our group took together, although it was far from being a hardship trip. We were pampered by the crew of the *Silonona*, enjoyed the open bar on board, had our daily massages, consumed freshly caught seafood and slept in air-conditioned suites with clean sheets.

Looking back, our close to 20 years of travelling together produced many pleasant memories. Raj passed away peacefully while meditating on one of her retreats in Rishikesh. The rest of us do get together periodically, to talk and laugh about incidences, such as Beet being run over by a motorcycle while crossing the road in India. The motorcyclist sustained more serious injuries than her. And Beet falling off a ledge while backing up to take a group photo. "It had to be you," we would say. Kim Lean's nonstop giggling when she had taken a few drinks in a restaurant in Xinjiang. Linda screaming and crying when she found a leech stuck to her ankle in Bhutan. Raj trying to get us some Indian hemp when we were in Delhi. Dora and her canned pig's trotters, because she could not do without pork. Me, any cold beer would do.

Chapter 12

FOOD

I like to think of myself as being extremely adventurous when it comes to food. I will eat anything *once*. However, there have been occasions when I wish I could have eaten my words instead of having to eat what was being served to me.

Naturally, the country where I have found the most exotic types of food is China. There is a saying: "The only thing that a Chinese would not eat is something whose back does not face the sky." The implication is that the only thing off-limits to a Chinese person's palate is a fellow being, because humans stand erect.

Once, I was visiting some customers of mine in southern China and they invited me to lunch. They told me that it was my lucky day because wheat worms were in season and these were available only for one week in a year. Naturally, they asked if I would try some, and my answer was that I would try anything once.

The dish was served in an opaque porcelain bowl and looked like steamed egg custard. I was told that these wheat worms had been steamed with hen eggs and some very expensive sun-dried mandarin orange peel. The custard looked harmless enough, until I dug my spoon into it. Buried underneath the custard were what looked exactly like maggots. Hundreds of them. It was too late to pull my spoon away from the contents in the bowl so I had to take a spoonful of it back onto my plate. I made sure I had a big glass of cold beer on standby when I put that spoonful of maggots into my mouth. I did not even dare to chew it, so I just gulped it down with a mouthful of beer, followed by the whole glass of beer. I was not sure whether my host was amused or insulted.

One of my favourite snacks is found in Beijing, and it is associated with poison and venom. Deep-fried scorpions are crispy on the outside and crunchy on the inside, and a handful of them goes very well with beer. You can usually find them in roadside stalls, bars and restaurants. The scorpions are full-sized adults, measuring about 10 cm in length. They are served whole – with pincers and tail intact – and scattered over some shrimp crackers. Cooking scorpions neutralises their toxins, although some people prefer to remove the stingers and venom glands before putting the scorpions into the frying pan.

Among the best known spice-loving Chinese provinces, three stand out in particular. There is a food-related saying or tongue-twister[1] that describes the people in these provinces: "Those in Guizhou like their food to be spicy, those in Sichuan are unafraid of spicy food, and those in Hunan fret if their food is not spicy (貴州人辣不怕, 四川人不怕辣, 湖南人怕不辣)".

I was with a colleague in Jingdezhen, the porcelain capital of China, and we went out for dinner at a restaurant. The owner asked if we had ever tasted their local duck which had the basal knob of a goose on its head. She brought one out to show us and we agreed to order a dish of it.

Just before she went back into the kitchen, she turned around and asked if we could tolerate spiciness. Like a macho warm-blooded Chinese, I told her that I would only worry if it were not spicy enough.

---

1 Variations of this saying exist, and they play on the juxtaposition of the provinces.

That was a fatal mistake. When the dish was served, it was so spicy that it was simply inedible. We had a small piece of the meat each and she had to take the rest of it away.

The people in other parts of the world are no less daring when it comes to eating birds, big or small. In Thailand's capital Bangkok, braised duck tongues are tasty and cheap. I would order them from a particular restaurant whenever I travel there. The same dish would cost 10 times or more in Singapore and Hong Kong. In many western countries, ostrich meat is a substitute for lean red meat, and ostrich eggs are often made into omelettes.

During my trip with the Hardship Group on the Silk Road, we stopped in Xinjiang, China, and saw a dish with the curious name of "Snow Mountain Camel's Hoof" listed on our dinner menu. How could we possibly pass up on an opportunity to savour something so exotic? The restaurant required 24 hours' notice to prepare the dish, and since we were doing some local sightseeing the following day, we pre-ordered the dish for dinner at night. Of course, we prayed that they did not have to cut off a live camel's hoof just for us.

When the dish was served, it came on a big plate and the whole hoof was covered with whipped egg white. The hoof was just a big lump of cartilage but it tasted very gamey. Each of us took only a small portion and left the rest untouched. We paired the dish with a glass of Loulan, a red wine made from locally-grown grapes in Turpan. At that time, a bottle of Loulan was less than RMB100[2]. Today, Loulan red costs more than RMB1,000 a bottle!

On that same trip, we had dinner in a small town in Xinjiang. Because the people were predominantly Muslim, lamb/sheep/goat was

---

2   The RMB–US$ exchange rate in the early 1990s fluctuated quite a bit, but RMB100 was approximately equivalent to US$12 at that time of my trip.

their main staple meat. There was a dish cooked in a big pot. All the sheep offal – brain, eyeballs, tongue, sweetbread, lungs, heart, tripe, liver, spleen, kidneys, intestines and testicles – was just stewing in this big pot. The broth smelled so strong that I was sure they did not need to add any spices. Most of my friends did not touch the stew. I tasted a few pieces of recognisable organs from this special gumbo, such as tripe and intestines. When we were in Pakistan some 11 years later, we went to a street where all the food hawkers had a hot plate over a charcoal fire with dozens of sheep testicles sizzling on it.

During a work trip to Kunming, a major city in Yunnan province, I was offered grilled field rat over dinner. It looked no different from grilled pigeon. I have to say, it tasted pretty good too. It was just the thought of eating a rat that makes one hesitate a little.

Snake gallbladders are believed to improve vision and relieve arthritic pain, according to ancient Chinese folklore. One day, while strolling on a sidewalk in Hong Kong, I saw a snake seller with a few cages full of snakes. He pulled out a snake, and slid his hand over its body until he reached the section where the gall bladder was located. With a sharp knife, he cut open the snake's stomach and dropped the gall bladder into a glass. Then he offered the gall bladder for HK$100[3].

When there were no takers, he pulled out another snake, added its gall bladder into the glass and offered the two gall bladders for HK$180. He kept adding fresh snake gall bladders but decreased the incremental price.

When the glass had five or six gall bladders, someone in the crowd finally agreed to pay the asking price because it was a bargain by then. The snake seller poured some strong Chinese white liquor (*baijiu*) into

---

3 The exchange rate was approximately HK$100 to US$13 at that time.

the glass, stirred the concoction well, and handed it to the buyer, who swallowed the mixture in one gulp. I watched this for a while, but did not have the guts to buy any.

However, snake meat is a different – and delicious – matter. There was a snake restaurant in Guangzhou that I used to frequent. The main entrance was flanked by two upright 2-m-tall cobras, carved out of wood. The menu included all types of snakes cooked in many different ways. My favourites were salt-baked snake, shredded snake soup and grilled snake.

MORE FORBIDDEN FOOD: CRANKING UP THE SHOCK FACTOR

There are other exotic dishes in China which I have not personally experienced but are worth a mention:

Monkey brain: A live monkey is presented in a cage where its head would be the only thing sticking out of a hole on the table. A machete is used to slice off part of the skull, exposing the brain. XO brandy is poured into the scalp and everyone is invited to dig in with a spoon.

Live newborn rats: This is called the "three squeaks" meal. First squeak – when the live rats are picked up by chopsticks. Second squeak – when they are dipped into the accompanying sauce. Third squeak – when they are bitten by the diner.

Cobra venom: My friend was invited to a banquet where a cobra was brought out before the attendees and had its poisonous venom extracted into a bowl. Strong *baijiu* was then added. Anyone interested to have a sip would be offered some in a small porcelain teacup. But first, they were asked if they had any sores in their mouths. If they did, they were advised not to consume the mixture. According to Chinese folk medicine, cobra venom supposedly improves one's eyesight.

Sweet and sour live garoupa: The chef is supposed to know how to numb and immobilise the fish by acupuncture. If the fish is not sufficiently immobilised, it could flick boiling oil all over the chef who is trying to make the fish into a gourmet dish. Holding the fish by the head, the chef would lower the rest of the limp fish into a wok filled with boiling oil. Sweet and sour sauce would then be poured onto the deep-fried fish. The fish would still be alive while it is being eaten.

Some types of reptile meat are neither tender nor palatable. Once, I tried an alligator steak in Florida, and found it to be very tough. On a diving trip to Pulau Tioman in Malaysia, my group of fellow divers caught a monitor lizard (iguana). It so happened that one of the guys had been a commando during his National Service days. He skinned the creature and roasted it over an open fire, all the while smearing honey and soya sauce over its body. It smelled absolutely delicious, but the meat was extremely tough.

On a working trip to Dalian which is famous for its seafood – both fresh and preserved – I had dinner in a Japanese restaurant. At the next table was a young couple who ordered live fish sashimi. The fish was alive and its mouth was gasping for air, but the fillet on its back had already been carved out and cut into pieces of sashimi. After a while, the lady could not stand looking at the fish, so she covered the fish head with her serviette before working up the courage to eat the sashimi. Incidentally, we ordered the same dish but had no problems finishing the sashimi.

While on the subject of fish, I once visited a food street in Taipei called Snake Alley. This is a night market where all kinds of local snacks and exotic treats are sold. Vendors would skin live snakes, let the blood drain and serve up shot glasses of snake blood and bowls of hot snake soup[4] to those with a gutsy palate. Apart from reptiles, I also saw a tray of what looked to be raw meatballs that were 2 cm in diameter on display. There had to be at least a hundred of them. On closer examination, I realised that these were fish eyeballs. The muscle of the eyeballs made for a very delicious dish, especially when deep fried.

There have been tamer food experiences during my travels, but some are just as memorable to me. As a student living in America, I was invited

---

4 The last snake meat restaurant in Snake Alley closed in 2018.

to join some Nigerian students in California to savour their national staple food, "fufu", which is made from boiled cassava (tapioca). Although different West African countries have their own version of fufu and some are served as a soupy dish, my Nigerian friend's version was dry and yet sticky.

The whole thing looked just like a big lump of off-white dough. All of us tore out a small piece with our fingers and ate it accompanied by a bite of a jalapeno chilli pepper. I have to admit that it was quite tasteless but for the fiery sting on my tongue from the jalapeno. Incidentally, the jalapeno reminded me of the pickled jalapeno served with the homemade Mexican food that my friends and I had when we were picking oranges in Santa Paula, California, back in 1965. Just licking on the chilli pepper was enough to numb my tongue.

I have had some gloriously good and some atrociously bad meals on planes. I remember being upgraded to First Class on flights by Singapore Airlines, United Airlines and Cathay Pacific; the quality of their inflight dining was impressive. Meals were served with caviar, accompanied by chilled vodka. There was also an array of premium wines and cheese to choose from.

One of my worst inflight meals was the one on Nigerian Airlines, when I flew from Port Harcourt to London in the early 1980s. A fellow passenger had railed against the dried-out and unchewable chicken served, and I have to say he was right – it was truly "bounce-off-the-floor" hard. I also had some horrendous meals on regional airlines in China, where they believe quantity is more important than quality. There would be dinner rolls, biscuits and rice for starch, nuts and dried fruits for snacks, and different types of pickles to accompany the meals.

In the course of my travels, I have come to understand that people from different cultures develop different cuisines. Some are more adventurous about the food they eat, but others can be very closed-minded. I had an American friend who told me that she would eat fried calamari rings, but would never touch a slice of the body of a squid even it is fried in batter.

Chapter 13
HASH HOUSE HARRIERS

One activity which has taken me to many places around the world is running with the Hash House Harriers. These "Hash clubs" are known to be drinking clubs with a running problem. They are very loosely held-together organisations functioning as social clubs, whose members meet once a week to do some running and then imbibe on the amber liquid, a.k.a. beer, after the run.

The Hash is based on the ancient running sport of "Hares and Hounds". The Hares would set a trail and the Hounds are supposed to sniff it out. The trails could be marked with shredded paper, flour, chalk marks or even flowers. The Hares could set false trails to throw off the Hounds. There are no set rules, so each chapter may have some peculiar traditions handed down by the founding members through the years.

Started in Kuala Lumpur, Malaysia in 1938 by some British officers, Hashing soon spread to the world over. Expatriates who came to work in the Far East joined the local Hash club to meet like-minded people and widen their social circles. When they returned home after their posting, many of them started their own chapters. Because it all started in Kuala Lumpur, the local chapter there laid claim to be the "Mother Hash".

There are now thousands of chapters around the world. I am a member of a Singaporean chapter known as the Seletar Hash House Harriers. In some cities, there are more than seven Hashes, so there would be at least a run on each day of the week. Some are male only, and some are of mixed genders. There are even dog Hashes where the Hashers bring their four-legged best friends on the run, and bicycle Hashes where the "runs" are done on bicycles. There are Hash House Horrors, organised specifically for children of Hashers, and Hash House

Hazards for seniors who do not wish to kill themselves running with other macho young Hashers.

All of us are given a Hash name which is meant to stick with us for the rest of our lives. The name is supposed to have something to do with one's profession, appearance, real name, etc. For example, I was given the name "Nuts" by the Medan Hash, because I was dealing with palm oil when I ran with them for nine months.

As time goes by, we may not even know the real names of our fellow Hashers because our Hash names are the only names we are supposed to use on the Hash. Sometimes, this could create an embarrassing situation. I remember an incident when one of our members was stung by a swarm of wasps on the run and was sent to the hospital. We wanted to inquire about the seriousness of his condition, but none of us knew his legal name. He was only known as "Nurse F*cker" to us and it was most inappropriate to use that name to track him down in the A&E department.

In 1978, the Hong Kong Hash organised an Interhash where all the Hash chapters around the world were invited. Mother Hash did not want to be left out so, they organised the second Interhash in 1980. Thereafter, an Interhash would be held every two years, mainly in the Far East so as to make it more affordable to the chapters in Asia, where the standard of living is generally lower. Pretty soon, Pan Asian Hash, Pan Borneo Hash, Pan American Hash and many other more localised Interhashes sprang up all over the world. There are also events like Nash (National) Hashes. However, many of these became very commercialised, and seemed like they were organised solely for financial gain.

In 1967, I was back home in Sabah from America for the summer holidays. My mother told me that if I were looking for something to do, I could join the Sandakan Hash to get some exercise and make some friends. That was my introduction to the Hash. My mother was the personal assistant to the managing director of a trading firm known as

"Harrisons and Crosfield"; her boss's alter ego was the Grand Master of the Sandakan Hash. So she used to send out the weekly newsletter telling the other members where the run that week was going to be held.

As it turned out, Harrisons and Crosfield was the distributor for Anchor Beer and F&N Aerated Water. How convenient! Every Monday, the Land Rover belonging to the company would be loaded with a tub filled with Anchor Beer, F&N Ginger Beer and ice. Whoever was the Hare and setting the run that week just had to collect the vehicle from the distributor's warehouse and drive it out to the runsite. At the end of the run, we congregated around the vehicle and consumed a copious amount of beer and ginger beer. Afterwards, we adjourned to a restaurant where we had dinner, sang rugby songs and drank more beer. The following morning, the Hare would return the vehicle to the warehouse and pay for what had been consumed. I am not sure my mother knew what she was getting me into when she introduced me to the Hash.

In 1970, I spent the summer in Sandakan again. By then, I had my driver's licence, so I too, could drive the Land Rover out to the runsite. They did not give me a Hash name, as Hash names were not prevalent then. One evening, a Hasher did not return from the run, so we mounted a rescue team to look for him. We found him perched on a tree because it was dark and he needed protection from wild animals.

When I spent nine months working in Medan, Indonesia in 1979, I met some local Hashers and was invited to join them for their weekly run. Soon, I became more involved with the Hash in Medan. It was here that I was conferred my Hash name "Nuts". On Mondays, there was the men's run. On Wednesdays, there was the Harriettes' run. Although the committee of the Harriettes was composed of only women, the men were welcome to run with them to provide protection. On Fridays, I would join some Hashers for a game of rugby.

The majority of the Medan Hashers were working expatriates. Thus they were all driven to the runsite by their company cars. There was one run where the drivers were told to drive their cars to another ending point after the pack had set off, so that "short cutters" who turned around without completing the run would return to an empty carpark.

During the Interhash in Kuala Lumpur in 1980, I met several of my ex-air force colleagues who told me about a new Hash chapter they had formed in Singapore. As the founding members were mostly air force personnel, they named their Hash the "Seletar Hash House Harriers", after the air base in Seletar. I was invited to join them for their runs on Tuesdays, so when I relocated back to Singapore from Medan, I became a full-fledged member of the Seletar Hash. The Hash name given to me in Medan was carried over to Seletar.

In our Hash, apart from the Grand Master, the committee consists of his assistants, the Joint Masters; the Cash who takes care of money matters; the Brew who is in charge of making sure there will be ice-cold beers at the end of the run; the Sweep who ensures no one becomes lost on the trail; the Bard who leads the singing after the run; the Interhash Secretary who is our point man in dealing with other Hashes around the world; and finally, the almighty Hash Whip who maintains discipline within the club (what discipline?), especially during the circle when the Hashers gather around to talk about the run, the runsite for the following week's run, any other club matters and finally all the "offences" committed by the members on the run or outside of the Hash.

In some other clubs, the Hash Whip is called the Religious Advisor. During the circle in the Brussels Interhash, the Religious Advisor from the local Hash was dressed in a nun's habit, still wearing her dirty running sneakers, no less. In our Hash, the Whip carries a whip stick which is a voodoo stick that I brought back from Nigeria in 1981.

I have been running with the Seletar Hash for over 40 years now, and I have joined them on many Interhashes: Jakarta (1982), Pattaya (1986), Manila (1990), Phuket (1992), Kuala Lumpur (1998), Perth (2008), Borobudur (2012) and Bali (2016). I have also served three terms on the Hash committee. Whenever we travel to these Interhashes, all the beers carried on the plane would run out within the first hour. For the trip to Jakarta, most of us were on a Qantas 747. The beers ran out even on that two-hour flight.

In the course of my work, I have travelled to many places with Hash chapters. Because they are such sociable and friendly clubs, they welcome all visitors to join them for their run, especially Hashers from other

THE DELICATE ART OF MARKING TRAILS IN SINGAPORE

In the beginning, the Seletar Hash (my home Hash) used shredded paper to set our runs. However, we were cited by the police for littering. So we switched to marking our trails with chalk, but that was only possible if we were running on a hard surface. For other terrain types, we used flour to mark our trails. The National Parks Board then complained that our flour was killing their trees. Once, some civic-minded citizen alerted the police that someone was spreading anthrax in an MRT (Singapore's subway) station. Our Hares for that run were fined $1,000 because the authorities actually shut down the station for three hours until some forensic expert declared that the white powder was harmless. Most recently, our Hares have been using flowers bought from shops that supply Hindu devotees with flowers for worship at the temples.

countries. Nowadays, most of the Hash chapters have their own websites, so it is easy to contact the local Hash chapters during my visits. All I have to do is to contact the equivalent of the Interhash Secretary, identify myself as a visiting Hashman from Seletar Hash of Singapore, and they would gladly tell me where and when they are running next. Where practical, they would even offer to give me a ride out to the runsite, just as we would do for any visiting Hashman.

However, in the old days, before the Internet became prevalent, I was advised to call the British High Commission and ask to speak to a Hasher. Chances were, a Hasher would come to the phone. If I were travelling in the Middle East, I would also try the Standard Chartered Bank. Of course, nowadays, this trick does not work anymore, because the automated answering system would not be able to put me through to a Hasher. Speaking from personal experience, I was able to run with the Kathmandu Hash in the 1980s, by calling the British High Commission. A British Gurkha officer actually came to the phone and told me the runsite for the week's run. Similarly, I was able to run with the Abu Dhabi Hash by calling the Standard Chartered Bank.

In the US, I ran with the Washington D.C. Hash when I spent four months there from 1986 to 1987. Part of that time was during winter, and the trail was marked with red food colouring, sprayed in the snow. One of their members was "Hash Willie", and I spent a few nights in his house, having pizza and beer while watching a football game together.

When I was sent to Fort Worth, Texas for orientation after I joined Bell Helicopter, I ran with the Dallas Hash. After one particular run, we were told to bring a dollar note for the following week's run. When I checked out the location, I found that it was near the Coors brewery, so I assumed that the dollar was meant to buy a plastic cup during the visit to the brewery, so as to enjoy a free flow of beer. Instead, the run led us to a strip joint. Many mugs of beer were waiting for us on the bar, and the dollar was meant for us to tip the strippers by slipping it under their g-strings.

When I visited San Diego, I was brought to a San Diego Larrikin Hash. There, I met a lady, "Ice Box", who used to live in Singapore. She told me that her ex-husband used to run with the Seletar Hash, and she knew quite a few of our members. She asked me how "Crotch Croft" was doing. I had to tell her that he had an asthma attack while hiking and died. "That is too bad, and how is 'Ah Meng'?" Hated to tell her, but he died too, of cancer. She reached into her memory and asked me how "Han Solo" was. At that juncture, I had to tell her that he had also gone west and that she should stop asking me about anyone else in our Hash.

Although the emirate of Abu Dhabi has a predominantly Muslim population, alcohol was readily available there. I was picked up from the hotel by a local Hasher and brought to their run. After the run, there were loads of beer and singing just like in other Hashes.

However, Saudi Arabia was the complete opposite. As the motto of the Hash House Harriers is "A drinking club with a running problem", the "dry" kingdom was not an ideal location for such a club to operate as per normal. Not only was there no alcohol[1] on the Riyadh Hash, the members also had to run way out in the desert, away from prying urban eyes…in case the religious police raided the gathering. The vastness of the

1 However, once a month, there would a Hash party in one of the diplomatic compounds where alcohol would be made available.

sandy terrain afforded sufficient privacy for the female members to run in shorts and all members to uphold the post-run rituals and traditions, including mingling between unmarried couples.

The trails were marked by flour, but I was told that sometimes a herd of goats would pass by and eat up the flour, causing confusion for the Hashers looking for the trail. Once, a Hare was lost in the desert while setting a false trail, and his dehydrated dead body was found under the overhang of a boulder three days later by the police searching the area with their helicopters. I joined the Riyadh Hash run on a few occasions, but I would not swap it for my home Hash club in Singapore.

From the 1990s to 2006, I made many trips into China. Knowing that the Beijing Hash runs on Sundays, I would take the Sunday morning flight up there in time to join them for their Hash run. One memorable run was a weekend outing to the Jinshanling section of the Great Wall. Pak Seng, who used to run with the Hash House Horrors occasionally when he was younger, joined me on that trip.

We were supposed to spend that Saturday night in a camp. However, as things turned out, all of us grabbed a mattress from the camp and proceeded to spend the night up on the Great Wall. In the middle of the night, it started to rain and all of us huddled into the nearest watchtower on the wall to stay out of the rain. In the morning, we were told that those watchtowers were full of scorpions. At one point during that weekend, one of the regular Hashers asked me why I was constantly hanging around with "that young man" (Pak Seng). I told him flatly, "*That young man* is my son, that's why."

One peculiar tradition in the Beijing Hash is that when the Bard is leading the hash in a song, he or she would ask for a note. All of the Hashers made a throat clearing noise to give him a note. In the Beijing Hash, anyone who committed a "crime" had to drink beer from a rubber chicken. In the Seletar Hash, the punishment for a more serious "crime" was to drink beer from a bed pan which we called the "Piss Pot".

I also had the opportunity to do a run in London with one of the London Hash clubs. Pak Seng took me out to the runsite, which was a pub. The run was set in a park, so the two of us had a relatively clean run with the other Hashers. At the end of it, we spent the next hour or so in the pub, before we took the subway home. Because it was in a public place, the drinking and singing was relatively subdued. Some of the other Hashes were not so kind. They would set a run through the dirtiest trenches or muddiest tracks. Sometimes, we had to crawl through tunnels and even swim across rivers.

Hashing has become a way of life for me. On Tuesdays, come rain or shine, I will be out there with the Hash. I play soccer with my Hash team members. Many of our Hash Horrors have grown up and joined our Hash as full-fledged members.

For an expat living in a foreign land, joining a local Hash will greatly widen his or her circle of friends. This is true even for a local born and bred in Singapore. We also get to see parts of the country that we would never set foot on, had we not been running with the Hash. Our Seletar Hash members come from all walks of life. We have a brain surgeon and a dentist. We have lawyers and accountants. We have airline pilots and ship captains. We have policemen and military personnel. We even have a used car salesman and an ice-cream seller. We have multi-talented members who can sing, play the guitar, write and perform in a skit. What's more, our kinship extends beyond Tuesdays. There will be a group that meets for drinks on Fridays. Some of them would travel together to see other parts of the world and run with the Hash there.

I have been Hashing for more than 50 years. With the deteriorating condition of my spine, I have been advised by the doctors not to partake in any activity where my spine is subjected to pounding. So nowadays, I would only walk on the trail, but that has not slowed down my beer drinking.

Chapter 14
EPILOGUE

The last long-distance trip I took before the whole world came under the COVID-19 lockdown was to England, at the beginning of 2020. Kwan and I flew into London three days before the Chinese New Year, had our family reunion dinner with our children and grandchildren, and then flew home at the end of the following week. I even managed to slot in a trip back to Sabah with my younger sister Pat and her husband Kwok Leung to see our elder sister Shuk Tak and pay our respects at our late parents' grave. Three days before Singapore completely shut down her borders on 7 April, I returned home safely.

What followed was a series of cancelled trips. Firstly, our planned trip to return to Purdue University for Kwan to receive the outstanding alumni award on 17 April was postponed.

Secondly, the bi-annual Worldchefs Congress and Expo that was to take place in the fall of 2020 at St Petersburg, Russia, was cancelled. We had already bought the expo tickets and planned on meeting up with Pak Seng and his family in St Petersburg after the event. We wanted to travel on the Trans-Siberian railroad up to Ulaanbaatar in Mongolia. That train journey, of course, had to be called off as well.

As the pandemic raged on, plans for my 55th anniversary Menlo School class reunion in the fall of 2021 had to be shelved. To make up for the disappointment, one of my classmates arranged for a virtual reunion on Zoom, which was attended by around 15 to 20 classmates.

We finally made our first trip out of Singapore in the last week of September, 2021. When we left Singapore, we were prepared to be quarantined for two weeks upon our return. Because of that, we planned for a 6½-week trip, visiting both the US and UK. The flight from Singapore to the US was less than 20% full. Other than the periodic P.A. system messages reminding passengers to keep their masks on, the flight was quite uneventful.

We switched carriers in Tokyo, and I was looking forward to having some sake in the All Nippon Airways lounge in Narita Airport. I was very disappointed to see a sign displayed at the bar in the lounge that said: *Due to the National State of Emergency, no alcohol will be served in the lounge.* Not even beer!

The domestic flights in the US were quite routine. However, on-time departure was strictly adhered to. The gates would be closed half an hour before a scheduled departure, and as a matter of fact, I missed my flight from Oklahoma City to Chicago because I was a couple of minutes late to check in.

The 3½ weeks in the US saw us attending a series of events and business meetings. I accompanied Kwan to the Distinguished Alumni Award dinner at Purdue University, where she was presented with her award. After that, we went on visits to Johnson & Wales University in Providence, Rhode Island; George Washington University in Washington D.C.; and Rutgers University in New Jersey.

After we had completed our business meetings, we flew out of Newark International Airport to Heathrow, London. Instead of the customary long queues at the UK immigration border control at Heathrow, we were greeted by the sight of quite a short queue. Somehow, the electronic gates were not functioning properly, so we were directed to the counters manned by immigration officers and were cleared in no time.

Kwan and I were both happy to see the children and grandchildren after more than 1½ years! We rented a seven-bedroom villa overlooking the beach in Cornwall for a week, and celebrated Oi Leng's 44th birthday. The week-long family vacation was packed with plenty of activities. On one of the days, we walked across the causeway together at low tide to visit the tiny tidal island of St Michael's Mount. The grandchildren also spent a couple of days learning how to surf on the waters of St Ives. Before we left Cornwall, the family posed for photos at the iconic Land's End Signpost.

While in London, I saw the news that the Singapore government had set up designated Vaccinated Travel Lane (VTL) flights with selected countries and their respective cities. Under this scheme, fully vaccinated passengers who test negative with a polymerase chain reaction (PCR) test on arrival in Singapore from specific flights on certain airlines would not have to be quarantined. So, our gamble on the quarantine being lifted paid off. The only trouble was, the London–Singapore flight on which we were booked was not a VTL flight.

Calls to the Singapore Airlines office in London were greeted with the recording message that because of this new travel directive from Singapore, I might have to stay on the line for more than an hour in order to speak to a ticketing agent. To escape from the excruciating automated phone system ordeal, I took the trouble to travel to the Singapore Airlines ticketing office in Heathrow in person to change our flight to a designated VTL flight.

Even though we had to stay in London for an extra two days because the earlier VTL flights were full, we were able to return to Singapore without being quarantined, and were free to move about as soon as the results of the PCR test proved negative. We made another trip to London in early 2022, for our customary Chinese New Year reunion dinner with the children and grandchildren.

In April 2022, Kwan and I were invited to India for the opening of one of our partner schools in Delhi. The temperature was a scorching 43°C during mid-day. We also made side trips to Mumbai, Kochi and Kolkata while we were there.

One of my good friends, Jackson, has an employment contract in the Maldives for two years and that gave me a golden opportunity to visit the nation of islands again for some good scuba diving in May. I would definitely like to make another trip to the Layang Layang resort in Sabah to dive at the 6,000 feet drop-off wall.

In July, we went to Bangkok to spend a weekend with Kwan's cousin, Norman. He took us up to his weekend villa in Khao Yai, north east of Bangkok. On our return, I managed to slot in a trip to Sabah with Oi Leng's family to visit Shuk Tak, whom I have not seen for two years. We visited my parents' grave and paid our respects. Oi Leng and family climbed Mount Kinabalu while I gathered my St. Michael's Secondary School classmates for a dinner.

In September, we made a short trip to Hong Kong where I met up with my Menlo schoolmate Wing Ning as well as Linda, a member of the Hardship Group. There were still some restrictions in Hong Kong due to COVID, so I could not meet up with Dr Chan Sik, whom I have not seen since 1988. I was also not able to see my Aunt no. 9, who is the only surviving sibling of my father. Some of my cousins are still living in Hong Kong, although most have migrated to the US and Canada.

For October, we have planned and booked a trip to go diving in the Red Sea with Pak Seng and two of his sons. After that, we will follow him back to London to see the new house that he had moved into, as well as spend some time with Oi Leng and her family.

To wrap up the year, in December, we are going to the US to visit my brother Fred in the San Francisco Bay area, my ex-boss Mike in Oklahoma, and Kwan's sister in New York. If time permits, I would like to visit Lorena, the daughter of Uncle no. 5. She is now living in South Carolina. I would also like to track down Philip. He is the younger son of Uncle no. 4 and the last time I saw him was in New York 16 years ago. Kwan and I are planning to spend Christmas and New Year in the British Virgin Islands with a side trip to Puerto Rico.

Over the years, we have been attending the class reunions of Kwan's Bangkok Seventh-Day Adventist classmates. They are planning for another reunion in early 2023 after a three-year hiatus. Another regional trip would be a short visit to Luang Prabang, an UNESCO World Heritage Site in Laos.

I would definitely like to visit more places in China. I have always enjoyed tasting the local food in the different provinces and expanding my gastronomic horizons. On the other hand, Kwan would like to visit the wine-producing regions in France. As long as she is still involved with her culinary academy, we will have a lot of opportunities to visit other culinary academies around the world and participate in food shows because she will continue to sign up for the bi-annual Worldchefs Congress and Expo.

Sometime in the near future, I would like to meet up with Raphael and Kan, sons of Uncle no. 3. I have not seen them since 1966 and they still live in Vancouver, Canada. New Zealand is bidding for the 2024 Interhash. If they are successful in their bid, I would join the gathering and then make a side trip to Wellington to visit my friend Joe Keegan, who was an exchange RNZAF officer to Singapore back in the 1970s. We have been keeping in touch all these years.

Finally, as travel restrictions around the world further loosen up, my priority would be to cover the one continent I have not been to: South America. Kwan and I have a standing invitation to visit our good friend, the ex-Ambassador from Argentina to Singapore. When we do make that trip, it will be natural to hop across to Chile and Peru as well. We have a similar standing invitation to visit Ukraine from another good friend, the ex-Ambassador from Ukraine to Singapore.

Appendix A

United States Travel Timetable 1964–1971

This is a summary of how I managed to cover all of the 50 states in America during my years there. The superscript denotes the sequence of my first visit to a state.

When	Where	Why
Sep 1964	Honolulu, **Hawaii**[1]	Airport transit (en route to San Francisco)
	San Francisco, **California**[2]	Started school in Sunnyvale
Apr 1965	Denver, **Colorado**[3]	Easter holiday ski trip with dorm mate
Dec 1965	Phoenix, **Arizona**[4] **Colorado** **Utah**[5] **New Mexico**[6] Las Vegas, **Nevada**[7]	Christmas/New Year holidays with Cousin John
Jun 1966	Seattle, **Washington**[8]	Transit (en route to Vancouver)
	(Canada) Vancouver, British Columbia	Summer holiday visit and job at Uncle no. 4's shop
Sep 1966	(Canada) British Columbia; Alberta; Saskatchewan; Manitoba (America) Fargo, **North Dakota**[9] Noyes & Minneapolis, **Minnesota**[10] Madison & Milwaukee, **Wisconsin**[11] Chicago, **Illinois**[12] West Lafayette, **Indiana**[13]	56-hour bus ride from Vancouver to West Lafayette to begin college education

When	Where	Why
Dec 1966	St Louis, **Missouri**[14] Tulsa, **Oklahoma**[15] Dallas, **Texas**[16]	Sharing a ride, from Indiana to Texas on Route 66
	Oklahoma City, **Oklahoma** Wichita, **Kansas**[17] Kansas City, **Missouri**	Driving without license on day trip with Cousin John
Jan 1967	Cincinnati, **Ohio**[18] **Kentucky**[19]	Weekend visit to dorm mate's house
May 1967	**Michigan**[20]	Short trip from Elkhart, Indiana
Jun 1967	Davenport & Council Bluffs, **Iowa**[21] Omaha, **Nebraska**[22] Cheyenne, **Wyoming**[23] Salt Lake City, **Utah** Reno, **Nevada**	Sharing a ride, from Indiana to San Francisco
Nov 1967	Dayton & Columbus, **Ohio** Wheeling, **West Virginia**[24] Pittsburgh, **Pennsylvania**[25]	Thanksgiving holiday at dorm mate's house
Dec 1967	Louisville, **Kentucky** Nashville, **Tennessee**[26] Atlanta, **Georgia**[27] Jacksonville, Fort Lauderdale and Miami, **Florida**[28]	Christmas/New Year holidays with dorm mate in the Bahamas (bus ride from Indiana to Miami, followed by short flight)
Apr 1968	Detroit & Ann Arbor, **Michigan** Toledo, **Ohio**	Visit to Barry Green's house
Jun 1968	Route 66 **New Mexico** Las Vegas, **Nevada** Los Angeles & San Diego, **California**	Summer job in California
Dec 1968	Newark, **New Jersey**[29] New York City, **New York**[30]	Christmas/New Year holidays with Wally and his family
Jun 1969	Sioux City, **Iowa** Rapid City & Mount Rushmore, **South Dakota**[31] Yellowstone Park, **Wyoming** Butte, **Montana**[32] Coeur D'Alene, **Idaho**[33] Seattle, **Washington**	Summer job with Sze Yin

When	Where	Why
Aug 1969	Portland, **Oregon**[34]	Drive down the Pacific Coast
Dec 1969	Key West & Everglades National Park, **Florida**	Christmas/New Year holidays with Wing Kee, his brother and cousin
Jan 1970	Return via Montgomery & Birmingham, **Alabama**[35] **Tennessee** **Kentucky**	
Jan 1970	McLoud, **Oklahoma**	Semester break
Mar 1970	The Deep South: Gulfport, Jackson & Greenville, **Mississippi**[36] New Orleans, **Louisiana**[37] **Arkansas**[38]	Road trip with grad school classmates
Jun 1970	Anchorage, **Alaska**[39]	Airport transit
Jun 1971	Baltimore, **Maryland**[40] Washington D.C. Richmond & Virginia Beach, **Virginia**[41] Kitty Hawk & Hatteras, **North Carolina**[42] Charleston, **South Carolina**[43] Tallahassee, **Florida**	Last lap south to cover the Carolinas
	Wilmington, **Delaware**[44] Philadelphia, **Pennsylvania** New Haven, **Connecticut**[45] Providence, **Rhode Island**[46] Boston, **Massachusetts**[47] Portsmouth, **New Hampshire**[48] Kittery, **Maine**[49] Killington, **Vermont**[50]	Back up north to cover New England

Appendix B

My Top 3 Travel Pet Peeves

Much as I enjoy travelling, there are some things which I consider to be a major pain in the neck.

Bureaucracy

The Number One thing that has always bothered me, even till today, remains the bureaucracy encountered when getting in and out of a destination, especially with respect to immigration and customs procedures.

Certain places and its people are notorious for making it very difficult to do things. Afghanistan, for example. How could I have known how laborious it was to get an exit permit to leave the country? I bounced around from ministry to ministry, department to department, before I could get my hands on the requisite paperwork.

China was another case in point. The enormous visa stamp used by the immigration and customs officers was bad enough. But the manner in which the officers stamped my passport upon entry or exit – directly over the visa impression and covering important information – annoyed me to no end.

In Delhi, I was barred from going into the airport terminal for check-in because my air ticket to Singapore did not have the correct date printed on it. I explained to the officers at the door that I had brought forward my flight date at the last minute by calling the Singapore Airlines (SQ) office in Singapore directly. Having just flown in from Kathmandu 15 minutes earlier, I hadn't had a chance to get a new ticket printed. If they would just get the SQ counter staff to verify it on their computers, they would see the updated information. Unfortunately, all the SQ staff were inside the terminal checking-in the passengers! It was a Catch-22 situation…

Again, recently in India (this time in Kochi), Kwan and I were almost barred from our flight by an airport security guard who conducted a bureaucratic nitpicking exercise on us. Although our names were on page 1 of our printed e-ticket, the guard insisted that we produce page 2 for his inspection after he saw the words "page 1 of 2" at the bottom of the ticket.

I told him that I did not print out that page because it was merely a list of airline terms and conditions (such as the cancellation policy and luggage allowance), but he just refused to let us in. It so happened that a ground hostess from the airline walked by, so I waved her over and told her our problem. She looked at page 1 and told the guard that it was sufficient to show that Kwan and I had tickets on that flight. Only then did the guard relent and let us in.

Obviously, travel red tape is not endemic in Asia. Once, I faced a nasty American immigration officer who made me go to the back of a (long) line again, just because I forgot to sign the back of a form. Then shortly after 9/11, when I was entering Los Angeles, I was made to X-ray my luggage again, all because I touched it when I moved it closer to the check-in counter by less than 2 m after it had been X-rayed the first time.

Corruption

The Number Two thing that I dislike is having to deal with corrupt officials who are constantly on the lookout for ways to extort money. Some of them are very direct – no excuses needed – like the Nigerian security guard at the airport when he demanded US$10 from me.

Yet there are others who take advantage of unsuspecting travellers in a hurry, all in the name of invoking the law. When you enter Malaysia from Singapore via the Causeway, you might have seen a notice posted on the immigration booth, advising travellers to check that their passports have been stamped with a valid entry date before continuing on their way.

This is because there had been cases where an officer "forgot" to stamp the entry chop on random passports, but it did not occur to the travellers to examine their passports closely. On their way out of the country, these travellers would face the consequences of their carelessness: the missing entry stamp offered the attending immigration officer an opportunity to impose an instant fine on them, because they had entered the country "illegally".

In most countries, the tradition of tipping is widely accepted. You pay a gratuity for a service that someone provides you, say, for being given preference in queues, or seating. Unfortunately, this practice is also prevalent in officialdom in many countries, where foreign business travellers are expected to take the initiative and grease someone's palm when they are applying for things such as licenses or permits, so that their applications would float up to the top of the pile.

However, in one country I know, it worked the other way round. The office cleaner came into the office first thing in the morning, riffled through the documents on the table to see whose application was sitting at the top of the pile, and gave that person a call. The message to the applicant? If he did not deliver a certain amount of money to the cleaner's house, his application would mysteriously sink to the bottom of the pile. In other words, he would be downgraded, served last, sent to the back of the queue, etc., unless he paid an upfront "tip".

Having spent a fair amount of time travelling in and out of Medan, Indonesia in the 1970s, I have had many encounters with mercenaries in the government service.

For example, an immigration officer would take my passport, look it over, set it aside and wave an entire plane load of other passengers to clear immigration and customs. During that time, I would be waiting by the side, seething with indignation. He would then pick up my passport again and start looking for "problems" in a leisurely manner.

First, he would ask me all kinds of questions, such as "You were born in Hong Kong, so why are you holding a Singapore passport?" or "Why don't you look like the photo in the passport?" Finally, he would say, "If you pay me Rp10,000[1], you can have your passport back". One officer even told me, "Usually, I only charge Rp10,000 but Hari Raya is around the corner, so the price just went up to Rp30,000".

I didn't have a choice but to pay. But I didn't want to take it lying down, so I went to the Singapore consulate to complain about the incident. The embassy staff who attended to me said, "Next time, you let us know and we can get your passport back for Rp5,000".

It is customary for Chinese people to give out little red envelopes containing cash – we call them *ang pows* – during Chinese New Year to kids.

1   Rp10,000 was approximately US$17 in those days.

However, an immigration officer in Medan once asked me, "Where is my *ang pow?*" He frowned when I told him that I did not have any.

The problem extended beyond the immigration department. Once, I went with my business partners to meet with a government official. After the meeting, I was about to return to our vehicle, when one of my partners said, "Let's go to the men's room". But I don't need to go, I told him. "Just come with me", he insisted. In the toilet, he asked us how much cash we had. All of us emptied our wallets into a white envelope, which he then went back to hand over to that official.

On another occasion, I visited a park with two other local friends in Medan. The posted entrance fee was Rp200 per person. One of my friends took out a Rp500 note and told the attendant at the ticketing office, "Three persons". The attendant gave us two entrance tickets, took the Rp500 note and let all three of us in. He pocketed Rp100 and my friend saved Rp100. The whole transaction was so spontaneous without hesitation, one would think it was rehearsed.

Those who had worked or done business in Indonesia also shared with me their encounters with crooked officials. I met a Singaporean woman who was doing some research in Medan. She was married to an Australian man. Communications were difficult for the couple whenever he travelled. One day, she received a message from the telegram office saying that she had a telegram from Australia. She was very excited, knowing the telegram would be from her husband.

When she called the telegram office, she was asked whether she would like to see the telegram. "Of course," she replied. But she was told that if she did not pay a fee of Rp10,000, she would not get to see the telegram.

Still on the subject of communicating via telegram and telex, I met the general manager of the German Behn Meyer office in Medan. He told me that he had to submit his sales report to Germany at 4 p.m. every day. He had been paying someone in the telex office a sum of money every month so that his telex line would remain trouble free.

On one occasion, that regular technician was on leave. The general manager received a call from the telex office demanding a new payment or else his telex line would not work anymore. He refused, so promptly at 4 p.m. that day, the telex line in his office went dead, and he was unable to send out his sales report. Reluctantly, he called the technician in the telex office and agreed to pay that "ransom". And miraculously, the telex started humming again.

I had a friend who owned a fleet of trucks plying the road between Medan and Belawan, the port. Somewhere along this road was a weighing station, where all trucks were required to drive in to be weighed before they could continue to their destinations. It was customary to pay a "service fee" to the weighbridge operator. No matter how much zinc ingots you were carrying in your truck, the reading from the weighbridge would show 5–10 kgs below the maximum allowable weight. In order to speed up the weighing process, my friend had to pay the person in charge of the motor vehicle department a monthly fee so that his trucks did not have to pay the customary "tax".

One day, one of his trucks failed the weighing test because the officer administering the test was new and just posted in. When the driver explained that his company already had a "special arrangement" with the person who was overall in charge, the new officer said that he also had a family to feed, so the driver had to pay up or he would issue a summons to the company.

Because he did not have to pay off anybody under normal circumstances, the driver did not have enough cash on hand, so he grudgingly accepted the summons. When he brought the summons back to the office, my friend went down to see the person overall in charge, who angrily denounced the issuing officer for insubordination. "If he does not respect me, I can get him posted to some outpost where he will rot!" So, he wrote a note to the issuing officer instructing him to pay the fine instead.

Queue-jumping

In many countries that I have been to, I would invariably experience people attempting to cut in line. Some of them may have valid reasons for doing it, maybe because they are trying to catch a train or a flight. They would politely ask for permission from the other people in the queue. But then, there will be some thick-skinned people who would inconspicuously sneak into a queue and pretend that they had been there all along.

Once, I was in a taxi queue in Guangzhou, China when a well-dressed young man butted in at the head of the queue. From 20 m away, I shouted, "Comrade, please join the queue!" In a communist country, calling him a comrade in such a situation embarrassed him enough that he gave me a nasty look and then left the queue.

In the late 1980s before Hong Kong was returned to China, I was at the Beijing International Airport, queueing up to check into a flight headed for Hong Kong. The flight was delayed, but the airline would not start the check-in process, so the queue stretched to 100 m long. At the head of the queue was a Caucasian who would chase away anyone who tried to cut into the line. When I boarded the plane, I discovered that he was seated in the economy section! After we landed in Hong Kong, a Rolls-Royce bearing the British Royal Coat of Arms and no license plate actually came out onto the tarmac to pick him up as he walked down the passenger airstairs. I never found out if he had to go through the immigration process like the rest of us. Probably not.

On another occasion, I was checking in for a flight in Tawau, Sabah, East Malaysia, and the queue was quite unruly. There was an Asian man holding an Australian passport who told his wife quite loudly in the local Sabah Hakka dialect, "Let's cut into the queue here". Obviously, he had not discarded his old ways even though he had migrated to Australia and become an Australian citizen. I wonder whether he would dare to do something like this back in Australia.

I have also experienced the other extreme while queuing to check into a flight in Yemen. The whole queue had more than 50 people, and it extended to not much more than 10 m! There was just no way anyone could have cut into the line. You can imagine how uncomfortable I felt, being squeezed in between two Arab men in a non-airconditioned terminal.

Appendix C

Remembering My Firsts...

I have always been fascinated with flying and would like to dedicate this section to my first experiences inside aeroplanes.

First flight

My first flight on an aeroplane took place in 1959. I was about 10 years old, visiting relatives in Hong Kong with my mother and my siblings. Riding in a DC-3 from Sabah to Singapore was uneventful, but the onward journey from Singapore to Hong Kong was something else. While the other airlines were using jet aircraft such as Convair 880s and Boeing 707s, Malayan Airways was still operating the same route with unpressurised DC-4s. In the passenger compartment, we had cold air blowing from the overhead air outlets, and hot air blowing from the floor level outlets.

There were also strange sounds coming from the first-class compartment. When I ducked through the curtains to find out who or what was making the noise, I saw crates and crates of young chicks. Not the human type but the feathered type! While the jets would have taken 3 or 4 hours, our flight in a four-engine (no less) propeller aircraft took 8 hours!! That was a memorable experience.

First flight in a jet aircraft

In 1963, I had my first experience in a jet aircraft, a deHavilland Comet 4 jetliner. The same sector, Singapore to Hong Kong, was supposed to take 3½ hours. However, not long after taking off from Kallang Airport, I noticed that one of the engines on the left-hand side seemed to be operating on and off. Some passenger even claimed that fire was spewing out of one of the engines.

So we turned back to Singapore and waited on the ground for several hours while the ground crew changed the engine. We arrived in Hong Kong 8 hours later than the scheduled time, no faster than the DC-4 which we took four years ago.

First flight in a Boeing 707

In 1964, I stepped into a Pan American Airways (Pan Am) Boeing 707 in Hong Kong, for my first trip to America. In those days, the range of the 707 did not allow the aircraft to fly non-stop from Hong Kong to San Francisco, so we had to make a refuelling stop in Honolulu.

Over the next seven years, when I was studying in the US, I did not do much travelling by air. The era was before Reagan deregulated the skies, so air travel was unaffordable. However, the father of one of the students in my boarding school was a captain with Pan Am. Every now and then, we would hear about Todd hopping onto a Pan Am flight, to Europe or Asia, over the weekend, because he "enjoys flying".

With the limited range of the Boeing 707, to fly from San Francisco to Hong Kong on a summer trip home with my college pals, I had to transit overnight in Honolulu and Tokyo. This offered me an opportunity to explore more countries and cities especially since we were put up in high-class international hotels and issued with coupons for our meals.

First few flying lessons

I took my first flying lesson in a motorised glider. Powered by a converted 42hp Volkswagen engine with a manual pull cord starter, these gliders had fabric skin and wooden frames. We would climb to 3,000 feet, shut off the engine and then glide around a training area. The feeling of gliding without the engine was so sensational. When the aircraft descended to 1,000 feet, we would hold the cyclic stick between our knees, pull start the engine with our two hands, and climb out again.

One day, I was paired up with a new instructor. I had accumulated just a few initial hours of flying then. During the lesson, my landings were very rough and the aircraft was bouncing all over the place. After one such landing, without warning, the instructor told me to stop the aircraft in the middle of the runway. He climbed out of the aircraft and said, "I don't want to die with you. Now you take the aircraft up yourself." He then calmly walked back to the control tower, while I took off and performed my first solo flight. He was experienced enough to see that I was ready for my first solo.

One of the emergency manoeuvres that we practised when flying our gliders was to take off on the runway, climb to 200 feet, pull back the engine throttle into idle to simulate an engine failure, also known as a fan stop, make a 180° turn and land the aircraft on the runway again.

On my second solo flight, I was assigned a different instructor. As I was executing a touch and go (where I was to take off again after touching down on the runway), he called me over the radio from the tower and instructed me to make a *full* stop, meaning that I should land the aircraft and end the sortie. Somehow, I heard the command as a *fan* stop. Without questioning him, I proceeded to pull the throttle at 200 feet, and then turned the aircraft around and landed.

I received some strong reprimand from him after that incident. I was told that simulating a fan stop at 200 feet and turning the aircraft around to land was not a manoeuvre that one should carry out on the *second solo flight*. Several months later, another very experienced pilot was executing the same manoeuvre at 200 feet when the wing of his glider clipped a coconut tree and he crashed onto the ground, with fatal consequences.

From the glider, I transitioned into a Cessna C-150 trainer. Over the years, I have accumulated more than 400 flying hours, flying all around East and West Malaysia. When I was in Sandakan, I made up some excuse to the control tower so that I could fly over my parents' house and take some aerial pictures of the building and its compound. I even had the good fortune to fly into Thailand and Indonesia.

When I joined Bell Helicopter in the late 1980s, I was given lessons on the Bell 206 Jetranger. I needed a few hours to un-learn some of the flying techniques to transition from a fix-wing pilot into a rotary-wing pilot, but I managed to progress to the solo stage.

As an aviation enthusiast, I continue to maintain a passion in most types of flying machines. However, I have never been interested to get into a hot-air balloon because it does not offer the pilot full directional control.

Appendix D

How To Breeze Through Airport Queues

Inevitably, much of my long-haul travel now and in the future is likely to be in the air. As I am someone who travels frequently, be it for business or pleasure, I always prefer swift and hassle-free immigration clearance procedures. It often boils down to knowing which immigration counter to select, and whom to avoid queuing behind. The shortest line is not necessarily the fastest line to get cleared.

In the US, when it comes to checking-in at airports, I always try to avoid lining up behind someone who is oblivious to the long line of passengers waiting to check in behind him or her. From my experience, they would demand their right to sit as far away as they can from the toilets, or as far away as they can from the galley because of the noise. They also want the best connecting flight at the next destination but would not pay the extra fees. They would be haggling with the check-in staff over the best combinations till the cows come home.

When it comes to gauging which immigration counters are speedier, I would usually try to choose counters where female immigration officers are stationed, because I find that female officers usually type faster on the keyboard than male officers.

For international flights, when I first arrive in a crowded arrival hall, I would try not to queue up behind argumentative travellers. If there were any problems with their documentation, they would invariably argue endlessly with the government officials and hold up the line. I also avoid students who usually have to produce all kinds of supporting documents, which take much longer for the inspecting officer to go over.

When travelling in Asia, I avoid lining up behind any African-looking travellers. Based on my observations over the years, they tend to be treated by airport authorities with high suspicion (as drug smugglers?), no matter how well dressed they might be. Their travel documents would be scrutinised with a fine-tooth comb, and their luggage would be X-rayed and sniffed by police dogs. If you were to stand behind them in a queue, be prepared for a long wait. Once, I witnessed a customs officer banging the shoes of an African man on the inspection counter, perhaps hoping that the heels would fall off and white powder would come gushing out.

Now that countries are loosening up restrictions and learning to live with COVID, I expect travel to be even busier than in pre-pandemic times – bigger crowds, more queue-jumpers, and overworked immigration and customs staff. Try my travel tips on your next trip!